Producing in the Home Studio with
PRO TOOLS

SECOND EDITION

DAVID FRANZ

Berklee Media

Associate Vice President: Dave Kusek
Director of Content: Debbie Cavalier
Marketing Manager: Jennifer Rassler
Senior Graphic Designer: David Ehlers

Berklee Press

Senior Writer/Editor: Jonathan Feist
Writer/Editor: Susan Gedutis
Production Manager: Shawn Girsberger
Product Marketing Manager: David Goldberg
Production Assistant: Louis O'choa

ISBN 0-87639-008-4

1140 Boylston Street
Boston, MA 02215-3693 USA
(617) 747-2146

Visit Berklee Press Online at
www.berkleepress.com

DISTRIBUTED BY

HAL•LEONARD®
CORPORATION
7777 W. BLUEMOUND RD. P.O. BOX 13819
MILWAUKEE, WISCONSIN 53213

Visit Hal Leonard Online at
www.halleonard.com

Printed in the United States of America by Vicks Lithographic and Printing Corporation

10 09 08 07 06 05 04 03   5 4 3 2 1

CONTENTS

ACKNOWLEDGMENTS

A fantastic bunch of people and organizations really helped and supported me through the entire book-writing process.

Berklee Press was like a family to me: Thanks to Dave Kusek (Associate Vice President, Berklee Media) for seeing the vision through to reality (you are the man); Debbie Cavalier (Director of Content, Berklee Media) for your guidance, encouragement, and for simply being my favorite person on the planet; Sue Gedutis for your Frisbee-throwing, friendship, and inspirational editing; Jonathan Feist for your conceptual input and moral support; Kate Klapfish for your many marketing talents, the Underground Sun ale, and for being chill; Barry Kelly for your indomitable energy, your studio building skills, and for being a good friend; Jennifer Rassler for cab rides, good spirits, and awesome vocals; Milan Kovacev for your friendship, good ears, and your work on the protoolsbook.com Web site; graphic designer Shawn Girsberger for making this book look even better than what I imagined; David Ehlers for your friendship, delicious Mexican food, and great work on the book's cover; Carin Johnson for your ever-supportive guidance and infectious smile; the Berklee Press workstudy staff (namely Dan Chen, Joe Tangari, Louis O'choa, Adam Conrad, Kevin Plessner) for putting up with my many requests; and Linda Chase, Michael Serio, Max Lord, John Mileham, Craig Reed, Cliff Anderson, Jeff Barsky, Maria Leggett, Boriana Jeleva, Rob Heath, Ann Woody, Amie Karp, Steve Krampf, David Goldberg, Marilyn Bliss, Ola Frank, Ami Bennitt, Ann Thompson, and Chris Buttner for your hard work, support, and friendship.

Digidesign did everything they could to make this project successful: Paul Foeckler (Director of Marketing) was responsible for nothing short of everything and made it all happen. Thanks for your encouragement and camaraderie. Claudia Curcio was driven and provided assistance at every turn. Claudia — you rock! Additionally, I salute the entire Digidesign organization for their vision, energy, and remarkable products.

Thanks to Berklee College of Music for providing the creative environment where ideas can flourish and where projects like this book come to fruition. Thanks in particular to Lee Berk (President of Berklee College of Music) for being a wonderful benefactor. Immense thanks go out all of the teachers I studied with at Berklee College of Music, namely Rob Jaczko, Terry Becker, Mitch Benoff, Carl Beatty, Stephen Webber, Michael Farquharson, Mark Wessel, Dan Thompson, Jon Aldrich, Ivan Sever, Tony Carbone, Michael Bierylo, and Ben Elkins. You have all illuminated me in countless ways and I'll never forget your influence on my life. Also, I am indebted to my friends at the Berklee Studio office, particularly Scott Mabuchi, Carrie Adase, Jon Berkowitz, Vassily Izumchensky, Hun-Min Park, Michael Conti, Alexia Rosari, Jonny Morrow, Sam Branch, Assen Stoyanov, Todd Smyth, Rachel

Juozapataitis, Aaron Heitmann, Pete Boynton, and Andres Botero, as well as fellow students Jeff Svatek, Alex Wann, and Will Robertson.

This book would be nothing without the editorial and structural contributions of Marvin Sanders and Sue Gedutis. Thanks for putting up with me and my bounteous keystrokes as well as for shaping this book into its final form.

I owe a large debt of gratitude to the musicians I worked with while writing the book: Andrew Stern and the Flat 5 Blues Band, Fat Little Bastard, Christie Zarlengo and Trio Zarlengo, Steve Yawnick, Chris and John Reynolds, Burt LaFountain, Danielle Miraglia, Tina Dawn, my old-school friends in the Cool Grape Goodness (Scott Elson, Alex Evans, and Dan Lincoln), and my new brothers in Lipfloater (Mike Coen, Michael Gilday, Barry Kelly, and Keith Pierce). Your creativity and musicianship consistently inspired me and further illuminated the purpose for this book.

Special thanks to my good friend Simon Heselev for the countless good times, laughing fits, and general silliness while learning. Our discussions about and sessions using Pro Tools really helped make this book possible.

Also, some great folks at several terrific organizations really contributed to this project: Michelle Kohler at Shure Inc., Dave McCarthy at Line 6, Larry Berger at Glyph, Marko Alpert and Michael Logue at Antares, AJ Bertenshaw and Steve Hoek at Serato Audio Research, Eric and Lorey Persing at Spectrasonics, Robin Whitcore at MultiLoops, Greg Giametta at IK Multimedia, Ben Chadabe at GRM Tools, Rich Courtney at PreSonus, Bob Reardon at Waves, and Clint Ward at Emagic.

And finally, the underlying foundation for anything that I accomplish is rooted in the love and support offered unconditionally by my family— Mom, Dad, Mike, Grandma, Grandpa, Barb, Bert, Kevin, Ruth, Korkut, Marion, John, Peter, and Karen. Thank you for all you've been to me.

CD SONG CREDITS

Rock

"Slip and Fall"

Written by David Franz and Mike Coen

Performed by Lipfloater (Barry Kelly, Michael Gilday, Keith Pierce, Mike Coen, and David Franz)

Recorded, mixed, and mastered at Underground Sun Studio by David Franz

For more information on Lipfloater, visit www.lipfloater.com

Jazz

"Inception"

Written by Noah Jarrett

Performed by Fat Little Bastard (Andrew Stern, Eric Platz, and Noah Jarrett)

Recorded, mixed, and mastered at Underground Sun Studio by David Franz

For more information on Fat Little Bastard, visit www.fatlittlebastard.com

Electronica

"Last Mistake"

Written by David Franz and Tina Dawn

Performed by David Franz and Tina Dawn

Recorded, mixed, and mastered at Underground Sun Studio by David Franz

For more information on Tina Dawn, visit www.tinadawn.com

Hip-hop

"Payback"

Written by David Franz and Reflekt

Performed by David Franz and Reflekt with samples from Fat Little Bastard

Recorded, mixed, and mastered at Underground Sun Studio by David Franz

For more information on Reflekt, visit www.gildaymonster.com

For more information on Underground Sun Studio and David Franz, check out www.undergroundsun.com and www.davidfranz.com

INTRODUCTION AND
THE BASICS OF PRODUCING

I'm a songwriter and performing musician at heart, but like many home studio recordists, I'm also an engineer and producer. Experience aside, I'm probably like you in many ways: We are musicians and students of life. We share the desire to create and learn. Moreover, we want to improve our musical creations.

Maybe you've just begun recording, or maybe you've been doing it for years. Either way, you've decided to take your music to the next level. You've invested in Pro Tools. Digidesign created Pro Tools LE, Pro Tools Free, Digi 002, Digi 001, Mbox, and ToolBox with home recordists in mind—they brought their professional, industry-standard software and hardware to the home market. With these products you can create incredibly high-quality recordings provided you have sufficient inspiration, drive, and expertise. Inspiration and drive are entirely up to you, but this book is a resource for developing the skills you need to create top-notch productions—to make sure your music shines.

You may already be proficient with Digidesign's software and hardware, or you may have just purchased it yesterday. Regardless of prior Pro Tools experience, this book can help. It was created for artists, songwriters, bands, and aspiring engineers and producers who want to better understand how to engineer and produce their own recordings using Pro Tools and Digidesign's home recording hardware.

As artists and/or songwriters, it may not be clear what specific functions engineers and producers perform in the creation of music (though you probably already perform many of these functions). For you, the delineation between one function and the next will disappear because you'll learn to do them all at the same time! But for the sake of clarity, here are some brief examples. . . .

What does an engineer do? In the realm of music, an audio engineer does everything from setting up microphones and pressing Record to mixing and mastering the final tracks of a song. An engineer's duties range from the completely mundane (like running mic cables across a room) to those of the utmost importance (like editing vocal takes to create a lead track with great energy and emotion). In this book I'll cover engineering topics such as creating and automating mixes, choosing and placing mics, using effects and plug-ins, editing audio files, and mastering—to name a few.

What does a music producer do? A producer is responsible for nothing less than everything in a project. This means a producer must play many roles. He or she has to facilitate the musical vision, arrange the songs, schedule the rehearsals, lead the studio sessions, and perform many, many other roles as described in The Basics of Producing segment later in this introduction and throughout the book.

As you can see, the roles and tasks of the engineer and producer are distinctly different from those of the artist or songwriter—but in most cases you can play all of these roles at any given moment in your musical lives. Knowing that, this book is meant to serve as an all-encompassing Pro Tools home studio self-production guide. The following chapters will demonstrate engineering techniques and production skills necessary to realize the full potential of your (or your client's) songwriting and artistry using Digidesign hardware and software.

This book has four sections: Getting Started with Pro Tools, Preproduction, Production, and Postproduction. The order of the sections outlines an effective process for bringing projects to completion. Within each chapter of a section, production and/or engineering techniques are explained, examples are given, and "doing it like the pros" tips are offered. Alongside the normal text, breakout boxes and sidebars highlight specific aspects of the chapter. The examples in each chapter appear in text form and some are on the included CD-ROM.

Also included on the CD-ROM are four production projects (Rock, Hip-hop, Jazz, and Electronica) that you can follow as you read the book. At the end of each chapter, these projects will illustrate production techniques covered in the chapter, as well as some additional production techniques specific for each musical genre. QuickTime movies accompany some of the chapter projects to further help you learn the techniques.

Chapter 1 takes you through setting up your Digidesign hardware and software with regard to your home studio equipment. You'll get started immediately with recording in Pro Tools in chapter 2. Chapter 3 goes deeper into recording audio, chapter 4 covers the tools and techniques of editing audio, and chapter 5 discusses recording and editing MIDI. In chapters 6 and 7, you'll delve deep into the details of what producers and engineers attend to during preproduction. Chapter 8 discusses expanding your studio with new gear and chapter 9 covers many of the ways to maximize the performance of your Pro Tools-driven computer. Chapters 10 and 11 go into detail about the roles that producers and engineers play during a recording session. The last two chapters cover mixing and mastering concepts and techniques.

I'll assume you're a novice producer and engineer — at least in the realm of recording using Pro Tools. I'll demonstrate how to use many of the features found in Pro Tools and show you ways to essentially use it as a musical instrument. This book, however, is not a Pro Tools manual. The folks at Digidesign have created thorough documentation for their hardware and software, and I will reference their manual from time to time. Instead, this book will mainly describe production and engineering techniques based on the Berklee College of Music curriculum, via Digidesign's home studio products.

Berklee College of Music is the world's largest independent music college and the premier institution for the study of contemporary music. Digidesign products have become the industry standard for audio professionals who produce material for music, multimedia, radio, and film.

Both Digidesign and Berklee realize that the music industry is changing. The home recording climate is booming and you're right in the thick of it! These days, people in home studios are producing a lot of great music that rivals music produced by major record labels in expensive professional facilities. And with the Internet providing a worldwide distribution network, you can send high-quality digital home recordings anywhere in the world. Is your music ready for this exposure? Are you ready to take your productions to the next level? Do you have the drive?

With Digidesign's audio products, Berklee's expertise, and your energy, you'll be ready for the music when the inspiration arrives.

THE BASICS OF PRODUCING

This segment provides a foundation for the rest of the book. It lays out the activities that a music producer goes through in the production process and provides a big picture view for any Pro Tools recording project.

Music producers at all levels, whether they're recording themselves in a home studio or producing a platinum-record-selling artist in a huge recording facility, have many responsibilities in common. But no matter what the scale of the project is, the producer is involved in three main stages of the record production process: preproduction, production, and postproduction.

Preproduction consists of all the activities that take place before a recording session. During preproduction, the producer meets with the artist and listens to their material. The producer and artist discuss identity, image, purpose, and sound. To help focus the project from recording through marketing and promotion, they must discern who will buy this artist's music. They then choose which songs to record. Some songs may be ready to record today, while others may need work. Knowing which ones are which will help set the schedule and budget for the project.

In many cases the bulk of real preproduction lies in the writing, rewriting, and arranging. A song arrangement consists of three main components: instrumentation, song form, and mood or attitude of the song. A big part of a producer's job is figuring out how to obtain a particular sound on a song or project, because the instrumentation significantly affects the mood or attitude of a song. Many times this means hiring an instrumentalist, vocalist, arranger, orchestrator, programmer, recording engineer, or mix engineer for their specific skill...as long as it's within the budget. The more skills you develop for yourself in any of these areas the more desirable you will be to potential clients because you will save them money... and potentially make more for yourself in the process. Be careful though—trying to do

The CD-ROM that came with this book has example Pro Tools session files with audio and QuickTime movies that demonstrate many of the techniques presented throughout the book. Use these examples to follow a Rock, Hip-hop, Jazz, and/or Electronica project from start to finish. The CD-ROM also includes session templates, worksheets, and Pro Tools software documentation as PDF files that you can print out and use while working on your productions.

things that aren't in your skill set might hurt the project more than help it, especially if your time could be better spent in other areas.

The producer determines how many rehearsals and sessions are necessary, as well as the schedules for the rehearsals, recording sessions, and mixing sessions. In most cases, the producer should be at all of the rehearsals and studio sessions. Rehearsals provide the perfect place to analyze all aspects of the songs, tweak them, and get them into final forms for the upcoming sessions. More time spent rehearsing pays big dividends when the Record button is pushed in the actual session.

The final step of preproduction for the producer is to do everything in their power to make sure the recording sessions go well. That means (a) calling the musicians to make sure they'll be at the session on time, (b) checking that you have the necessary equipment and that it's in good working order, (c) creating a plan so everyone knows what's going to happen, and (d) whatever else it takes for you to feel confident that the recording session will go off without a hitch.

Production refers to all of the elements involved in capturing performances during a recording session. This includes creating a comfortable studio atmosphere, focusing the artist's energy, evoking and capturing the best performances, recording the best sounds (for every instrument and every vocal), providing creative and practical input, listening critically to everything (analyzing both the fine details and the big picture), commending good performances, making difficult but firm decisions when something isn't working, and mediating differences of opinion.

Postproduction is anything done to the recorded performances after the session. The producer generally directs the mixing and mastering sessions, when the tracks from the recording session(s) are mixed together to create a final stereo or surround sound mix. Track levels are adjusted, stereo imaging (panning) is manipulated, and EQ and effects are added. Though the mix engineer certainly has some creative latitude, in most cases the producer directs the session and has the last word. The producer has to keep the original vision for the project in mind, and the sound of the mix should both reflect the artist's identity and be accessible by their potential demographic.

Mastering involves getting the final mixes ready for the CD master that's duplicated. This includes choosing song order, determining how much time there should be between tracks, making the volume of each track similar, and adding EQ and/or compression/limiting, among other things. Many professional producers aren't directly involved in the mastering process. They send the final mixes off to an experienced mastering engineer with trained ears and special, high-end mastering equipment. However, schedules and budgets might make this impractical in a home studio, so you'll probably play the role of mastering engineer in addition to everything else. If you have good ears, the right equipment, and an accurate monitoring environment, mastering your own recordings can be done well using Pro Tools!

Presenting the finished product is the moment of truth: The producer must deliver copies of the project to the artist. If working for a record company, he'll also deliver the final masters to the label. He may also oversee creating artwork or providing lyrics for the CD jacket.

There are many other important jobs producers perform that influence the final recordings:

- Negotiating contracts with the artist and/or record label

- Copyrighting the songs

- Developing and promoting the artist

- Building a solid team (finding a good manager, music publisher, accountant, and lawyer)

- Counseling and being supportive to the artist

PRODUCING YOUR OWN MUSIC

Even if you are not a professional producer, you should find many parallels from these duties to producing in your home studio. Many of the top professional producers use Pro Tools when making records, and they utilize the same techniques and procedures you'll use on your projects. Yet, not everyone aspires to produce big name artists. You may be happiest when you're producing your own music, not someone else's. Whether or not you perform the tasks listed above is entirely up to you. Nevertheless, being aware of (and practicing) them can help you avoid many problems and improve your productions.

This production process will be reinforced throughout the book, making this book useful for learning Pro Tools production techniques as well as developing your sense of how the techniques fit into the big picture of the production process.

Let's get to it....

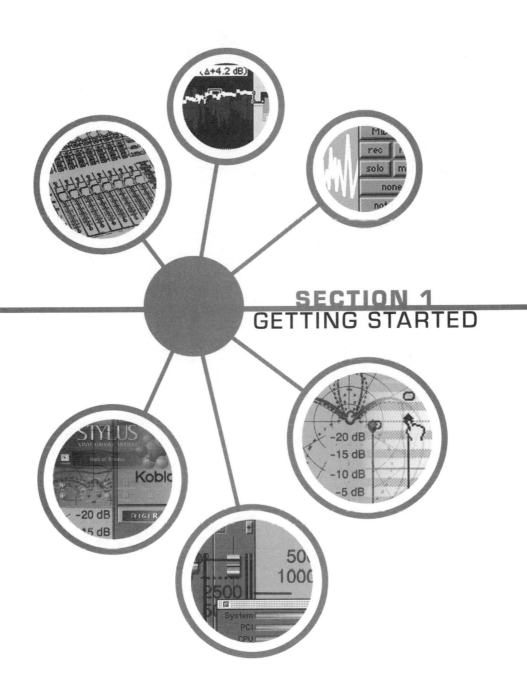

SECTION 1
GETTING STARTED

Setting Up Your Studio

In this chapter:

- **Documentation to read**
- **The Pro Tools interface**
- **Equipment setup**
- **The ins and outs of signal flow**
- **Smart speaker placement and acoustics**

Congratulations . . . you have Pro Tools! You're now a member of a rapidly expanding community of musicians around the world who use this state-of-the-art software to compose, record, and produce their music. This book was written to help you get the most out of Pro Tools, introduce the arts of digital recording and editing, and start you down the path towards better productions.

Chapter 1 will introduce you to the Pro Tools software interface and help you set up your home studio (including speaker placement and acoustical treatment).

If you have Pro Tools LE already installed on your computer, do not install Pro Tools Free. Pro Tools LE will not launch and will have to be re-installed to function properly.

LET'S GET STARTED...

If you haven't already, please read the Introduction section in this book as well as first few chapters in the *Quick Start/Getting Started Guide* that came with your Digidesign product. The introduction lays the groundwork for learning using this book and the guide will help you to correctly configure your computer, install the Pro Tools software, and connect your Digidesign hardware.

If you don't have Pro Tools, you can download a free version from Digidesign's Web site for either Mac or PC. Visit **www.digidesign.com** and click on Pro Tools Free. Be sure to check that it is compatible with your computer and operating system.

Throughout the rest of the book, unless specifically noted I'll refer to Pro Tools LE (both 6.X and 5.X versions) and Pro Tools Free simply as Pro Tools because most techniques described in this book apply to all versions of Pro Tools. Also, many directions in this book apply specifically to both Digi 002 and Digi 001, so I will often collectively refer to those pieces of equipment as 002/001.

PRO TOOLS SOFTWARE

What is Pro Tools?

Pro Tools is a software application that enables digital audio and MIDI recording, editing, and mixing on your personal computer. It utilizes **non-linear** hard disk recording and **non-destructive** digital editing to help you create your musical masterpieces, with the help of another program called DAE.

Non-linear recording means your audio files are recorded and stored in chunks on your hard drive and not linearly as they would be recorded on tape. **Non-destructive editing** means that any cutting, pasting, trimming, separating, or clearing of audio data occurs virtually... the source audio files are not harmed in any way. Pro Tools only performs editing functions on a map of the actual audio data, never touching the recorded source data.

What is DAE?

When you launch the Pro Tools software, another application called DAE (Digidesign Audio Engine) also launches in the background. (In Pro Tools 5.3 and above, DAE is actually built into Pro Tools itself.) This program is an additional operating system that enables advanced digital recording. Pro Tools and DAE run simultaneously to provide hard disk recording, digital signal processing and mixing, and MIDI functionality.

If you've never used Pro Tools before, the Pro Tools interface may seem a bit daunting. However, it will soon become second nature to you. Here are some of the basic terms and elements you'll use in Pro Tools.

Sessions

Every time you launch Pro Tools, you can create a new session or open a pre-existing session. A Pro Tools session is much like a word processing file...it's a document that contains information. A Pro Tools session contains maps of all the data associated with a project, including audio files, MIDI data, edit and mix information, as well as comments and titles. You can only have one session open at a time, but as you work you can save multiple versions of the session for backups and for trying new ideas. The user interface of a Pro Tools session consists of two separate screens called the Edit and Mix windows.

The Edit and Mix Windows

The Edit window displays audio waveforms, MIDI data, timeline information, and all of the tools for editing the waveforms and data. All other pertinent track data (volume, panning, solo, mute, blocks, and automation data) can also be viewed in this window. Almost all editing tasks are performed in this window.

The Mix window is designed like a mixing console. Its primary function is for mixing multiple tracks down to a stereo (2-track) mix. There are vertical channel strips for each track, with sections for inserts, sends, input/output routing, and volume faders, as well as automation, pan, solo, and mute controls.

■ Fig. 1.1.
Pro Tools Edit Window

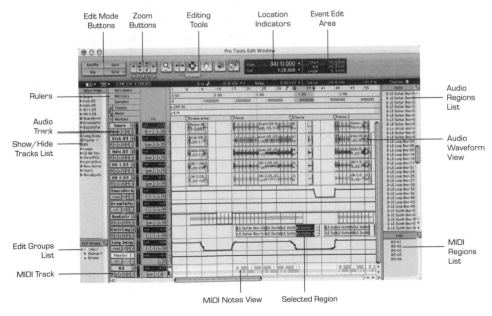

Fig. 1.2.
Pro Tools Mix Window

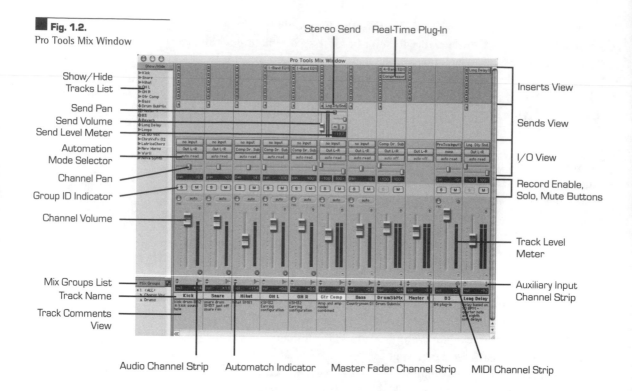

Stereo Send   Real-Time Plug-In

Show/Hide
Tracks List

Send Pan
Send Volume
Send Level Meter
Automation
Mode Selector

Channel Pan

Group ID Indicator

Channel Volume

Mix Groups List
Track Name

Track Comments
View

Inserts View

Sends View

I/O View

Record Enable,
Solo, Mute Buttons

Track Level
Meter

Auxiliary Input
Channel Strip

Audio Channel Strip   Automatch Indicator   Master Fader Channel Strip   MIDI Channel Strip

The Transport Window

The Transport window has controls like those on a cassette player or analog tape machine and is used to play, stop, record, fast-forward, and rewind your recorded material, as well as some more advanced functions. You can use the buttons in this window to control playback, recording, and navigation in Pro Tools.

To view any of these windows, select the window name from the appropriately titled Windows menu at the top of your Pro Tools screen.

In the following chapters, we'll cover many of the important features and functions found in these Pro Tools windows while keeping a broad perspective on the concepts and realities of producing music in your home studio.

Fig. 1.3.
Pro Tools Transport Window

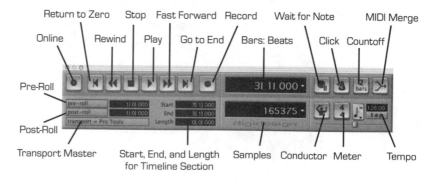

Return to Zero   Stop   Fast Forward   Record   Wait for Note   MIDI Merge

Online   Rewind   Play   Go to End   Bars: Beats   Click   Countoff

Pre-Roll

Post-Roll

Transport Master   Start, End, and Length   Samples   Conductor   Meter   Tempo
for Timeline Section

CONNECTING YOUR STUDIO

After you have connected your Digidesign hardware and you've installed your Pro Tools software, what's the next step? Plug in the rest of your gear, of course! Some of you may have just a microphone and a MIDI keyboard. Others may have a small rack of gear and a couple of instruments. Those who are blessed have racks and racks of gear and many acoustic, electric, and MIDI instruments. For those in the last category this chapter may be of help — but also consult chapter 8, "Advanced Studio Setup," for more information on larger rigs.

The Basic Setup

- 002/001/Mbox, keyboard and/or guitar, mic, computer, home stereo
- Audiomedia III card, keyboard and/or guitar, mic, computer, home stereo, mic pre-amplifier or small mixer

Because Pro Tools software has advanced mixing capabilities and the Digi 002/001 have many inputs and outputs, you really don't need an outboard (external) mixer to use Digi 002/001, though there may be benefits depending on how you like to work. You can also use the Mbox, ToolBox, or Pro Tools Free without an outboard mixer. See the discussion on inputs and outputs later in this chapter.

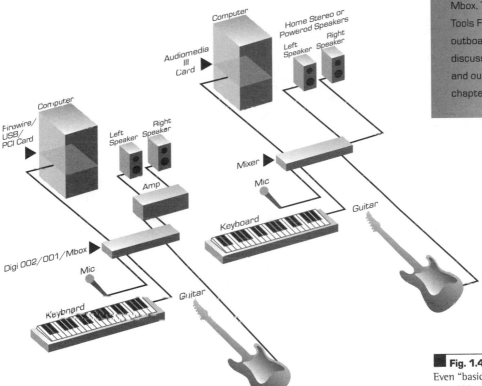

Fig. 1.4.
Even "basic" setups can be incredibly powerful in tandem with digital recording tools.

If you're using home stereo speakers as studio monitors, I recommend connecting the monitor outputs from Digi 001, the RCA outputs from Digi 002, the TRS line outputs from your Mbox, or the RCA outputs from your Audiomedia III card to your home stereo amplifier on an open line-in jack. For example, I've connected my 001 monitor outs to the VCR input on my stereo amp so I can still listen to my CD, tape, and record players without having to reconnect them. The Vol knob on the front of Digi 001 controls the monitor volume to your stereo. Set the level of this knob close to the output of your CD or tape player, so if you switch between devices the levels will be matched and you won't get any ear-splitting surprises.

Most home stereos use RCA connectors, however Digi 001/Mbox has 1/4" outputs. This means you'll need to buy a pair of 1/4"-to-RCA adapters (or cables) to monitor your 001/Mbox through your home speakers. These adapters are available at most audio dealers. Digi 002 and ToolBox XP have stereo RCA outputs so you don't need an adapter. A stereo RCA cable will do for this purpose.

Using your home stereo for monitoring can work very well, but watch out if you apply a lot of equalization. You may have a graphic EQ built into your amplifier, or even a stand-alone unit. You might consider flattening the settings (by positioning the EQ levels to 0dB boost/cut) to hear exactly what your mix sounds like on nonequalized systems. Also, home stereos often have preset EQ settings for increased low- and high-end response. In fact, some systems have settings that make your music sound like it's coming from a different ambient space (e.g., a jazz hall or sports arena). I recommend turning off all of these features (bass boost, surround, and EQ presets) and setting everything to normal. This will ensure that you're listening to an accurate representation of your music — the way it really sounds in Pro Tools.

Fig. 1.5.
If there's a graphic EQ in your monitoring chain, you'll probably want to "zero" all of the settings while recording and mixing.

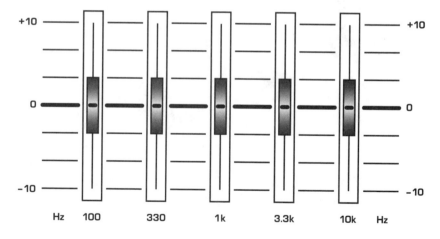

To use a microphone, electric guitar, or any other instrument that has a magnetic pickup, plug the XLR or 1/4" cable into a mic/line input on Digi 002/001/Mbox. To plug these devices into the Audiomedia III card, you'll need a piece of gear that has a mic preamplifier (or "preamp"), such as a mixer. A **preamplifier** boosts the mic signal to *line level*, the required level that the inputs to the Audiomedia III card can accept.

Line-level instruments with 1/4" cables (e.g., keyboards, preamps, and mixer outputs) can be plugged directly into any of the inputs on Digi 002/001/Mbox. All of these inputs can be used with balanced or unbalanced cables. However, because the Audiomedia III card has RCA inputs, 1/4"-to-RCA converters should be used for direct inputs to the card. Otherwise, you can run line-level instruments into a mixer that has RCA outputs connected to the Audiomedia III card.

In addition, every Digidesign home studio product has digital 2-channel S/PDIF inputs, and Digi 002/001 also has an 8-channel optical (also referred to as "lightpipe") input. Advanced studio setups (including digital inputs and outputs) are discussed further in chapter 8.

OH YEAH? WHAT'S IN **YOUR** STUDIO?

My current studio can be described as a mid-level setup—falling somewhere between the basic setup described previously and a fully decked-out system. I have a Mackie 16-channel mixer (1604-VLZ Pro), Mackie HR824 monitors, a Line 6 Guitar Pod Pro, a Line 6 Bass Pod Pro, a General MIDI keyboard (Yamaha PSR-410), a small MIDI sound module (Roland JV 1010), a home stereo system with several pairs of speakers, a Macintosh G4 computer (500MHz and 768 megs of RAM), a PreSonus Digimax, a headphone amplifier, and several pairs of headphones. I also have numerous Shure microphones, a Line 6 Flextone II XL guitar amp, an acoustic drum set, an electric guitar, an acoustic guitar, and an electric bass. (Information about Shure, Mackie, PreSonus, and Line 6 and their products is included in appendix D.)

Self-powered monitors (like the Mackie HR824s) have amplifiers built into them, thus you don't need to run them through an amplifier as you would for your home stereo speakers. You can connect self-powered monitors directly to the outputs of your Digidesign home studio product, or to an outboard mixer. Even if you're using self-powered monitors, I suggest also connecting Digi 002/001/Mbox to your home stereo. This way you can listen to your mixes through at least two different sets of speakers for comparison. In my home studio, I have a set of Mackie powered monitors (HR824s), a set of Fisher home stereo speakers, and a set of Sony boombox speakers. With the flip of a button or two, I can switch between sets of speakers, making it easier to create a mix that sounds good on multiple systems. (More information on the importance of using several sets of speakers for mixing can be found in chapter 12.)

To set up your studio like this, connect your home stereo to the monitor outputs of Digi 002/001 and your mixer to the main outputs of Digi 002/001. For the Mbox, you can connect your mixer, amplifier, or self-powered monitors to the line outputs and your home stereo to one of the headphone outputs. If your home stereo amp has speaker A and B outputs, connect a different set of speakers to each of the stereo amp outputs. If not, your mixer may have several stereo output options. My Mackie 1604-VLZ Pro has main outs, tape outs, submix outs, control room outs, direct outs, and a mono output, all of which can send audio to other sets of speakers if configured correctly.

This setup enables me to easily switch between my powered Mackie monitors and two different sets of home speakers. How? When you press the Monitor Mode switch on Digi 001, this stops the stereo signal from reaching the monitor outs (to my home stereo), but allows it to pass through the main outputs. The main outs (connected to two channels on the mixer) pass signal to the powered speakers. Muting those channels on the mixer and unpressing the Monitor Mode switch swaps the sound output back to my home stereo, which can also switch between two sets of speakers. So in total, I can hear my audio on three different pairs of speakers. (For stereo mixing, make sure you're only listening to one pair of speakers at a time!)

Fig. 1.6.

The Digi 001 provides flexible speaker connectivity. Here, the monitor outs are connected directly to a home stereo and the main outs are connected to two inputs on the mixer, allowing you to monitor using two different sets of speakers.

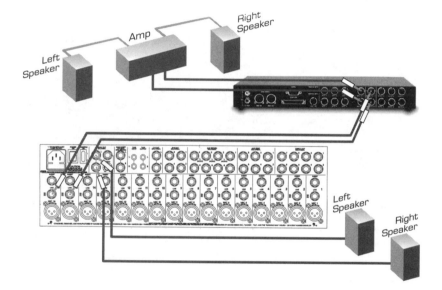

If you want to record more than two microphones at once with Digi 001 (or four with Digi 002) you'll need additional preamps – the outputs of the preamps can be patched to the line inputs of Digi 002/001. If you want to record more than eight mics or instruments at once and you can't access the other 002/001 inputs (S/PDIF and optical inputs, discussed in chapter 8), you'll have to set up a submix of the inputs in your mixer (because there are only eight analog inputs on Digi 002/001). A **submix** combines multiple signals and allows you to use fewer input tracks. For example, if you're recording a guitar amp with three different mics, you can combine the three mic inputs to one output on the mixer and send that submix to just one track in Pro Tools. Consult chapters 9 and 11 for more detailed explanations of submixing.

MIDI SETUPS WITH YOUR DIGIDESIGN GEAR

Setting up MIDI instruments can be confusing, but Digi 001 makes connections simple with a one-in/out MIDI interface. If you have a MIDI device, simply connect the MIDI out of your device to the MIDI in of Digi 001 and the MIDI in of your device to the MIDI out of Digi 001. Digi 002 has a one-in/two out interface that allows you to hook up one MIDI controller as the input to operate two MIDI sound modules through the two MIDI out ports. If you have several MIDI devices, you can build a daisy-chain MIDI setup (as discussed in chapter 5) or you'll need some sort of MIDI interface to connect and route your MIDI data. The MIDI interface will connect to your computer through a port (e.g., parallel, serial, USB, etc.); it does not connect to Digi 002/001. To use MIDI with the Mbox or AudioMedia III card, you also need a MIDI interface.

Information on the basics of MIDI, setting up your own MIDI network, and setting up Pro Tools for MIDI is provided in chapter 5, and chapter 8 explains MIDI interface connections.

SEPARATE LIVES — PARTITIONING YOUR HARD DRIVE

If you're just getting started with a new computer and don't have an external hard drive for audio, it's a good idea to create two (or more) hard drives from your one existing internal drive. This is called **partitioning** your hard drive, and is done to separate audio files from all of your other files (system software, applications, documents, etc.) so that it's easier to locate them — not only for you, but also for the computer. If a computer has to look all over the place for different files, jumping back and forth between areas on one hard disk, it will slow down and the audio playback and recording performance may suffer. For example, separate a 40GB internal drive into a 10GB drive (for applications, documents, etc.) and a dedicated 30GB drive for audio. Partitions are useful for external drives as well. For instance, consider partitioning a 120GB external drive into four partitions of 30GB to improve hard drive performance and project organization. Consult your computer's manual to learn more about partitions.

INPUTS AND OUTPUTS

How you approach the signal flow in, out, and through your Pro Tools software is integral to your studio setup. The internal signal routing in Pro Tools software is very flexible, and the number of choices far outnumber what's available in outboard mixers. A **signal path** is the way you route audio or MIDI signals through Pro Tools and your gear.

Outboard mixers usually have hard-wired signal paths used specifically for one of the following functions: inputs/outputs, sends, inserts, and/or auxiliary routing. In Pro Tools software, outputs can be used for all of these signal paths; they can be assigned to feed aux inputs, send inputs, busses (a **bus** carries several signals on one path), other software inputs, and outboard hardware inputs. You can essentially route any signal anywhere and – if you're not using outboard gear – you won't need any patch cords to do it! You can label, format, and map all Pro Tools inputs, outputs, inserts, and busses to your liking and then save the entire configuration with your session – it's a total recall system. That means you can always pick up right where you left off with a session, even if you don't work on it for months.

The I/O Setup dialog is where you create the routing for your signal paths by assigning track inputs, outputs, inserts, sends, and plug-ins. It can be found by choosing I/O Setup from the Setups menu.

Fig. 1.7.
The I/O Setup dialog for the Digi 001. Notice that inputs 3 and 4 are carrying a stereo signal, but can also be split off as individual mono sub-paths.

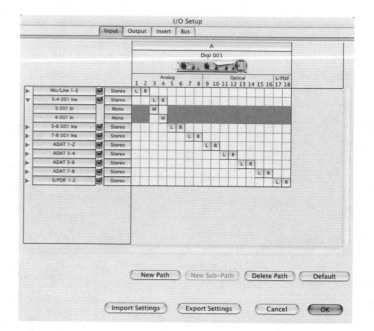

Audio signals are routed internally in Pro Tools on **paths**. *Main paths* are groupings of inputs, outputs, inserts, or busses and are most often stereo pairs. *Sub-paths* are the components of the group from the main path. For example, inputs 3 and 4 ("3–4 001 Ins," as seen in figure 1.7) are connected to the left and right outputs from a synthesizer; "3–4 001 Ins" represents a main path (stereo), while the individual "3 001 In" and "4 001 In" are mono sub-paths of the main path.

You can customize Pro Tools signal paths in the I/O Setup and save them to match your studio configuration. (Notice how I've labeled the inputs for my home studio Pro Tools setup in figure 1.7.) To save an I/O setup, select Export Settings from the I/O Setup dialog and name the I/O Settings file. You can then import these settings to other sessions by choosing Import Settings in the I/O Setups dialog or by selecting the I/O Settings file in the session parameters when creating a new session. More information on routing is presented later in this book.

As you can see, Pro Tools software has a flexible mixer. But if you still want to use an outboard mixer you can do so (if using the Digi 001) by assigning all of your tracks to outputs 1–8 and connecting those outputs to eight inputs of your mixer. Or you can keep the audio inside Pro Tools, but use MIDI control surfaces to get that "hands-on" feel (more on this in chapter 8). Even cooler, Digi 002 itself is a mixer. You can assign any tracks and/or parameter controls to any of its faders and pots to control the software mixer entirely with your hands.

GAIN STAGES

It is important for you to understand the gain stages in your equipment. A **gain stage** is any amplifier (or attenuator) that boosts (or cuts) the level of an audio signal. On Digi 002/001/Mbox there's one input gain stage: the Gain knobs for inputs 1 and 2 (plus 3 and 4 for Digi 002). However, the Input Gain window in Pro Tools (shown in figure 1.8) controls the gain for the other line inputs. To open this window, select Hardware under the Setups menu. Adjust the controls as necessary to get high enough levels into Pro Tools. (See chapter 2 for details on getting good recording levels.) Again, because Pro Tools is a total recall mixer, these settings — and all other internal Pro Tools gain stages such as fader levels — are saved with every session.

Always be aware of the signal path! If you find your input levels are too high or low, check every point in the path and adjust the mixer and software settings to achieve optimal levels. (Consult your mixer manual for assistance in proper gain staging.)

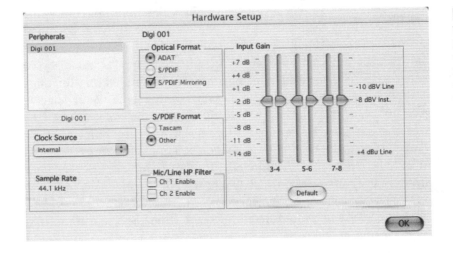

Fig. 1.8.
Digi 001's Hardware Setup (Input Gain) is used to control the input gain for channels 3–8. If you're using the Audiomedia III card, Digi 002, or Mbox, the window's a bit different.

If you have an outboard mixer it's important to understand the gain stages on it, too. A mixer will have a preamp gain control (usually a rotary knob located near the input area) and a mixer channel gain control (usually a vertical fader located at the bottom of each channel's input/output module). Additionally, a mixer has a master fader and possibly some submix, auxiliary, and control room gain controls. Depending on how you set your mixer to interface with your 002, 001, Mbox, or Audiomedia card, you may use some or all of these gain stages.

SETTING UP YOUR LISTENING ENVIRONMENT

When setting up your home studio, one of the most important things to consider is where to place your monitors (i.e., speakers). Whether you'll be listening through one pair of speakers, switching between multiple pairs, or using a surround sound setup, there are some accepted configurations.

SURROUND MIXING USING THE DIGI 002/001

Although Pro Tools LE does not officially support surround sound panning, you can still set up a surround speaker system using Digi 002/001 to create surround sound mixes. The only thing you really can't do is some of the crazy panning available in Pro Tools|HD and Mix systems. Information on surround configurations is presented later in the chapter and in the *Pro Tools Reference Guide*, and information on surround mixing using Digi 002/001 is presented in chapter 12.

Standard Stereo Systems

When listening to two speakers, your goal is to hear the optimal stereo image. Also called the **phantom image**, this occurs in the middle of two speakers placed at equal height from the floor. To hear the phantom image your head should be on the **median plane**, an imaginary line equidistant from each speaker (see figure 1.9). Ideally your head and the two speakers should form an equilateral triangle — the distance between you and each speaker is the same, and equal to the distance between the two speakers. This ensures that you're hearing the most accurate stereo image from your speakers. In this setup you'll perceive the sound coming from the area directly between the two speakers. (The way I have my studio set up, it often seems like the sound from my speakers is actually coming from my computer monitor, which is placed directly between them.) Additionally, if at all possible try to keep your speakers away from walls, which (along with the floor and ceiling) have a tendency to magnify bass frequencies.

The reason you should be equidistant from the speakers is that you want the sound from each speaker to reach your ears at exactly the same time, or you may experience the precedence effect. The **precedence effect** (or Haas effect) occurs when the listener is off the median plane (by as little as six inches). It shifts the phantom image toward the speaker closest to the listener. As a result, the sound from the closer speaker arrives at the listener's ear first, which may fool them into thinking it's louder. If you're basing a mix on this kind of false imaging, you may have to redo the entire thing!

To create the proper listening setup I recommend using a tape measure to accurately position your speakers. First sit down where you'll normally be listening in your studio, then use the tape measure to approximate an equal distance from your head or chest to a spot on your left and right sides where your speakers could be placed. A good distance is 3–4 feet, which is the same distance the speakers should be apart from each other.

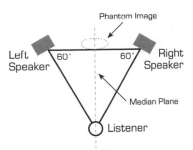

Fig. 1.9.
Properly placed stereo monitors should form an equilateral triangle with the listener.

In fact, the closer you are to your speakers, the less the room acoustics will color the sound. (This is called **near-field monitoring**, and is the most common approach for mixing.)

Next place your speakers at equal height from the floor in your approximated positions. If possible, the speaker height should correspond to your sitting height (or at least be pointed to that height). Angle the speakers at approximately 60 degrees toward the median plane. Finally, sit down again, use the tape measure, and precisely position the speakers to achieve the equilateral triangle setup. Now listen to some music and find out if you hear the phantom image. Try moving back and forth along the median plane and moving your head side-to-side. Can you hear the difference?

If you think you've placed your speakers correctly but still don't hear the phantom image, your speakers may be out of phase. Fortunately, this is an easy fix. If you're running speakers through an amplifier with positive (+) and negative (–) connections, make sure your speaker wire is attached correctly; that is, negative connector on the amp to negative connector on the speaker, and positive to positive. If this doesn't fix the problem, your speaker cables could be wired out-of-phase so try different ones. Correctly connecting your speakers with properly wired cables should eliminate speaker phase problems.

Surround Sound Systems

Unlike stereo (two-speaker systems), surround sound systems consist of five or more speakers. However, some of the same principles from two-speaker stereo apply. For instance, all speakers should be equidistant from the listener. (The subwoofer is an exception to this; see explanation below.) There's also a median plane and a phantom image in a surround sound system; the amount of musical material presented in the front and back speakers can move the phantom image along the median plane.

Most surround sound systems include a subwoofer, though there's no subwoofer shown in figure 1.10. Because of their low frequency, bass audio signals are difficult to localize spatially so precise placement of the subwoofer typically does not affect the phantom image. In most surround sound setups, however, the subwoofer is placed on the floor beneath and between the center and one of the front speakers.

There are many surround sound formats with different speaker placements and track layouts discussed in the *Pro Tools Reference Guide*. Although Pro Tools LE does not support true multi-channel mixing, there are other cool ways to mix for surround systems using Digi 002/001, covered in chapter 12.

Fig. 1.10.

A 5.1 surround speaker configuration (without the subwoofer, which is what the ".1" stands for). In this configuration, notice the back speakers are approximately 70 degrees off the median plane.

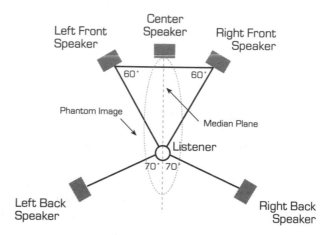

THE ACOUSTIC TREATMENT

Once your equipment and speakers are set up, you should consider the acoustical treatment of your room(s). Every room has its own sound, which has to do with its shape, the materials on the walls, floor, and ceiling, and the objects in the space. Each of these factors affects the way sound waves travel and how they're reflected or absorbed. For example, tiled bathrooms sound more "live" (i.e., they have more sound reflections, or reverb) than "dead" bedrooms with absorptive curtains and carpeting.

When setting up your studio, test the room where you'll record and listen to your tracks for the room's acoustical properties. Snap your fingers and talk aloud in different areas (you might want to make sure nobody's around when you do this). Listen for strange flutter echoes in those spots, and play some of your favorite music to listen for any frequency boosts/cuts in different areas (e.g., bass boosts in the corners). Finally, listen for noise within the studio, such as computer fans and hard drives, and for outside noise such as traffic or neighbors.

There are many things you can do to "treat" problems found while conducting your listening tests. Put diffusers, bass traps, or specially designed absorptive materials (like Auralex Studiofoam) in spots that have unwanted frequency boosts/cuts or echoes. These also help soundproof your room, to keep sound from both coming in and getting out. Also place absorptive materials (a) on hard surfaces to deaden the room and (b) around anything that's noisy. Do everything you can to isolate your studio from outside noise, like double-paning or covering windows and sealing door jambs. Finally, you can remove or add objects in your room (such as furniture) to change its overall sound. Heck, sometimes just throwing a blanket or hanging a tapestry on a reflecting surface can have serious acoustical benefits.

In most home studios it's best to create a "dead" environment for recording and listening. That way you have control over the sounds you record because you can always *add* "liveness" by inserting effects (reverb, delay, etc.), but it's hard to remove too much from an already recorded track.

Okay. Your gear is set up and plugged in, your speakers are placed properly, and your room is acoustically treated. . . . Your studio is ready for action. Let's jump into making music with Pro Tools! ▋▋

PRO TOOLS HANDS-ON

In every chapter of the book, I'll present projects that explore the techniques explained in that chapter. Let's get started with some general projects.

Install, Register, and Configure

- Install Pro Tools
- Register with Digidesign (if using Pro Tools LE hardware and software)
- Configure your computer's operating system the way Digidesign recommends

Set Up Your Studio Listening Environment

Once your hardware and software is working, test your studio setup and listening environment by opening up and playing one of the sample Pro Tools sessions provided by Digidesign. Sample sessions are included on the CD that came with your Digi gear as well as on the CD that came with this book. As covered in this chapter, accurately measure the distance between your speakers and listening position. Be sure your speakers are placed so that you can hear accurate stereo images. If something sounds funny, you may have a phasing problem. Try fixing the problem using the solutions presented in the chapter. If the output signal is noisy, you may have noisy gear and/or cables, or you may need to tweak your gain stages.

Test Gain Stages and I/O

Now test your gain stages. Start with the outputs. Follow the signal path starting from the output level in Pro Tools (check the Master Fader track) all the way to the speakers. Adjust any gain stages along the way to optimize the signal. This often means putting all volume faders/knobs at "0" and adjusting the last gain stage in the chain as your final volume control.

Next test your inputs. Plug an instrument or microphone into the first input of your signal path (e.g., input 1 of the 002/001/Mbox or channel 1 of your mixer/mic preamp). If using external mic pres or a mixer, route its output signal into an input on your Pro Tools hardware or sound card. With the sample Pro Tools session still open, assign the first audio track's input to the input where you've plugged in your instrument or mic, as in the figure below.

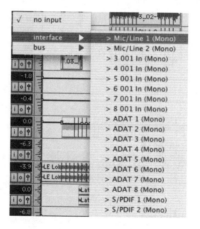

Record-enable the track by pressing the Record button on that track and check for an input signal. Follow the signal path from the instrument to the mic and examine the levels on all gain stages along the way. Tweak the gain stages so that you can get a good recording level into Pro Tools without a lot of noise and without distorting any part of the input chain. Do this every time you insert a new piece of gear into the signal path because the gain structure will change. That way, you'll always be sure to get the highest quality signal into Pro Tools.

Create an I/O Settings File

If you've already set up all of your gear, make a customized I/O Settings document. While still in the sample Pro Tools session, choose I/O Setup from the Setups menu. As described in the Inputs and Outputs section of this chapter, label inputs, outputs, inserts, and busses the way you want and save the I/O setup by choosing Export Settings. Anytime you create a new session, you can import this setup (or make it the default setup in a session template – see chapter 3) so that your I/O is always labeled correctly. Make an I/O Settings file now, even if it's basic. You can always edit it or make a new one later if your setup changes.

When you're done with all of this, close the sample Pro Tools session by choosing Close from the File menu, or pressing Shift + Control + W (Win) or Shift + ⌘ + W (Mac).

Now you're ready to start recording your own music.

Recording a New Idea

In this chapter:

- **Recording an idea**

- **Regions, record modes, and edit modes**

- **Punching and monitor modes**

- **Recording to playlists**

- **Recording with a click track**

If you're anything like me, when you come up with a new musical idea you want to record it right away. My memory is good, but trying to remember that cool lick I played last night can be quite difficult. And even if I remember it, many times I can't recreate the original feel even a day or two later. Capturing that fresh idea is the first step in the preproduction process for songwriting. Let's learn how to record that idea . . .

RECORDING A SONG IDEA

Here are the basic steps to setting up a new Pro Tools session and recording an audio track.

1. After launching Pro Tools, select New Session from the File menu, name the session, and select the session parameters. (More information on session parameters is presented in the next chapter.)

Fig. 2.1.
In the New Session dialog box, you can choose the session's title and location, as well as its audio file type, sample rate, bit depth, I/O settings, and whether it's compatible with both Mac and PC Pro Tools systems.

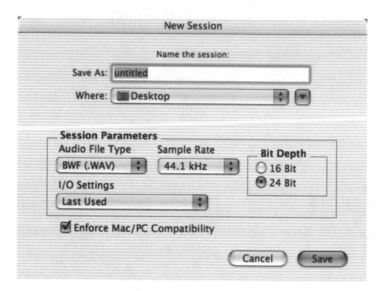

2. Create an audio track by selecting New Track from the File menu or by typing Shift + Ctrl + N (Win) or Shift + ⌘ + N (Mac).

Fig. 2.2.
The New Track dialog box allows you to create mono or stereo audio tracks, aux inputs, and master faders, as well as MIDI tracks.

3. Select the input source that your instrument or microphone is plugged into, as in figure 2.3.

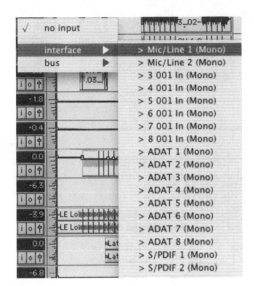

■ **Fig. 2.3.**
The input selector is used to assign which 001 input will be routed to the track.

4. Record-enable the track by pressing Record (figure 2.4).

5. Set the input level.

   a. To set recording levels in Pro Tools using Digi 002/001/Mbox:

      • Adjust the Gain knob for the mic line input on your Digi gear, or

      • For other line inputs, adjust the fader in the Input Gain section of Pro Tools. Do this by choosing Hardware from the Setups menu.

   b. To set recording levels in Pro Tools using the Toolbox:

      • Adjust the **trim** (also called line trim, mic trim, mic gain, etc.) on your external mixer or standalone mic preamp to get a good level into your Audiomedia III card, and

      • Adjust the faders in the Input Gain section of Pro Tools. Do this by choosing Hardware from the Setups menu.

6. Record your idea by clicking the Record and Play buttons in the Transport window. Click the square Stop button when you're done.

■ **Fig. 2.4.**
Press the Record-Enable button to "arm" the track.

■ **Fig. 2.5.**
With your track record-enabled, hit the Record button first and it will blink red, then hit Play. Pro Tools will start recording (the Record button will stop blinking).

You can record while looking at the Edit window or the Mix window. Both have their advantages. The Edit window shows the waveforms as they are being recorded. The Mix window allows you to see all (or many) input levels at once. To quickly switch between the Edit and Mix windows, press Ctrl + = (Win) or ⌘ + = (Mac). Perform this keyboard shortcut by pressing and holding down Ctrl or ⌘ while pressing the = key.

Try to think of Pro Tools not just as a computer interface, but as a creative tool or even an instrument — my suggestion is to plug in and be ready to record every time you play or practice. If this causes too much pressure to play something good, don't plug in but at least make it easy to do so later. You should be ready to record quickly if inspiration strikes.

Whether working on your music or someone else's, you probably won't be satisfied recording just one track at a time into Pro Tools. One of the most powerful (and fun) parts of using Pro Tools is taking advantage of its powerful multi-track recording capabilities to record multiple musicians at one time.

With the Audiomedia III card you can record four tracks simultaneously using its two analog and two S/PDIF inputs, while the Mbox allows you to record two tracks at the same time using either its two analog or two S/PDIF inputs. With Digi 002 and Digi 001 you can record up to 18 tracks at a time using eight analog inputs, eight optical (lightpipe) inputs, and two S/PDIF inputs. And once you have the raw tracks, you can combine and edit them in just about any way imaginable.

I've done recording projects where I've maxed out all of the inputs into every piece of Digidesign gear to see if my computer, Digidesign's hardware and software, and additional hardware could handle the load. To my delight everything worked fine (see chapter 8 for more about advanced setups). But before you max out your Pro Tools system, let's cover some basic Pro Tools recording concepts.

Fig. 2.6.
The Audio and MIDI Regions lists are usually visible on the right side of your Edit Window, unless they've been hidden by clicking the double arrow button on the bottom right corner. To unhide these lists, click the double arrow button.

REGIONS

Pro Tools calls each recorded portion of a track a **region.** Every time you record, Pro Tools creates a new region on each record-enabled track. New regions are also created when you edit tracks by cutting and pasting, resizing, separating, and recapturing existing regions. Each region name appears in the Audio Regions list (for audio tracks) or the MIDI Regions list (for, you guessed it, MIDI tracks), as in figure 2.6.

You can drag regions from these lists onto tracks and arrange them in any order. You can also audition an audio region (listen to it) by Option-clicking (Mac) or Alt-clicking (Win) on the region name in the Audio Regions List.

There are several types of regions that you'll work with in Pro Tools: Whole-File Audio regions, User-Defined regions, Auto-Created regions, Offline regions, and Multi-Channel regions.

Whole-File Audio regions are created when you record or import an audio track, as well as when you consolidate existing regions or process a region with an AudioSuite plug-in. They reference an entire audio file on your hard drive and are displayed in bold on the Audio Regions list.

User-Defined regions are created when you specifically name a region, such as when you (a) record or import a pre-named region, (b) capture, separate, or consolidate a selection, (c) trim a whole-file audio region, or (d) rename an existing region.

Auto-Created regions are created when Pro Tools automatically makes new regions, such as when loop recording, punch recording, and editing.

Offline regions are regions that cannot be located or are unavailable when opening a session or importing a track. They are displayed in italics and are dimmed in the Audio Regions List and appear in playlists as light blue regions with italicized names. Despite being "offline," these regions can still be edited, yet they cannot be processed with AudioSuite plug-ins.

Multi-Channel regions reference multiple regions and audio files for stereo or surround tracks. They are displayed as a single region name in the Audio Regions List and can be expanded (by clicking the triangle next to their name) to see the individual channels. Each region can be dragged independently to a track. These regions are only present in Pro Tools 5.1 and above.

RECORD MODES

Once you've recorded some initial tracks you might want to fix a few things. There are many ways to capture alternate takes or record over mistakes in Pro Tools:

- Record on an entirely new track.

- Record destructively or non-destructively over an existing track.

- Try another take (or re-record a section) on a different playlist.

- Use loop record to record several takes one after another.

- Punch in and out at certain times.

I'll cover all of these techniques in this section.

■ **Fig. 2.7.**
The record modes, clockwise,
from top to bottom left:
Non-Destructive, Destructive,
Loop, QuickPunch.

There are four record modes: Non-Destructive, Destructive, Loop, and QuickPunch. The current record mode is indicated by the Record button icon in the Transport window (see fig. 2.7). By Control-clicking (Mac) or right-clicking (Win) the Record button in the Transport window, you can change between record modes. You should familiarize yourself with all of these modes, because you'll probably use each one sooner or later.

Non-Destructive Record Mode

You'll typically record in Non-Destructive mode. In this mode you can record a new audio file over an existing region on a track, but both the new and old regions are saved. Any region can be used simply by selecting it from the Audio Regions list and dragging it into a track. For example, if you like the fifth take of the stereo guitar solo better than the sixth take, select and drag take 5 of the "Gtr Solo" region to the "Gtr Solo" track. (To highlight two regions at once, select one region and Shift-click the second region.)

■ **Fig. 2.8.**
The full Transport window in
Non-Destructive Record-Ready
mode.

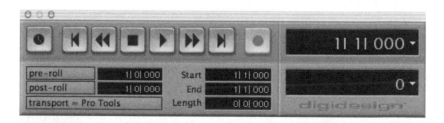

■ **Fig. 2.9.**
Non-destructive recording
makes it easy to keep multiple
takes and choose the best one
later. Here we're going to drag
the fifth take of the guitar
solo from the Audio Regions
list to the solo guitar track.

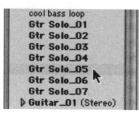

PLACING REGIONS IN TRACKS

Regions are placed according to the current edit mode:

Shuffle	Spot
Slip	Grid

- In Shuffle mode existing track regions are slid as necessary to make room for the new region.
- In Spot mode you're prompted by the Spot dialog box to enter a location for the dragged region.
- In Grid mode the dragged region snaps to the nearest Grid boundary.
- In Slip mode the regions are placed freely anywhere in the destination track.

  To switch between edit modes use the F1–F4 function keys: F1 = Shuffle, F2 = Spot, F3 = Slip, and F4 = Grid.

  Get to know the differences and best uses for each of the edit modes. Try them all out . . . you'd be surprised how big a difference they can make to the quality and efficiency of your work.

Destructive Record Mode

If you record over a region while in Destructive record mode, the new region will permanently replace the old audio region. This allows you to save space on your hard drive, but it also makes it really easy to accidentally record over good tracks. Be careful using this mode – in fact, I advise not using it unless it's absolutely necessary.

Loop Record Mode

In Loop mode you can record multiple non-destructive takes over the same section of music while the section repeats. This is particularly useful if you want to stay in a creative moment and capture several takes in rapid succession. I use this mode for vocals on a regular basis as it creates a comfort level for the musician . . . the repetition allows the vocalist to really get into the flow of the part. It's also useful to capture multiple takes on a jam or solo section.

While in Loop record mode, simply highlight a section of time (must be over one second) in the Ruler or on a track, then hit Record. (Note: Pre-roll will only be active on the first take and post-roll only on the last.) After you've finished recording, select the current take then ⌘ + click (Mac) or Control + click (Win) the track, and choose which take you want from the Takes list popup menu (as in figure 2.10).

Fig. 2.10.
After recording multiple passes of a part using loop record, you can choose the "keeper" from the Takes list.

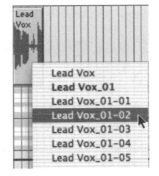

> When recording, pre-roll is the amount of the track that's played before it's record-enabled, and post-roll is the amount that plays after actual recording has stopped. To set pre-roll and post-roll times, type the amount of time into the pre-roll and post-roll area of the Transport window, pressing the forward slash key (/) after each amount. ⌘ + K (Mac) or Control + K (Win) activates or deactivates pre-roll and post-roll.

QuickPunch

In this mode you can use simple key commands (or a footswitch with Digi 002/001) to non-destructively punch in and out. You can do this up to 100 times during a single run through a song. QuickPunch is instantaneous; the instant you click the Record button or press the ⌘ + Spacebar (Mac), Control + Spacebar (Win), or footswitch during playback in QuickPunch mode, Pro Tools immediately punches the track in or out without delay. (Note: Though you can click on the Record button to punch in and out, the key commands and footswitch are much easier.) To use QuickPunch just choose it as your record mode, play the track, and punch in and out to your heart's content.

AUTOMATED PUNCHING

Using a footswitch to punch in and out with your 002/001 requires good timing. Unless you have a fair-sized margin for error around your punch point you may want to use another technique. A poorly placed punch can ruin a great take or create a noticeable change that might be difficult to edit. This isn't meant to discourage you from performing manual punches — some people love the feel of punching "on the fly" — but I've found that automated punching is simple to set up and less worrisome. Whatever method you choose, all punching can be undone. Ah, the beauty of hard disk recording!

Good Punch Points

Fig. 2.11.

An easy region to punch in and out. Notice the absence of signal on either side of the punch point.

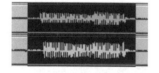

To find a seamless punch point, select a spot where there's little signal on the track or where the waveform crosses the x-axis (horizontal axis) and has no amplitude. Doing this will help make the crossfade around the punch point unnoticeable in many cases.

For more difficult punches you should zoom in (both vertically and horizontally) to accurately place the points.

Keep the selected area highlighted. Now figure out how much pre-roll and post-roll you'd like. From the Operations menu, choose the monitor mode you'd like to use — Auto Input Monitoring or Input Only Monitoring (see the sidebar on monitoring modes) — and you're ready to go.

Fig. 2.12.

A more difficult region to place your punch points.

MONITORING MODES — HEAR NO EVIL

You can monitor input signals using one of two options in Pro Tools: Auto Input Monitoring switches between the existing track and the new input signal while Input Only Monitoring (as its name suggests) monitors the input at all times. Auto Input Monitoring is very helpful for punching in and out of a track.

Monitor Modes in Pro Tools

Monitoring Modes in PT	When playback is stopped	Playback before punch point	While punched in	Punch out point and beyond
Auto Input Monitoring	Input Signal	Existing Track	Input Signal	Existing Track
Input Only Monitoring	Input Signal	Input Signal	Input Signal	Input Signal

When Input Only Monitoring is enabled, the Record button in the Transport window appears green. To easily switch between the two monitor modes, use the shortcuts Option + K (Mac) or Alt + K (Win). When using Auto Input Monitoring in Non-Destructive record mode, the switch back to monitoring track material on punch-out is not instantaneous. To get instantaneous monitor switching on punch-out, use QuickPunch.

To proceed with your automated punch, record-enable the track(s) you'd like to punch and press the Record button. Your Transport window will look similar to figure 2.13. Press Play and the computer will do the punch automatically.

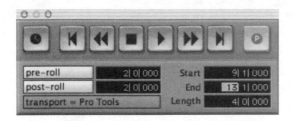

Fig. 2.13.
Automated punch record-ready with pre-roll and post-roll. If your monitor mode is set to Auto Input, you'll be able to hear the original track right up to the punch-in, at which point you'll hear what's being recorded.

Remember: When you record non-destructively like this, the original track remains and any newly recorded track can be erased or replaced. Also note that you can automate a punch-in like this in any recording mode (not just QuickPunch as indicated in figure 2.13).

PLAYLISTS

Playlist is a term that applies to several distinct features in Pro Tools. An **edit playlist** is a group of regions arranged on an audio or MIDI track. An **automation playlist** stores automation data for volume, pan, mute, and plug-in parameters on audio tracks, and mute data on MIDI tracks. Playlists can also act as virtual recording tracks for alternate takes.

When limited to a certain number of tracks, you can creatively use playlists to your advantage for both recording and editing. I use playlists most often to record additional takes of a track. For example, you can try another take of the guitar solo: simply click on the Playlist button (the arrow) next to the name of the track you want to record on and choose New. A dialog box will open asking you to name the new playlist. In the example shown in figure 2.14, I've recorded six takes of "Gtr Solo." Once you've recorded multiple takes (on a new playlist each time) you can easily audition them using the dropdown menu. In the figure, "Gtr Solo.03" and "Gtr Solo.02" were the two best takes, so I played each back several times to see which one I wanted to use.

Once all these takes have been recorded, it's easy to go back later and cut and paste the best parts from each playlist to create the master take. In fact, I often use this approach when recording an entire band, particularly if they're playing to a click track. By creating a new playlist for every take, all of the takes sit on top of each other (figuratively) and it becomes much easier to edit the takes together later.

Fig. 2.14.
Playlists allow you to easily choose the best take on any track.

KEYBOARD SHORTCUTS FOR RECORDING

Instead of pressing Record then Play, you can begin recording by:

• Pressing F12.

• Pressing ⌘ + Spacebar (Mac) or Control + Spacebar (Win).

• Pressing 3 on the numeric keypad if the numeric keypad mode is set to Transport (in the Operation Preferences page).

Sometimes I like to use Record Pause mode, which helps decrease the delay before beginning to record — particularly if you're recording a large number of tracks, or playing back a large number of tracks while recording new ones. Simply press Option + ⌘ + Spacebar (Mac) or Alt + Control + Spacebar (Win) then get comfortable and press the Spacebar when everyone's ready to roll.

And don't forget the Cancel record and Undo functions. Pressing Control + period (.) (Win) or ⌘ + period (.) (Mac) stops a recording and discards the take. Pressing Control + Z (Win) or ⌘ + Z (Mac) will undo a recording. These two commands can save you plenty of hard drive space and reduce the clutter of unwanted tracks in your sessions.

SOMETIMES THINGS JUST CLICK

So the engineer in you has recorded your idea into Pro Tools. Now the producer in you should evaluate the idea and the performance. How critical should you be of the initial recordings? If you're brainstorming or recording just for fun, don't be critical at all. However, if you think you might want to use this track later, try to get the best take (recorded version) of the idea that you can. Try a few more takes on new tracks (or playlists) if you're not happy with the first take, or you may want to keep several takes to critique later, or keep all of them to edit into one master take.

Even when recording fresh new ideas, you should also consider playing to a click track, because who knows . . . you may want to use the initial tracks later in the production process. This is especially important if you've captured the raw emotion or right feel on early performances; many times it's impossible to recreate everything that went into getting that dynamite first pass.

You might not be used to playing with a click track, but practicing with one can improve your timing and rhythm. And the benefit of recording with a click is you can overdub other parts later and not have to guess about the tempo. For example: If you record a guitar part today, two weeks from now your drummer friend can lay down some tracks without worrying about tempo fluctuations (not that drummers ever worry about a guitar player's time).

Pro Tools is equipped with a Click plug-in. To activate the click track in your Pro Tools session, insert the Click plug-in on an audio track by selecting Click from the Inserts list, as in figure 2.15.

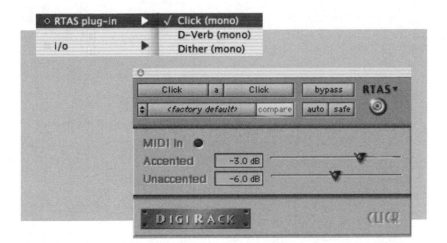

Fig. 2.15.
The Click plug-in uses tempo and meter information from the conductor track displayed in the Tempo and Meter rulers at the top of the Edit window.

The click track follows the tempo and meter of the session, which you can access through the Tempo and Meter dialog boxes. Double-click on the "4/4" button in the extended Transport window to open these dialog boxes.

Fig. 2.16.
The Transport window shows all of its functions when you check off "Counters," "MIDI Controls," and "Expanded" from the Transport Window Shows command in the Display menu.

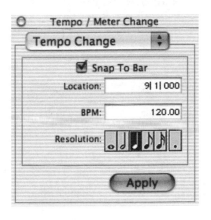
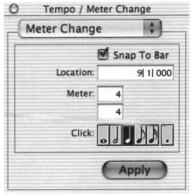

Fig. 2.17.
The Tempo and Meter dialog boxes help you create tempo and meter changes in your Pro Tools session. You can also open these by selecting Show Tempo/Meter from the Windows menu, Change Tempo.../Change Meter... from the MIDI menu, or by clicking on the tempo and meter icons in their respective rulers.

Don't know what tempo you want? Try tapping it in. Tap in a tempo into the Transport window by clicking on the "Tap" button, which only appears if the conductor button is not highlighted, as in figure 2.18. This turns off the conductor track and enables Manual Tempo mode.

Fig. 2.18.
Create a manual tempo by clicking your mouse on the Tap button, or use the slider to select a tempo.

In the following chapter, we'll get into more detail on conductor tracks as well as go deeper into recording with Pro Tools. But first, check out these projects. ▮▮

PRO TOOLS HANDS-ON

Create, Record, and Experiment

To start, create a new session, create several new tracks, double-click each track to label them and make comments describing what each one contains, record a few tracks, and try recording onto new playlists on those tracks.

Record to a click track. While recording, use pre- and post-roll as well as the punching techniques described in this chapter. Once you've got some tracks down, experiment with the different record and edit modes and learn the differences between them.

Personalize Your Edit Window

While you're at it, set up your Pro Tools Edit window the way you like it. You can choose whether to show or hide numerous pieces of information. On the top part of the Edit window, you can show any, all, or none of the rulers, including Bars|Beats, Minutes: Seconds, Samples, Markers, Tempo, and Meter, by clicking on the button shown in the figure below. Note: The Bars|Beats, Minutes: Seconds, and Samples rulers are called the Timebase Rulers, while the Markers, Tempo, and Meter rulers are called the Conductor Rulers.

opens ⟶

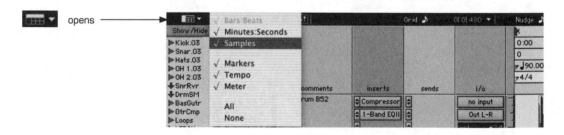

Besides showing the standard I/O and record, solo, mute, and automation buttons for each track, you can also choose whether to show or hide the Inserts, Sends, and Comments views as shown in the next figure.

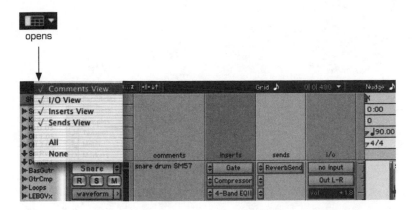

opens

By clicking on the double arrow at the bottom left of the Edit window, you can choose to show or hide the Tracks list and Edit Groups list. By clicking on the double arrow at the bottom right of the Edit window, you can choose to show or hide the Audio and MIDI Regions lists.

The First Step in Preproduction — Recording Song Ideas

The first step in the music production process while recording, editing, mixing, and mastering in Pro Tools is coming up with ideas for new songs. On the CD that came with this book, there are four example songs (in Pro Tools sessions) that you can follow through the production process. In most chapters, I will update each song, utilizing production techniques explained in the chapter. The Pro Tools sessions are named according to genres: rock, jazz "fusion," hip-hop, and electronica.

Copy the folder named "Book Projects" onto your audio hard drive. In addition to the audio and fade files, this folder contains Pro Tools sessions compatible with both Mac and PC users of Pro Tools 5.1 and above (including Pro Tools 6.X).

Open up any or all of the sessions titled "Chap2Rock," "Chap2Hiphop," "Chap2Jazz," and "Chap2Electronica" to find a basic song idea for each musical style. Examine the ideas and experiment with them. I will be building on these basic ideas throughout the book as each song moves from its initial idea to a complete production. The idea is for you to witness the production process in action.

Deeper into Recording with Pro Tools

CHAPTER 3

In this chapter:

- **Recording levels**

- **Sample rate and bit depth**

- **Buffer settings and latency times**

- **Conductor tracks, importing audio, and session templates**

- **The basics of sends, returns, and busses**

- **Headphones and headphone mixes**

Chapter 2 set you up with enough practical knowledge of recording in Pro Tools to be dangerous. The projects showed off the first step in the preproduction process for songwriting —song idea generation and recording. In this chapter I'll delve deeper into the recording process and explain some of the technology, theory, and advanced features of Pro Tools. I'll also take the projects further down the path of preproduction by expanding on the song ideas from the last chapter.

Always keep an eye on input levels! I often find that once the Record button is pushed, players play harder and singers sing louder than when you were first checking their levels. In Pro Tools LE, you can view large individual track meters by clicking the fader button near the volume and pan controls of any track. (The asterisk [*] button next to any track fader in Pro Tools 5.1–5.3 has the same function.)

SETTING RECORDING LEVELS

When recording to analog tape, most people try to push the recording level to the highest point they can without distortion. This is done to maximize the **signal-to-noise ratio** — in this case, the ratio of audio signal recorded to the amount of inherent noise on the analog tape medium. Recording at high levels on analog tape increases the clarity of the recording and keeps the inherent noise as low as possible. And in fact, many people even like the sound of slight analog *distortion*. This occurs when the tape is overloaded with audio signal (sometimes called "tape saturation"), and can create a pleasingly "warm" sound. The ability to do this is one reason that some people are still partial to analog recordings over digital ones.

However, recordings you make in your Pro Tools home studio can rival high-end analog recordings made in professional studios! In contrast to analog tape, there's very little noise associated with digital recording, so the signal-to-noise ratio is higher, providing very accurate representations of your music. As with analog, most people push digital recording levels, but in this case to allow for the use of greater bit depth. As you will see in the next section, using the entire bit depth provides the most accurate "picture" of an analog waveform. Unlike analog distortion, however, overloading a digital track causes digital clipping — the audio signal is literally cut off at 0dB, often creating a decidedly nasty sound. "Digital distortion" isn't pleasing like analog distortion can be, so digital levels should always remain below 0dB (the clipping point).

Yet, even if you see the red peak indicator on one or several of your tracks, that doesn't necessarily mean your signal has been digitally clipped. Pro Tools has a certain amount of headroom between when the red peak light is activated and when the actual audio is clipped. Watch the meters, but also use your ears to experiment with recording levels and find what works well for your system. In general, if a signal peaks very occasionally that's usually fine. However, if the signal peaks often, then decrease the input level.

SAMPLE RATE AND BIT DEPTH

Now that you've had some experience recording digitally into Pro Tools, let's talk about two primary determinants in the accuracy of a digital recording: sample rate and bit depth. These two parameters provide a grid onto which the analog audio signal is plotted and determine how well the digital recording represents the original sound.

■ **Fig. 3.1.**
Here we see an analog waveform and a digital representation of it. Faster sampling rates and larger bit depths provide more accurate digital representations of analog sounds.

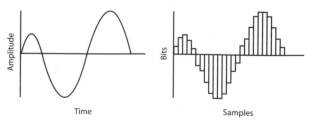

In discussing **sample rate**, consider photography as an example. If you set up a camera to take a picture of the sky once every hour, you could follow weather patterns in a very rough way. With this low "sample rate" you would probably miss many significant events. However, if you took pictures every second you would see much more detail (like the moment rain began to fall or when sun broke through the clouds).

Digital recording is like taking pictures of music at a speed determined by the sample rate. If the sample rate in your session is 44.1kHz, Pro Tools takes 44,100 pictures of your input audio every second. Each picture captures the amplitude (level) of the audio signal at that moment.

Each sample is digitally "mapped" to an exact digital value and converted into binary digits (or bits). The number of bits in the system is referred to as bit depth. The higher the bit depth, the more accurate the digital representation of the analog sound.

The precision of the amplitude value depends on the **bit depth** — small bit depths yield less precise representations of the audio signal. Back to our photography example: In color photography, a photo taken with a bit depth of 4 bits (2^4) would only allow 16 different colors ($2^4 = 2 \times 2 \times 2 \times 2 = 16$). If the color of a photographed object is not precisely one of the 16 colors allowed, the closest color would be assigned to it. Obviously, 16 colors can't possibly describe all of the shades and hues found in our colorful world. The same logic applies when describing the myriad nuances of sound with an audio signal — usually, the more bits the better. That's why depths of 16 bits and 24 bits are offered in Pro Tools: 16-bit resolution offers 65,536 (or 2^{16}) levels of audio amplitude and 24-bit resolution offers 16,777,216 (or 2^{24}). With bit depths this high, it's like having thousands (or millions) of colors to choose from instead of only 16.

For each new session you open in Pro Tools you're asked to choose between 16-bit or 24-bit recording, as in figure 3.2. Be aware that you can't mix bit depths and sampling rates within sessions; you'll need to convert any audio being imported if the file was recorded at a different bit depth or sampling rate than the session.

CDs are recorded with 16-bit resolution and a sample rate of 44.1kHz. However, faster sample rates and higher bit depths yield more detailed audio representations and improve the accuracy of your recordings. The most accurate digital representation of music that Pro Tools LE software currently offers is 24-bit resolution with a sample rate of 48kHz, with the exception that Digi 002 can record 88.2kHz and 96kHz tracks. Pro Tools Free (Win) supports up to 48kHz as well, while the Mac version only supports up to 44.1kHz.

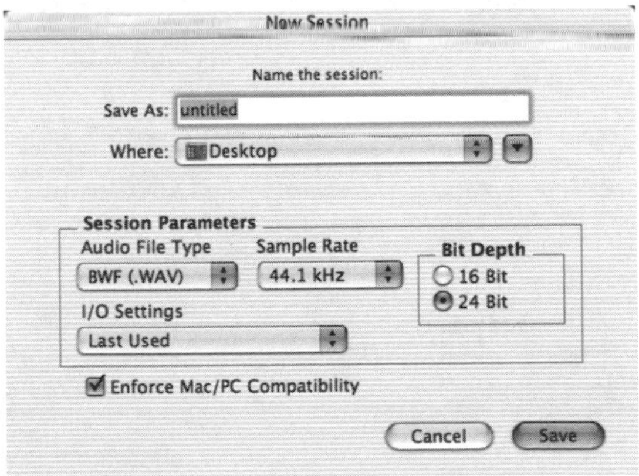

Fig. 3.2.
The New Session dialogue lets you choose the audio file type, bit depth, sample rate, and I/O settings, as well as Mac/PC compatibility.

Fig. 3.3.
Memory requirements for
different sampling rates and
bit depths. If you plan to do
a lot of hi-res recording, you
may need to stock up on hard
drives.

Fig. 3.4.
The Disk Allocation window
enables you to choose the
exact location where each
track you record will be stored.
To assign all tracks to a
specific drive, press Alt (Win)
or Option (Mac) while selecting
a drive name.

Beware: Recording at 24-bit resolution requires 50% more hard disk space than 16-bit recording. For example, a mono audio track recorded at 16-bit resolution and 44.1kHz sample rate requires 5MB per minute of hard disk space; the same track recorded with 24-bit resolution requires 7.5MB per minute. Using a sample rate of 48kHz or higher also increases the memory needed to store files. If you do a lot of high-resolution recording, you may need an extra hard drive or two. (The "Support" section of Digi's Web site lists approved drives.)

Despite the bit depth and sample rate you use when recording, you must convert the files to 16-bit/44.1kHz to burn them to a CD. I often record at the highest sampling rate and bit depth available to ensure the highest recording quality, then apply dither during mixing and mastering to convert tracks to 16-bit. More on file conversion and dithering is found in chapter 13.

Number of tracks and length	16-bit at 44.1 kHz	16-bit at 48 kHz	24-bit at 44.1 kHz	24-bit at 48 kHz	16-bit at 88.2 kHz	16-bit at 96 kHz	24-bit at 88.2 kHz	24-bit at 96 kHz
1 track, 1 minute	5 MB	5.5 MB	7.5 MB	8.2 MB	10 MB	11 MB	15 MB	16.4 MB
2 tracks (stereo), 5 minutes	50 MB	55 MB	75 MB	83 MB	100 MB	110 MB	150 MB	165 MB
2 tracks (stereo), 60 minutes	600 MB	662 MB	900 MB	991 MB	1.2 GB	1.3 GB	1.8 GB	1.9 GB
24 tracks, 1 minute	120 MB	132 MB	180 MB	198 MB	240 MB	164 MB	360 MB	396 MB
24 tracks, 5 minutes	600 MB	662 MB	900 MB	991 MB	1.2 GB	1.3 GB	1.8 GB	1.9 GB
24 tracks, 60 minutes	7 GB	7.8 GB	10.5 GB	11.6 GB	14 GB	15.6 GB	21 GB	23.2 GB

DISK ALLOCATION

Every audio track you record is stored on either an internal or external hard drive. Tell Pro Tools where to record each track by specifying the location in the Disk Allocation window. Choose Disk Allocation from the Setups menu to open a window like figure 3.4.

Audio files folder are kept in each session's Audio Files folder. However, spreading these files over several drives can improve your entire system's performance because one hard drive won't be doing all

Disk Allocation		Maxtor 75 GB Disk
		Lip RT Burt
Track	Root Media Folder	Lipfloater RT
Gtr Solo.03	DigiDrive:Trancendental:	DigiDrive
Click	Maxtor 75 GB Disk:Trancendental:	AweD-O #2
Guitar	Maxtor 75 GB Disk:Trancendental:	AweD-O #1
Bass DI	AweD-O #1 :Trancendental:	Macintosh HD
Bass Pod	AweD-O #1 :Trancendental:	
Vox	DigiDrive:Trancendental:	

☐ Custom Allocation Options
  Root media folder: <volume>:<root folder>
☑ Create subfolders for audio, video, and fade files   (Change...)
☐ Use round robin allocation for new tracks

(Cancel)   (OK)

the work. But don't worry about losing track of your files. DigiBase, the file management utility in Pro Tools, can help you keep track of all of these files. Chapter 9 has more information on DigiBase.

WINDOWS AND MACINTOSH SESSION COMPATIBILITY

Pro Tools now lets you save your sessions and audio so they can be opened on both Windows and Macintosh computers. Checking the Enforce Mac/PC (or PC/Mac) Compatibility box in the New Session dialog (figure 3.2) forces Pro Tools to create files that are usable on both Mac and Windows platforms. (The box can't be checked unless AIFF or WAV is selected under Audio File Type.)

Sound Designer II files were the standard file format for previous versions of Pro Tools, but they're only read by Macintosh systems. Thus, if you want your session and associated audio files to be compatible on both Windows and Macs, choose the AIFF or Wave file type. **AIFF** (Audio Interchange File Format) and **Wave** (sometimes written WAV or .wav because of the file extension) can be read by both Windows and Mac software.

Note that some ASCII characters can't be used for naming regions, tracks, files, or plug-in settings in Mac/Windows-compatible sessions. These characters are slash (/), backslash (\), colon (:), asterisk (*), question mark (?), quotation marks (""), less-than and greater-than symbols (< >), vertical line (|), and any character typed with the Mac's Command (⌘) key. If you type one of these characters, a dialog will appear to prompt you for a new name.

I recommend making all of your Pro Tools sessions Mac/PC compatible so that if you ever need to take them to another studio, there'll be no compatiblity hassles.

BUFFER SETTINGS AND LATENCY TIMES

Through the process of digital recording, analog audio signals are converted into digital data, the data is recorded, and then the data is converted back into an analog signal for playback. Although very fast, this conversion process is not instantaneous. The time it takes your computer to receive an input signal, process it, and send it to an output is called **latency**. Latency values can be as low as 3.0 milliseconds (essentially unnoticeable) or as high as 50 milliseconds on up (quite noticeable). These times vary depending on the hardware buffer size (H/W Buffer Size) that you choose from the Hardware window in the Setups menu.

Anytime you convert an analog signal to digital or vice versa, the analog-to-digital (A/D) or digital-to-analog (D/A) converter delays the signal by about 1.5 milliseconds. Thus, when a signal is converted on the way in to your computer (A/D) and then converted as it's played back out of the computer (D/A), the conversion delay adds up to 3.0

milliseconds. Your computer also takes some time to process the audio (depending on the buffer size set in Pro Tools) as it comes and goes, which means the total latency of your system equals the conversion delay (3.0 milliseconds) plus double the latency amount given in the following chart (figure 3.5). For example, recording with a sample rate of 44.1kHz and a buffer size of 128 samples, the total latency is 2.9ms × 2 plus 3.0ms, equaling 8.8ms.

Fig. 3.5.

Latency can be a groove killer if it's not properly accounted for during recording.

Sample Rate (kHz)	Buffer Size (samples)	Latency Amount (ms)	Total Latency (ms)	Use for:
44.1	128	2.9	8.8	Recording drums and other
48		2.7	8.4	timing-critical instruments
44.1	256	5.8	14.6	Recording vocals and
48		5.3	13.6	instruments with slower attack times (guitar, bass, etc.)
44.1	512	11.6	26.2	Mixing with 24 tracks
48		10.7	24.4	
44.1	1024	23.2	49.4	Final mixdown or many
48		21.3	45.6	plug-ins

While recording you'll often want to operate with the lowest possible level of latency. Unless you're using an Mbox, Pro Tools LE offers **Low Latency Monitoring** (under the Operations menu) as an excellent option. It provides a latency time of only 3.0 milliseconds (the converter delay), because the audio you hear never actually goes into the computer for processing – there's a mixer in your 002/001/AM III card that returns the audio immediately. The following restrictions apply when using Low Latency Monitoring:

- You can only record tracks with inputs set to an audio interface (not a bus).

- You can only listen to tracks assigned to outputs 1 and/or 2.

- All plug-ins and sends assigned to record-enabled tracks (routed to outputs 1–2) are automatically bypassed, and must remain bypassed.

- Record-enabled tracks will not register on meters for master faders.

These restrictions are easy to work around. I use Low Latency Monitoring during many of my sessions and it works great. In fact, the only time I don't use it is when I absolutely have to hear the output of a plug-in while recording.

The Mbox handles latency in a different way. It allows you to monitor the input signal before the signal leaves the Mbox, thus creating no latency. This zero-latency feature is controlled with the Mix knob on the front panel, which allows you to blend and adjust the monitor ratio between the Mbox inputs and Pro Tools playback.

OK. Enough heady stuff. Let's get into some more Pro Tools recording and production techniques. In chapter 2 I covered the basics of recording with Pro Tools providing enough knowledge to get your initial song ideas onto your hard drive. Here I'll cover some topics that you can use to expand upon your initial song ideas and start to create "demos" of your songs—the conductor track, importing audio, session templates, send and return effects loops, and headphone mixes.

THE CONDUCTOR TRACK

In chapter 2, you learned about the conductor rulers and how to create a simple click track. Well, what if your song is not so simple? What if it has tempo and meter changes...and maybe even tricky rubato sections where time is flexible? No problem. In Pro Tools speak, a conductor track is basically a click track with changes in its tempo and/or meter. And you can program in any changes you want. In short, the conductor track refers to the combination of the tempo and meter events in the session.

For instance, say you want an accelerando (an increase in tempo) at bar 23 and a change in meter at bar 27 in your song. To do this, open the Tempo/Meter dialog (using one of the ways you learned in chapter 2), enter your tempo and meter changes, and click Apply after each one. The new changes will appear in the Tempo and Meter rulers (as in figure 3.6).

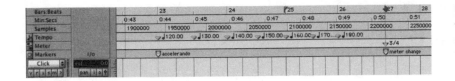

Fig. 3.6.
The Tempo and Meter rulers show all of the conductor track information.

Although it is very easy to make a complicated conductor track in Pro Tools, that doesn't mean you always should. Some songs are not suited for recording with a click, particularly very rubato songs. Also, clicks can be detrimental to the feel of some songs. As always, let your ears be the judge.

IMPORTING AUDIO

What if you've got some killer samples (e.g., drum loops, bass lines, sound effects, etc.) that you want to add to an existing Pro Tools session? Pro Tools makes it easy to bring in samples and tracks from other sessions. To import an audio file to its own track in your session, choose Import Audio to Track from the File menu. To import an audio file into the Audio Regions list, choose Import Audio from the Audio Regions List menu, as in figure 3.7. Both commands open the same Import Audio dialog, as seen in figure 3.8.

Fig. 3.7.

Besides importing audio, the
Audio Regions list pop-up
menu has a lot of powerful
features, as you'll see in later
chapters.

Fig. 3.8.

The Import Audio dialog box
enables you to bring samples
and other audio files into
your current session and will
convert them to the session's
sampling rate and bit depth if
necessary.

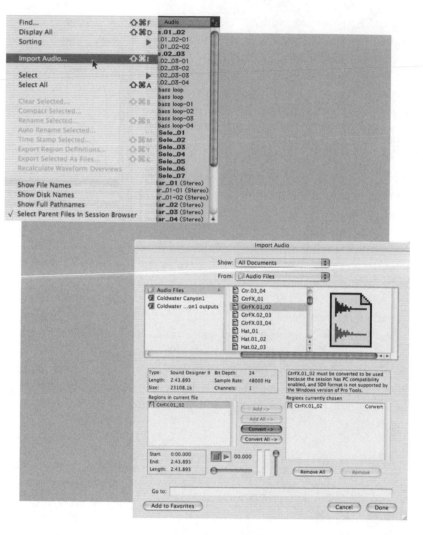

In the Import Audio dialog, choose the files you want to import,
audition them if you want using the Play and Stop buttons, and click
"Add" and/or "Convert." All files that are in the bottom right box will
be added to the current session when you click "Done" and will be
available in the Audio Regions list immediately after they are converted
(if necessary) to the current session's sampling rate and bit depth.

You can choose the quality of sample rate conversion used when converting and
importing audio into your session. Choose Preferences from the Setups menu,
and click on the Editing tab. From the Conversion Quality pop-up menu, choose
the conversion quality (as in the figure on the next page). With the choices come
tradeoffs between quality and time. "Good" and "Better " settings are usually fine and
the conversion time is not very long. "Best" and "Tweak Head" can take large amounts
of time and should only be used when the highest quality conversion is required.

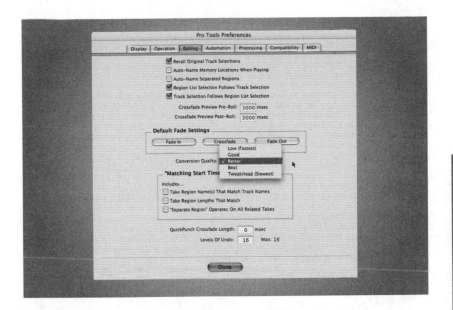

SETTING UP A SESSION TEMPLATE

When recording new song ideas and demos, don't let time hinder your creativity. To capture a new idea while in the moment, recording must be quick and easy. You don't want to spend 15 minutes setting up your studio gear, musical instruments, and a Pro Tools session to capture a fleeting idea or musical brainstorm – the moment will be lost. Make it easy to record your ideas by setting up a Pro Tools session template, and you'll only be 15 seconds away from capturing your stroke (or riff) of genius.

A session template is a customized Pro Tools session that includes track setups, mixer setups, window arrangements, and zoom level memory locations configured to your liking. Specifically, session templates save audio and MIDI track configuration, track names, shown/hidden tracks, track input and output assignments, MIDI channel assignments, track volume and pan, soloed and muted tracks, aux inputs, bus assignments, track width and color, track groups and group lists, click track settings, disk allocation, and keyboard focus. A session template also includes all session setups found in the Setups menu (i.e., Hardware, Preferences, etc.) including I/O Settings (remember those from chapter 1?).

To create a Windows session template, right-click the Pro Tools session that you've configured and choose Properties. Click the General tab and choose the Read-only check box. That's it. Close the Properties window.

To create a Macintosh session template, select the Pro Tools session by clicking it once, then choose Get Info from the File menu. In the window that appears, click on the Stationery Pad check box. That's it. Close the Get Info window.

You can have several templates for different occasions. For instance, you may create a setup for recording just two mics — one for voice and another for acoustic guitar. You may set up a template for doing a sequence using several pieces of MIDI gear, or you can have one for recording your entire band. I suggest setting up a template for any configuration you work with on a fairly regular basis, though it doesn't hurt to save templates from weird or complex one-off sessions as a jumping off point for other projects.

Once you've created your own template files, make them easy to find. I recommend putting an alias (Mac) or shortcut (Windows) on your computer's desktop. You may even want to create a folder with multiple templates for easy access to any setup you need.

When you choose to start a new project from a session template, you

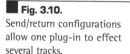

Fig. 3.9.

After opening a session template, Pro Tools will ask you if you want to create a new session based on the template, or if you want to edit the template.

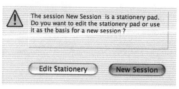

need to name the new session and save it as a different file, or you'll be editing your actual template. Pro Tools will warn you about this with an alert message like the one in figure 3.9.

THE BASICS OF SENDS, RETURNS, AND BUSSES

If you want to hear effects while recording or do some basic mixing in the preproduction process, it's important to understand sends, returns, and busses. If you're familiar with the signal routing of a mixer, you're probably familiar with these terms. Pro Tools uses sends, returns, and busses in the same way as a hard-wired mixer — you just have more flexible routing options in Pro Tools.

I'll explain with an example: Let's say you want to put the same delay effect on several tracks using a plug-in. Instead of putting that plug-in on each of the tracks, you can put one delay plug-in on an aux track and use it for any other tracks that need delay (aux is short for auxiliary input). You do this by sending copies of all the tracks that need delay (via a bus) to the aux input with the plug-in. The bus carries the tracks to the aux input, where they're processed using the plug-in. They are then sent out, usually to the main stereo outputs. In this case, the aux track is called an effects return. See figure 3.10 for a visual representation of the signal flow.

Fig. 3.10.

Send/return configurations allow one plug-in to effect several tracks.

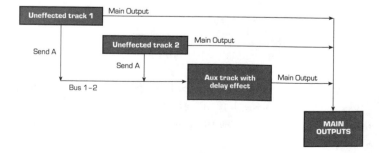

Here's how this delay send and return is specifically set up in Pro Tools:

1. Activate a send (the "diamond" buttons above tracks' Input selectors in the Mix window) on each track that you want to put delay onto — adjust the volume and panning. I recommend starting with the volume at 0.0. Select a mono or stereo bus output (e.g., bus 1–2) as the path to the aux track.

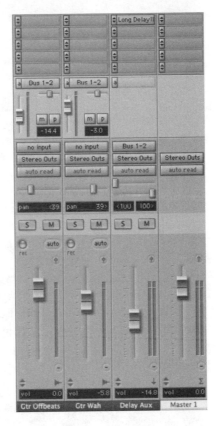

Fig. 3.11.
Effects loops like this offer flexible signal routing as well as a reduced load on your CPU.

2. Create a new aux track by selecting New Track from the File menu or by typing ⌘ + Shift + N (Mac) or Control + Shift + N (Win), and then choosing Aux Input from the dropdown menu above the Create button. Choose Mono for a mono return/mono plug-in or Stereo for a stereo return/stereo plug-in.

3. Choose the bus path (e.g., bus 1–2) as the input of the aux track from the track sends (in the Mix window). The output of the aux track usually goes to the main outputs, unless you want to route it somewhere else. See figure 3.11.

With this setup, the individual send faders control the amount of signal that's sent from each track to the delay plug-in on the aux input. The aux track fader controls how much of the delay effect on those tracks is added to the overall mix.

Sends, returns, and busses are integral parts of recording and mixing in Pro Tools. Their functions are explained in greater detail in chapters 11 and 12.

HEADPHONE MIXES AND HEADPHONES

A large proportion of recording in professional and home studios is done with headphones on to avoid feedback, create sound separation, and have separate mixes for individuals (if needed). As an engineer you need to be constantly aware of the recording and playback levels of the headphone mix, the routing of audio signals, the hardware you're routing it through, and how the overall mix sounds.

There are several ways to get multiple "feeds" to different sets of headphones. Here are some ideas:

After copying it to your hard drive, open up the Pro Tools session titled "Basic Effects Send Aux" on the CD-ROM and try playing around with the sends, busses, and aux tracks (effects returns). The signal flow of this setup is often misunderstood...take some time to really digest the concepts so you can use effects sends/returns easily.

- If you're using your home stereo as the monitor output, plug a splitter into the headphone jack and run your headphones from there.

- If you have the Mbox/002/001 you can split the headphone output.

- If you're using a mixer there are probably several stereo outputs that can feed headphones.

- If you're using a home stereo and a mixer, you can utilize the headphone jacks from both units (as well as the one from the Mbox/002/001), giving you a total of at least four headphone outputs. However, using all of these different headphones with separate levels might get confusing.

A better solution might be to buy a headphone amplifier specifically made to supply multiple sets of "cans." Simply plug any of the monitor outputs (home stereo headphone out, Mbox/002/001 headphone out, or mixer out) — or two direct outputs from the Mbox/002/001 (e.g., analog outputs 1–2) — to the input of a headphone amp. Each amp supplies multiple pairs of headphones with your stereo signal and every pair has its own volume control, allowing each person to adjust their own overall level. Headphone amps may also accept multiple input signals, so technically you could supply some headphones with one mix and other pairs with a different mix. (Creating two or more different headphone mixes is covered in chapter 11. This is a really cool feature — check it out. To jump right in, open up either Multiple HP Mix session on the book's CD-ROM.)

KEEP FEEDBACK IN CHECK

Except when they want Jimi Hendrix-like guitar feedback, most people try to avoid feedback in studio environments. Acoustic **feedback** is created when two magnetic pickups (e.g., microphone and speaker) feed each other the same audio signal. An audio signal going into the mic comes out of the speaker back into the mic and so forth, creating a loop. This **feedback loop** is the result of the signal building upon itself and creating a sometimes painful and injurious noise. Feedback at high decibel levels can cause hearing loss — not to mention damage to equipment — so be careful! It's a good idea to keep your monitor level down or *preferably off* when recording using microphones that are in the same room. Create a headphone mix instead.

Buying Headphones

Let's continue with the headphone topic. When buying headphones for your home studio it's most important to consider how they'll be used. Will you be using them during recording sessions? Consider buying closed-ear headphones so there's minimal sound leakage while tracking.

Will you be using them to mix? Consider buying headphones with a flat frequency response so you're sure of their accuracy. Will clients be using these headphones for extended periods of time during sessions? Consider comfort as an important factor in the equation.

There are three types of headphones: open-air, semi-open, and closed-ear (or sealed). These terms refer to how much sound isolation the headphones provide. Often the open-air or semi-open are more comfortable than closed-ear headphones because they don't fit so tightly. However, open-air and semi-open headphones allow some amount of sound to escape into the room. That means the sound could leak into microphones in the recording studio — particularly important to consider if you'll be recording with a click track. Sealed headphones allow very little leakage, so click tracks and other loud signals won't be picked up by mics in the room.

There are other factors to consider when choosing headphones:

- Long-term wearing comfort — people might have to wear them for many hours at a time

- Spatially accurate sound field — that is, they accurately reproduce the stereo image you've created

- Extended, smooth frequency response — at least 20Hz to 20kHz

- Reliability and durability — people tend to toss around headphones like they're indestructible

- The ability to produce high levels with very low distortion — some people like their headphones loud (see sidebar on noise levels at the end of this chapter)

Whatever headphones you buy, compare them to other products. Being aware of the characteristics of headphones will provide useful information during recording, critical listening, mixing, and mastering. (I'm not advocating using headphones to mix or master, but sometimes that might be the only option if your roommates, family, or neighbors are sleeping or otherwise sensitive to volume.)

For example, the headphones I use for recording sessions in my home studio are closed-ear, comfortable, loud, and bass-heavy. This information tells me that (a) I don't need to worry about leakage into microphones, (b) I should be careful of the overall volume of the headphone mix, (c) I don't need to pump the bass in the headphone mix, (d) I may need to bump up the mid and high frequencies in the headphones to compensate for the bass response, and (e) if I'm recording a bass part, I'll know that what I record into Pro Tools isn't as boomy as it sounds in the phones. For critical listening, I use a separate pair of headphones that are closed-ear, extremely comfortable, and have a softer volume and flat frequency response.

[DON'T] STICK IT IN YOUR EAR

Listening to high levels of any type of sound (whether it's music, jackhammers, or jet engines) can be dangerous if done even for short periods of time. OSHA (Occupational Safety and Health Act, 1970) has published the following data:

Permissible Exposure to Noise Levels

SPL (A-weighted)	Daily Exposure
90 dB	8 hours
92	6
95	4
97	3
100	2
102	1.5
105	1
110	0.5
115 dB	0.25 hours

Decibels (dB) are the units used to measure the ratio of sound pressure level (SPL) of an audio source to the lower threshold of human hearing. An SPL of 130dB is the upper threshold of human tolerance; a noisy factory might have an SPL of 90dB; your house or apartment has an SPL of approximately 45dB. (Apparently some Who concerts reached a noise level of 120dB . . . it's no wonder Pete Townsend is having difficulties hearing these days!)

Please be careful with listening levels and be sure to give your ears a break from time to time — allow them to recover from loud levels. If you *must* listen at loud levels try to protect your ears (using plugs, etc.), because permanent damage to your hearing could mean permanent damage not only to your career, but also to your basic enjoyment of music. ▮

PRO TOOLS HANDS-ON

Experimenting with Recording Levels and Different Sample Rates/Bit Depths

You always need to be aware of your recording levels and how each device that your signal is going through affects the overall recorded sound. And, because of what you now know about bit depths and sampling rates, it's imperative to maintain good levels when recording through those devices.

Revisit the gain stages along your signal path and optimize their levels to get the best possible sounds into Pro Tools. Also, try recording at different sampling rates and bit depths. Create a new session with a sampling rate of 44.1kHz and a bit depth of 16. Record a track. Save the session and create a new 48kHz/24-bit session. Without changing anything in your signal path, record a similar track. Import the track in the 44.1kHz/16-bit session into the 48kHz/24-bit session and compare the sound of each track. Even though the 44.1/16 track was converted into 48/24, can you hear a difference? Digi 002 owners can try this at even higher sample rates.

Creating a Conductor Track — Tempo, Meter, and Markers

Open a pre-existing session or create a new one. Once in the session, open the Tempo/Meter window and make a conductor track by inserting tempo and meter events. Push the limits: try extreme tempo changes and wacky meter changes. Turn on the click track and listen to the madness that you created.

We haven't talked about markers, the third part of the conductor track. Let's talk about them here in the context of recording demo material and so that you can use them to edit in the next chapter.

Markers (a subset of memory locations) are useful for identifying significant locations in your sessions for use in playback and editing. There are several ways to create a marker, the easiest of which is to press the Enter key on the numeric keyboard. Choose a location in the session with the Selector tool and hit Enter or create a marker on the fly by hitting Enter while playing back or recording. The memory location dialog box will open, as seen in the figure at right.

Name the marker. I usually give my markers short names so that I can still see their names in the Markers ruler on the top of the Edit window, even if I'm zoomed out in the session, as in the figure below.

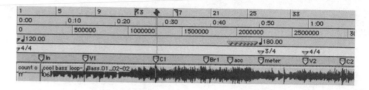

As seen in the memory location dialog, you can save General Properties (zoom settings, pre-/post-roll times, track heights, group enables, and which tracks are shown or hidden) with a marker. Experiment with General Properties and find out which are most beneficial to you.

Click on a marker in the Marker Ruler to recall its location and its General Properties. Select Show Memory Locations from the Windows menu to open the Memory Locations window (as in the figure at left). Click on a marker in the window to recall it.

You can move markers by dragging them in the Marker Ruler. You can delete them by Alt-clicking (Win) or Option-clicking the marker in the Memory Location window.

Try it. Play around with markers in a session. Create, move, and delete them. Assign General Properties to them and see how they affect your workflow. Markers will quickly become an indispensable tool for organizing your sessions and for improving your Pro Tools efficiency.

Further into Preproduction — Putting Song Demos Together

Those ideas and song demos from the last chapter have begun to take shape. Open up any or all of the sessions titled "Chap3Rock," "Chap3Hiphop," "Chap3Jazz," and "Chap3Electronica" to hear additional ideas for each of these songs. Check out the comments and experiment with the tracks. The new ideas are submixed together, and in some cases the submixes include effects and imported samples.

It's your turn to try importing audio samples and adding effects loops to your sessions. Also try creating conductor tracks in your sessions and creating a session template. These techniques can really increase the speed at which you transfer ideas from your head into Pro Tools. In the next chapter I'll show you how to edit those ideas once they're in Pro Tools.

In this chapter:

- **Non-destructive editing and edit playlists**

- **Edit modes and edit tools**

- **Comping tracks, fades, and crossfades**

- **Cutting, pasting, copying, and clearing**

- **Nudging notes and redrawing waveforms with the Pencil tool**

Now that you've got enough recording knowledge to get some demo material into Pro Tools, let's talk about how to edit that material. In my view, the most powerful features of Pro Tools lie within the software's extensive editing capabilities. Getting your head around all of the editing possibilities and techniques will take some time, but it's time well spent. You may need to refer back to this chapter as you progress through your projects because you'll probably be editing in every stage of the production process. But, before we get knee-deep in editing techniques, let's cover a few concepts that are crucial to your success in editing digital audio files with Pro Tools.

NON-DESTRUCTIVE EDITING AND EDIT PLAYLISTS

The reason that editing digital audio in Pro Tools is so powerful is that most editing functions in Pro Tools are non-destructive. What does that really mean? Non-destructive editing means that any cutting, pasting, trimming, separating, or clearing of audio data occurs virtually...the source audio files are not harmed in any way. Pro Tools only performs these editing functions on a map of the actual audio data, never touching the recorded source data. All edits that you perform simply help Pro Tools tell your hard drive where to look for data and how to arrange it for playback. Edit playlists are the mechanisms that do this.

As mentioned in chapter 2, an **edit playlist** is one or more regions arranged on an audio or MIDI track. The order and location of regions in a track define the track's edit playlist. The following examples will demonstrate the evolution of a track's edit playlist utilizing non-destructive editing.

When you first record a track, the edit playlist usually consists of just one entire whole-file audio region, as in the guitar track in figure 4.1.

Fig. 4.1.
This is the source audio file for a guitar track.

Say you like some parts of the track and not others, plus you want to get a bit creative with the track. So, you cut out some parts and move other parts so the track sounds really cool and ultimately looks like figure 4.2.

Fig. 4.2.
If you were recording with analog tape and had to chop up the file like this, the edit would take forever!

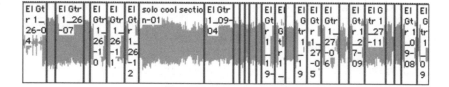

Once you begin editing a track, many distinct regions are created and the edit playlist becomes more complex. Yet, with non-destructive editing, instead of creating brand new audio files for each small part of the track shown in figure 4.2, Pro Tools simply directs the hard drive to the place where each part of the audio track is located on the original source audio file, in the order determined by the edit playlist.

Having a large number of edits on your tracks requires the hard drive to do a lot of locating. (That's one reason that you need a fast hard drive to have Pro Tools work properly.) For example, the edit playlist may first direct the hard drive to read the first two seconds of the source audio file. Then an edit occurs that tells the hard drive to read the last four seconds of audio on the source file. The next edit instructs the hard drive to read a different section, and so on. Thus, the original audio file is not actually cut apart and spliced together…it only appears that way on your computer screen. In reality, the source audio file is completely intact and untouched. Ah, the beauty of non-destructive hard disk digital audio editing.

EDIT MODES AND EDIT TOOLS

There are six edit tools you can employ for editing in Pro Tools: the Zoomer, Trimmer, Selector, Grabber, Scrubber, and Pencil tools.

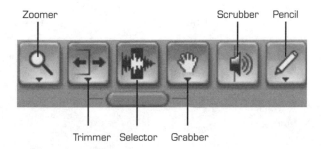

Zoomer   Scrubber Pencil

Trimmer Selector Grabber

Fig. 4.3.
By pressing the bar below the Trimmer, Selector, and Grabber tool icons, you can select the Smart Tool. This edit tool lets you use the Selector, Grabber, and Trimmer, as well as create fades and crossfades, all at once. Depending on where you place the cursor within a region or MIDI note, the Smart Tool automatically switches to the appropriate tool for the job.

The Selector Tool

The Selector tool will probably be your most used edit tool. Its primary functions are to place the cursor for playback at a specific point on the track (by clicking in the track) and to select specific track material for editing (by clicking and dragging in the track).

Here are some handy Selector tool features: If you double-click with the Selector on a region, the entire region will become selected (highlighted). If you triple-click with the Selector on a track, the track's entire edit playlist will become selected (highlighted). If you place the cursor somewhere on a track's edit playlist, then hold down the Shift key and select another part of the playlist, all of the area between the two points on the playlist will become selected.

The Grabber Tool

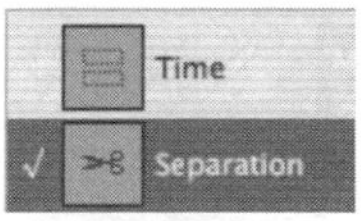

The Grabber Tool comes in two flavors: Time Grabber and Separation Grabber, as seen in figure 4.4.

You'll probably use the Time Grabber most often. Its primary function is to select or move entire regions, MIDI events, and Conductor track events. The Grabber can also be used to insert and edit automation breakpoints (see chapter 12). Read about creating and editing automation data in this chapter's Pro Tools Hands-On.

Time

√ Separation

Fig. 4.4.
The Separation Grabber separates selected material into new regions. This tool makes it really easy to grab part of a track, cut it automatically, and move it somewhere else.

⊞ The Trimmer Tool

The Trimmer's main function is to shorten or expand a region. It can also be used to lengthen and shorten MIDI notes as well as scale automation and controller data up or down. Being a non-destructive tool, it does not actually modify the original audio or MIDI data.

For editing audio, the Trimmer is most often used to cut off the beginning or end of a region or to extend a region's start or end point by clicking and dragging the beginning or end of a region left or right to shorten or lengthen the region. To reverse the direction of the Trimmer, press Option (Mac) or Alt (Win).

The Trimmer tool can also be used in Time Trimmer mode. The Time Trimmer uses the Time Compression/Expansion AudioSuite plug-in to alter the length of an audio region and create a new audio file. Use this tool to time compress or expand a region so that it matches the length of another region, fits better on a tempo grid, or for a special effect. Simply drag the start or end point of a region with this tool to expand or compress the region. Choose the default settings for the TC/E plug-in from the pop-up list in the Processing Preferences page or create your own by opening the plug-in itself and saving your settings.

EDIT MODES — OH, BEHAVE!

The Edit modes (Shuffle, Slip, Spot, and Grid) determine how regions behave on a track's edit playlist when edited by the edit tools. They provide you with different ways to manipulate your recorded tracks with the editing tools.

Shuffle mode: This mode restricts the placement of regions so that they snap to each other and are placed end to end.

Spot mode: In this mode, you're prompted to enter a location for the moved or trimmed region.

Grid mode: This mode constrains edits and selections to the nearest spaced boundary.

Slip mode: In this mode, regions can be moved and trimmed freely, and placed so that regions overlap or so there is space between regions in the destination track.

For example, the Trimmer tool, when used in conjunction with each of the edit modes, can be a very powerful editing tool. Often, you'll want to use the Trimmer tool in Slip mode. When in Slip mode, the regions are simply trimmed wherever you see them on the computer screen. However, when using Shuffle mode, adjacent regions are slid as necessary to make room for the edited region. If using Grid mode, the trimmed start/end times snap to the nearest grid boundary. And, if using Spot mode, the Spot dialog opens, where you can enter the new location for the trimmed region's start or end point. Try out all of the edit tools in each edit mode to see the unique editing features of every combination.

The Scrubber Tool

The purpose of the Scrubber in Pro Tools is to emulate the "scrubbing" technique used to edit analog tape. By scrubbing over a digital audio edit point, you can listen in closely to find the exact edit point, which may not be obvious just by looking at the waveform.

To scrub an audio track, select the Scrubber and drag within a track. To scrub two adjacent audio tracks at once, simply drag along the line between the two tracks. Zoom in on a track to scrub over a small area, or press Command (Mac) or Control (Win) to scrub at a finer resolution without zooming.

The direction, distance, and speed at which you drag will determine the sound of the scrubbed audio. Normal scrubbing allows you to scrub at regular playback speed or slower. If you want to scrub at speeds faster than regular speed, press Option (Mac) or Alt (Win) while dragging. This is called Scrub/Shuttle mode and allows for scrubbing at several times the regular speed. This feature is useful for scrolling through long tracks to find a specific part of the track.

The Pencil Tool

When editing audio, the Pencil tool has one function: to redraw waveforms. Often, this is done to repair waveforms, such as to eliminate a pop or click on the track. However, the Pencil has many other useful functions, including inserting MIDI notes, editing velocities for a range of MIDI notes, and drawing automation and controller events. And by pressing Option (Mac) or Alt (Win), the Pencil tool turns into an Eraser, which can be used to delete MIDI notes, or to program changes and sysex events. (Editing MIDI data is covered in chapter 5.)

As you may have already noticed, the Pencil tool comes in five flavors: Free Hand, Line, Triangle, Square, and Random. These represent the different shapes you can draw with the Pencil. I use the free hand and line shapes most often when editing audio. The other shapes are more useful when drawing or editing automation and MIDI data.

The Zoomer Tool

Primarily, the Zoomer tool helps you to enlarge a track (as you would with a magnifying glass or microscope) and find details within its waveforms. It's good for exposing problem areas in a track or locating good edit points.

To zoom in one level and center the Edit window at the zoom point, click once on a region with the Zoomer tool. To zoom back out to the previous level, Option + click (Mac) or Alt + click (Win) with the Zoomer; in this case, a negative sign "-" appears inside the Zoomer tool instead of the usual plus sign "+". Often, a more useful way to zoom is to click and drag on the specific part of a track that you want to magnify horizontally. In this instance, the zoomed area fills the entire edit window.

Scrubbing is a technique originally used in analog tape editing, where engineers would roll the tape back and forth over the tape machine's playhead at slow speeds with their hands to find a particular location on the tape . . . usually the location for a splice.

Fig. 4.5.
Click on the Pencil tool to choose between the five Pencil drawing shapes.

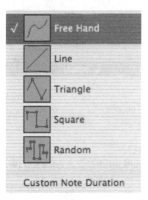

The Pencil is a destructive tool. It actually changes the original audio file permanently! Although pencil edits can be undone, be careful how you wield your pencil . . . it can be sharper than a sword when used on audio files.

Fig. 4.6.
The Single Zoom tool is
identified with an arrow to the
right of the Zoomer tool icon.
Normal Zoom mode doesn't
have the arrow.

In addition to the normal Zoomer tool, you can select the Single
Zoom tool that returns you to the previously selected tool after a zoom
has been performed. For example, when using the Selector you can click
on the Single Zoom Tool mode and, once the Zoom operation has been
performed, Pro Tools automatically switches back to the Selector.

KEYBOARD SHORTCUTS FOR THE EDITING TOOLS

You can use the function keys to switch between the edit tools. Simply press:

- F5 for the Zoomer (keep pressing F5 to toggle between the two Zoomer tools)
- F6 for the Trimmer (keep pressing F6 to toggle between the two Zoomer tools)
- F7 for the Selector
- F8 for the Grabber (keep pressing F8 to toggle between the two Grabber tools)
- F9 for the Scrubber
- F10 for the Pencil (keep pressing F10 to toggle through the five Pencil shapes)
- F6 + F7 for the Smart Tool

A PDF document listing all of the keyboard shortcuts was installed on
your computer with Pro Tools. Print out this document (appropriately named
"Keyboard Shortcuts.pdf") and become familiar with the shortcuts . . . they will
improve your Pro Tools efficiency immensely.

Tab to Transients and Link Selections

In the same area of the Edit window as the Edit modes, there are two
other useful buttons. Tab to Transients allows you to use the Tab key to
navigate from one **transient** part of an audio waveform to the next.

The other useful button found to the right of the Tab to Transient
button in figure 4.7 is the Link Selections button. This button links
Edit and Timeline selections, allowing you to set play and record
ranges by selecting in the track's playlist. When unlinked (the button
is unhighlighted), you can make Edit selections without disturbing the
Timeline selection. What that means is that you can select a portion of
the session to play in the Timeline (conductor ruler), but edit a different
section of the session. I usually just keep the Link Selections button
highlighted, but occasionally it's useful to unlink the Edit and Timeline
selections. For instance, when unlinked, you can loop a MIDI drum
beat and edit a few of the notes within the loop while it's playing back
without interrupting the playback.

Fig. 4.7.
Tab to Transients is particularly
useful for editing drums or
other percussive instruments,
where the transients are
usually indicative of the
beginning of a beat, measure,
or phrase.

Track Views

Pro Tools offers many options for viewing your regions and tracks. As
seen in figure 4.8, the Track View Selector, found in the Edit window
below each track's name, allows you to choose which data is displayed

in the track's playlist. Whatever data you choose to display is the data that you can edit on-screen.

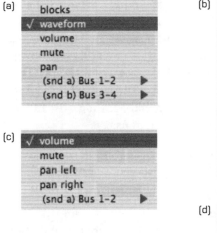

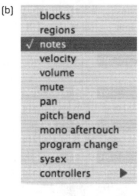

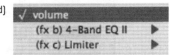

■ Fig. 4.8.
The Track View Selector for (a) an Audio Track, (b) a MIDI Track, (c) an Aux Track, (d) a Master Fader Track.

Audio and MIDI tracks have "Master views." That is, when a track is viewed in its master format, any edits performed on that track apply to all data on that track. For example, when an audio track is set to Waveform view, deleting part of the waveform data will also delete automation data on that section of the audio track. Here are the Master Views for each type of track.

Master Views

Audio	MIDI	Aux/Master fader
Waveform	Regions	*none*
Blocks	Blocks	
	Notes	

For most of your audio and automation editing, you'll probably use the Waveform and Volume views. To easily toggle back and forth between these two views, click in a track that you want to toggle (Shift-click for additional tracks), and press Ctrl + - (Mac) or Start + - (Win) on the alpha keyboard.

Creating New Regions

When editing audio, you will often need to select a portion of a region and delete it, move it somewhere else, or make multiple copies of it. For example, you may want to make multiple copies of a bass line to create a bass loop that repeats during a song's verse. In Pro Tools, there are several ways to select a portion of audio and create a new region, including capturing a new region, separating a region, or using the Separation Grabber tool.

I usually create a new region by selecting a portion of an existing region with the Selector tool and choosing Separate Region from the Edit menu (or typing ⌘ + E [Mac] and Ctrl + E [Win]). This command creates new regions by separating and renaming the affected regions on the playlist. Additionally, if you've placed the cursor somewhere on a region but haven't selected any part of it, the Separate Region command will split the region right where the cursor is. It is beneficial to automatically separate a region like this if you know you want to cut out and/or move the region, because it makes the region easier to select, grab, trim, move, or delete. I also recommend learning how to use the Separation Grabber to perform region separations.

Cut, Copy, Paste, and Clear

If you've used any piece of software (like a word processor or spreadsheet) other than Pro Tools, you probably have cut, pasted, copied, and cleared data before. Those actions are no different in Pro Tools, except that you are cutting, pasting, copying, and clearing audio or MIDI data instead of text or graphics. These commands are very useful for editing and can be used to edit any type of track material. The Track View determines what type of track material (e.g., volume data) is cut or copied from a track. Remember that you'll cut or copy all data that accompanies a track in its Master View, as mentioned previously.

As with most editing functions, the current edit mode determines how track material is affected by an editing action.

The key commands for copying, cutting, pasting, and clearing in Pro Tools are the standard commands in most other software programs.

	Mac	**Win**
Copy	⌘ + C	Ctrl + C
Cut	⌘ + X	Ctrl + X
Paste	⌘ + V	Ctrl + V
Clear	⌘ = B	Ctrl + B

DIGITAL EDITING TECHNIQUES

When cutting and splicing analog tape, you rely solely on your ears to find musical edit points. There are often hundreds of pieces of tape to keep track of and all razor-cut edits are destructive. It is an exacting and exhaustive process that yielded good results for several decades. However, it's fast becoming a dead art since digital editing has forever changed the way we think about production.

One of the best features of editing digital audio (in my opinion) is that you actually see the waveform you're trying to edit; you're able to combine your senses (hearing and sight) to get the job done. Obviously, music is heard, not seen, so we must continue to rely heavily on our ears to make sure anything we do sounds good. However, for visually oriented people like me, being able to see what I'm listening to helps me find accurate edit points much faster. In fact, most people rely on sight as their primary sense . . . even musicians.

With its variety of functions, there's really little you can't do in Pro Tools when editing audio or MIDI. In fact, because Pro Tools offers so many ways to edit your music, every Pro Tools user seems to utilize different techniques and functions to get their work done — an entire book could be written on Pro Tools editing techniques alone. That said, I'm going to cover just a few of the functions I use regularly. Additional information on all of the editing features of Pro Tools can be found in the *Pro Tools Reference Guide* and on the Digidesign Web site. I also recommend getting together with other Pro Tools users and exchanging tips — you'll be surprised how much you can learn. (Visit Digidesign's User Conference area or the DigiZine on their site for access to a knowledgeable and vibrant community of Digi users, from newbies to top pros.)

In its most basic forms, Pro Tools editing is cutting, pasting, copying, and clearing regions and files; being familiar with these commands is imperative. Editing also involves dexterity in creating regions, capturing regions, locking regions, placing regions in tracks, and sliding regions so you can manipulate them comfortably.

Usually I learn new editing techniques when forced to do so. For example, I needed to figure out the best and fastest way to comp a vocal part together. So I paged through the reference guide for information, asked some friends, and sussed out a few different techniques. After trying several methods, I chose to comp vocals using playlists because it worked best for my recording and editing needs. This technique might not be the technique that someone else would use first, but it works well for me. The moral: Don't feel like you have to be a total Pro Tools expert to edit like a pro. You can learn as you go!

Pro Tools has multiple levels of undo so you can step back through up to 16 of your previous edits.

Comping Using Playlists

"Comping" is the process of combining all the best parts from multiple takes into one master take. As I mentioned in chapter 2, I like to record multiple takes of tracks, particularly overdubs such as vocals or guitar solos, on new playlists on the same track. That way I can compare the parts I like from each and easily edit them to create a master take. To me, copying and pasting among takes on separate playlists is the fastest way to comp together the finished product because (a) it's not necessary to create or separate any regions (Pro Tools automatically creates them) and (b) the same selected audio or MIDI area stays selected when changing between playlists, making seamless comps a breeze.

To create a playlist for a new take, choose New from the Playlist selector and name the file accordingly (as in figure 4.9). To copy and paste between takes, select and copy the audio or MIDI area that you want from one playlist, then choose the "target" (master take) playlist using the Playlist selector and perform a paste — Pro Tools automatically creates a new region for the pasted part. If you need to create a crossfade between regions on a newly comped track to smooth out the sonic transition between two regions, choose Fades then Create Fades from the Edit menu (more on fades and crossfades in the section that follows).

Fig. 4.9.
Click on the arrow next to a track name to select or create a new playlist, then name the playlist.

Name for new playlist:

Gtr Solo-COMP

Cancel   OK

FADES AND CROSSFADES

A huge part of making your edits sound natural is your ability to use crossfades. Crossfading is the process of fading two regions of audio together to prevent pops, clicks, or sudden changes in sound. Crossfades have many applications, from smoothing transitions between regions to creating special audio effects.

Pro Tools makes it easy to create your own fades and crossfades. For those who've edited analog tape, you know you're basically limited to choosing one of a few different angles of tape cuts to create crossfades. But with Pro Tools you can actually draw your own crossfade curves and listen to how they sound, or choose from Equal Power, Equal Gain, and any of a number of different curves as seen in figure 4.10. You can even apply dither to fades.

Fig. 4.10.
The Fades window takes the pain out of creating seamless transitions between regions.

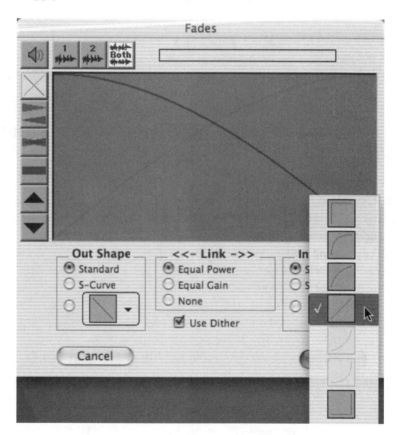

Note: When you're working with 24-bit files I recommend using dither on crossfades if levels are low, and that you always use dither on fade-ins and fade-outs. (Dither is fully explained in chapter 13.)

THE EASY WAYS TO FADE

As with most other major functions in Pro Tools, there are keyboard shortcuts that make creating fades easier. To access the Fades dialog box, simply type ⌘ + F (Mac) or Ctrl + F (Win). And even easier . . . to apply a crossfade to a selection without accessing Fades window at all, do this:

⌘ + Ctrl + F (Mac)   This uses the default fade shape defined in the Preferences.

Ctrl + Start + F (Win)   This uses the last fade shape that you selected.

And remember, you can also use the Smart Tool to create fades and crossfades. First, place the Smart tool near the beginning or end of a region. Then, to create a fade, mouse to the upper half of the track and the fade icon will appear. Click and drag where you want the fade to begin and end. Similarly, if you want to create a crossfade, mouse to the lower half of the region and the crossfade icon will appear. Click and drag where you want the crossfade to begin and end.

Nudging Notes

Sometimes you'll record a great take but one or two notes are just a bit out of time. A good example of this is when a bass player hits a downbeat slightly ahead of when the drummer hits the kick drum. (I'm not implying that bass players tend to rush; they just get overly excited sometimes.) To fix the syncopation, you can nudge the bass note slightly later in time to match the kick downbeat.

To nudge a note or several notes, first find the note(s) in the waveform in the Edit window. Zoom in close enough so you can see where the note begins and ends. Select the note(s) and create a new region by choosing Separate Region from the Edit menu. Now select the nudge value from the Nudge dropdown menu in the upper-right corner of the Edit window. You can choose from Bars:Beats, Min:Secs, or Samples. Pro Tools offers a list of values for each of these, but you can type in your own if you want. I recommend trying 10ms as a starting point and adjusting from there. Press the plus key (+) on the numeric keypad to move your selection forward by the nudge value or the minus key (–) to move the selection back. You may have to press either key several times to align the bass note with the kick drum.

And if you want to get really fancy.... If you nudge while pressing Control (Mac) or the Start key (Win), you can actually nudge the contents of a region without changing the region's start and end points. This only works if there's audio or MIDI material outside the region's start and end points. (It would work in our bass/kick drum example and could possibly yield slightly better results.) You should also note that the Nudge command works the same regardless of the Edit mode you're using at the time.

■ Fig. 4.11.
Use the Nudge dropdown menu to easily move selected regions without having to mess with ultra-accurate mousing.

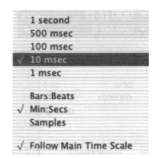

1 second
500 msec
100 msec
√ 10 msec
1 msec

Bars:Beats
√ Min:Secs
Samples

√ Follow Main Time Scale

Be careful using the nudge editing technique though. You can go crazy trying to align every note, killing way too much time and taking away from the real performance – the "vibe" – of the part. If the part needs that much fixing, re-record it!

Repairing Waveforms with the Pencil Tool

As mentioned previously, the Pencil tool allows you to redraw waveforms and make precise edits. This is particularly useful for repairing vocal plosives and pops or clicks that might randomly occur. Be careful when using this tool though; redrawing a waveform with the Pencil permanently alters the audio file on your hard drive once it's saved (i.e., destructive editing), so it's a good idea to make a backup of the original file before editing.

To repair a waveform by redrawing it you must view the waveform at the sample level. Zoom in all the way so the waveform appears as a continuous thin line. With the Free Hand Pencil tool, redraw the waveform by dragging the pencil over it. Try to keep the same basic form of the sound wave when redrawing or you might create an even nastier sound than the pop or click you were trying to fix. At the same time, you can create some wacky effects with pencil edits. Experiment with your waveform drawing technique . . . remember, you can always undo your edits (in this case, just make sure you're *very* happy or have a backup before you save).

Editing Automation Data with the Pencil Tool

I use the Pencil tool most often to edit automation data – it's so easy to draw volume fades and panning moves. I've found it very beneficial to create automation data first using the Mix window faders in Auto Write and Auto Touch modes, then fine tuning with the Pencil tool. (Automation is covered in chapter 12.) See the Pro Tools Hands-On section in this chapter for more info on creating and editing automation data.

Fig. 4.12

Volume automation data can be adjusted in fine increments using the Pencil tool.

This is particularly helpful when riding vocal levels. After you've recorded a good automation pass using the mouse or MIDI controller on a fader, go to the Edit window and select Volume from the Track View menu (as seen in figure 4.12). Use the Pencil tool to redraw any volume levels to make the track sound its best.

SEVERAL USEFUL KEY COMMANDS FOR EDITING

Key commands make your life a lot easier when using Pro Tools. Learn as many as you can and use them to improve your efficiency. More editing techniques and commands I find useful are described in chapters 9, 11, and 12, but here are a few I use often:

• You can slide a copy of a region to another location or track by pressing Option (Mac) or Alt (Win) while dragging.

- To retain a region's horizontal location when dragging to another track, press Control [Mac] or right-click [Win] while dragging.
- To zoom in/out horizontally, press ⌘ +] or [(Mac) or Ctrl +] or [(Win).
- To zoom in/out vertically, press ⌘ + Option +] or [(Mac), Ctrl + Alt +] or [(Win audio), or Ctrl + Shift +] or [(Win MIDI).

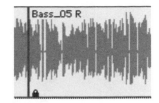

Fig. 4.13.
The keyboard shortcut for locking (or unlocking) a region is ⌘ + L (Mac) and Ctrl + L (Win).

Locking Regions

Once you've made some edits that you're happy with and don't want to unintentionally nudge or move the region, it's a good idea to "lock" the region in place. Locking a region or a group of regions ensures the region(s) cannot be moved, but allows you to still perform operations such as recording and automation editing on the region(s).

To lock a region, select the region(s) with the Grabber tool and choose Lock/Unlock Region from the Edit menu. A small lock appears in the region, indicating that it has been locked, as in figure 4.13.

It's a smart move to lock your regions once you've done some editing to a song. And, I highly recommend locking regions once you start mixing your song. You don't want to spend time realigning regions that you moved by accident while mixing.

Now let's move on to recording and editing MIDI tracks.... ▮▮

Fig. 4.14.
If you try to perform edits that would move the locked region, Pro Tools alerts you with this window.

▮ PRO TOOLS HANDS-ON

Experiment with Edit Modes and Tools

Experiment with each edit mode and edit tool on something you've already recorded, or choose a track from the CD-ROM sessions. Create new regions and move them around. Get familiar with the Smart tool by mousing over different parts of a region to see the many functionalities of the tool. Switch between edit modes and tools using the function keys. Also try dragging a region from the Audio Regions List and observe how the region is placed within a track's playlist, depending on the chosen edit mode.

Create Fades and Crossfades

Since crossfades are created by fading between overlapping audio material, a crossfade cannot be performed on regions that do not contain audio material beyond their region boundaries. Crossfades are written to your hard drive and stored in a folder named "Fade Files" within your session folder. When you play back your track,

Pro Tools reads and plays back the crossfade file from your hard drive.

The Link parameter in the Fades window (figure 4.10) enables you to choose the fade-out and fade-in curves used in a crossfade. Choose Equal Power when creating a crossfade between two completely different types of musical material. Choose Equal Gain when creating a crossfade between two identical types of musical material (e.g., on repeated loops).

You can also choose None when you want to edit the fade-out and fade-in separately. Press Ctrl (Win) or Command (Mac) while dragging to edit the fade-out section of a crossfade. Press Alt (Win) or Option (Mac) while dragging to edit the fade-in.

Try it. Create a crossfade between two regions. Listen to the difference between Equal Power and Equal Gain crossfades. Then, choose None in the Link section of the Fades window and try editing both the fade-out and fade-in sections of a crossfade. Finally, experiment with all of the other ways to create fades and crossfades, including the Smart Tool and keyboard shortcuts.

Create a Drum Loop

Why is creating a loop considered practice for editing audio? Because many of the concepts, techniques, and tools required to edit audio are used in creating a loop. Create a drum loop using the Naked Drums demo session included on the book's CD.

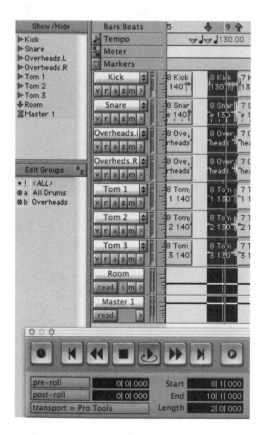

First, find and select a section of music that you'd like to loop, such as one measure of a drum beat, using Loop Playback. (Choose Loop Playback from the Operations menu.) Adjust the selection length so that the loop doesn't lose the beat. You may find using Tab to Transients helpful when selecting the material for your loop.

The next step is to separate the regions in each track so you can manipulate them using the edit modes and tools. Remember that you can separate a region by pressing ⌘ + E (Mac) or Ctrl + E (Win). To separate the regions on all tracks at once, highlight the section on all the tracks, then separate them. To select (highlight) multiple tracks at once, press the Shift key while selecting each track. An even easier way is to activate the "! <All>" Edit Group, as seen in the figure at left. Then, when you highlight one part of one track, all the tracks will be highlighted in the same places.

Move the loop to the end of the session, make several copies of the loop material, and paste them together. An easy way to make copies of a loop is to select all the loop material with the Grabber, then in Shuffle mode, select Repeat from the Edit menu [or press Option + R

(Mac) or Alt + R (Win)]. A dialog box will open that looks like the figure at right.

Type "3" as the number of repeats and click OK. This will paste three copies of the selected material next to the original material. As you learned earlier, Shuffle mode places regions right next to other regions so you don't even have to lift a finger to make the regions tight. You may need to crossfade each loop together to ensure there are no pops or other sonic inconsistencies between the end of the loop and the start of the next loop.

To quickly create a crossfade on all tracks at once:

1. Activate the "! <All>" Edit Group.

2. Position the Smart tool at the boundary between two regions.

3. Move the Smart tool to the lower half of a region to activate the crossfade tool.

4. Click and drag to create a crossfade on each track.

Use Memory Locations and Markers for Editing Audio

You can use markers to expedite moving large amounts of audio around in a Pro Tools session. For example, if you've got markers set up at the exact beginning and ending of a verse, you can make the verse twice as long by copying and pasting it in a matter of seconds. (Try *that* with analog tape!)

To do this, click on the beginning marker (in the Marker Ruler), press and hold Shift, click on the end marker, and copy the material. Click on the marker where you want to insert the additional verse and paste the copied verse (while in Shuffle mode). The audio files will line up snug to the previous verse and the following section of the song.

Try it. In any of the song sessions on the CD, create markers at the start of each section (e.g., verse, chorus, etc.). Use Loop Playback to make sure the markers are set up at the exact start and end points of the song sections so that they will flow together when combined. Cut and paste together a completely different arrangement of the song using the markers you created.

Edit Spoken Word

One of the most important and difficult editing tasks that you'll have to perform is editing speech and vocals. When editing speech (for a voiceover, a monologue, a rap, etc.), it's customary to edit the words so that there is no stuttering, stammering, hesitation, or mistakes (unless, of course, those effects are desired). Many times it's also beneficial to eliminate unnecessary pauses and open spaces between words and sentences. This will increase the pace of the performance and is often done when there are a lot of breathing pauses, or when you want to intensify the impact of the delivery (e.g., a fast-talking radio DJ).

When editing speech or vocals, it's always a good idea to have the script, text, or lyrics as a printed guide for making notes about where to place your edits. This also helps if you want to remove parts of the text while keeping the overall meaning.

A tricky yet interesting part of editing speech or vocals is figuring out the best edit points. Because language possesses such complex sounds and sound patterns, figuring out where words start and end can be challenging. There are many components of words that you need to be aware of when editing. They each have distinctive sounds and often sound totally different from each other, once you listen to them more closely and analyze their waveforms. As you get better at identifying waveforms, you will begin to hear—and also see—the differences between consonants and vowels, and you will learn the best ways to work with the unique characteristics of specific consonant and vowel sounds.

Try it. On the CD, there is a session called Voiceover. Copy it to your audio hard drive and open it. This session contains one audio file of voiceover material for you to listen to and edit. The audio is of me reading the first paragraph of chapter 4.

First, listen to the track at full speed to get a feel for it. Then, listen to the track at half-speed by pressing Shift-Spacebar. Try the Scrubber tool on some sections of the track. Listen to and look at the differences between consonants and vowels. Spend a minute or two scrubbing over different consonants and vowels to get a feel for where each word starts and finishes. Listen closely for the **sibilant** sounds of the letter "s" and also to the larger spaces left for commas and periods, as well as the smaller spaces between words.

There are some mistakes in the reading. This was done purposely. Edit out the mistakes and smooth out the timing of the performance so that you create a near-perfect reading. Then, shorten the open spaces between some of the words and sentences, thereby increasing the pace of the reading. Finally, check out my quick edit of the voiceover track on the track's second playlist and compare it to your edit.

Nudging the Groove

Use nudging to edit the offbeat guitar track in the Basic Effects Send session (on the CD) so that it lines up perfectly with the drum beats. Try this for four measures (or more). Listen to the differences between the original and your nudged version. Do your edits make the groove tighter or more sterile?

Record and Edit Automation Data

You can use all of the audio editing tools and techniques that you've learned so far to edit automation data. Used mainly in mixing, automation is data that automatically controls the parameters of a track (such as volume level or panning), the parameters of a plug-in (such as the ratio on a compressor or the wet/dry mix of a reverb), or any other automatable parameters within a Pro Tools session.

On audio tracks, you can control volume, pan, mute, send volume, send pan, send mute, and plug-in parameters. You can look at any automation data on a track by choosing it from the Track View Selector, as in the figure below (left).

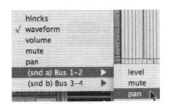

However, before editing automation, you've got to record it. The basic steps for recording automation are:

1. Put the appropriate track(s) in an automation writing mode (Write, Touch, or Latch mode) using the Automation Mode Selector, as in the figure above (right).

2. Press play to begin automation recording and adjust the controls (volume, pan, mutes, etc.) as needed. Pro Tools remembers all your moves.

You can also create automation data by drawing it with the pencil tool. Select the automation type you want to draw on a track from the Track View Selector, choose the Pencil tool and appropriate drawing shape, and start drawing. Check out the QuickTime movie "drawingautomation" on the CD to see this process firsthand. We'll get deeper into recording automation, including plug-in automation, in chapter 12.

Once automation has been recorded, you can edit it in three different ways.

1. Repeat the steps for recording automation to write new automation over the pre-existing data.

2. Graphically edit the automation data in the Edit window.

3. Cut, copy, paste, or delete automation.

When you edit an audio track while in Waveform view, edits affect the audio and all automation data playlists on that track.

That is very important to understand. Conversely, if the track display is set to show automation data, edits only affect the type of automation data displayed in the track. For example, with the track display set to "pan," the Cut command *only* cuts pan data from the pan playlist.

When you paste automation data, the data is pasted into the correct type of playlist, regardless of the track display setting. Audio data is pasted into the audio playlist; automation data is pasted into the appropriate automation playlist. Pasting new data replaces any previous data on the target playlist without shuffling, regardless of whether you are in Slip or Shuffle mode.

Try it. Record and edit automation in a Pro Tools session. Experiment with all of the edit tools to see how each one can edit automation. Create a fade-out manually by drawing it with the Pencil tool, then edit it with the Grabber, Trimmer, and Pencil tools. Draw mute automation on a track with the Pencil tool using the Square shape. Create auto-panning automation on a track with the Pencil tool using the Triangle shape. Experiment! Have fun!

Recording and Editing MIDI Tracks

In this chapter:

- **The basics of MIDI**

- **Recording MIDI and MIDI instruments**

- **Editing MIDI tracks, quantizing, and the Event list**

- **Importing and exporting MIDI files**

- **Creating realistic MIDI parts**

This chapter covers the basics of MIDI as well as most of the MIDI features in Pro Tools. For beginners and pros alike, it can serve as a guide for using MIDI in your productions. Even if you're an "old hand" with Pro Tools sequencing, be sure to check out the last section on creating real-sounding MIDI parts for some important production concepts.

MIDI in Pro Tools is treated essentially the same as audio so it's easy to transfer your recording, editing, and mixing knowledge from one realm to the other.

The Digi 002/001 has a built-in MIDI interface, but if you're using Pro Tools with the Mbox, Audiomedia III, or a third-party card, you'll need a separate MIDI interface to do your sequencing. Consult chapter 8 for more information on setting up an external MIDI interface.

THE BASICS OF MIDI

As you probably already know, **MIDI** (Musical Instrument Digital Interface) data is *not* audio data. Rather, MIDI performances are created using a MIDI controller such as a keyboard or drum machine, and used to trigger MIDI sound modules that produce audio (e.g., a MIDI sequence sends data to a sound module whose *audio* outs — not MIDI outs — are then recorded). MIDI devices send and receive MIDI data through **MIDI interfaces.**

MIDI connections are made with the MIDI in, MIDI out, and MIDI thru ports. As you might have guessed, MIDI in ports accept incoming data and MIDI out ports send MIDI data from the device. MIDI thru ports route a copy of all data received at the MIDI in port directly to another device in the MIDI communication chain. Not all MIDI devices have all three MIDI ports.

MIDI data messages are sent on channels, and each MIDI cable can transmit on 16 *different* channels. Each channel is used for a distinct instrument sound (e.g., channel 1 for a synth pad, channel 2 for piano, etc.), though channel 10 is often reserved for drums and percussion sounds. Many MIDI devices are multitimbral, which allows them to send or receive MIDI data on up to 16 channels or more at a time.

Setting Up Your Own MIDI Network

There are two basic ways to network your MIDI devices: daisy chains and hubs. In a daisy chain arrangement, a controller's MIDI out port feeds another device's MIDI in port, which feeds a copy of the data from its thru port to the next device's MIDI in port. In a hub-based network, each MIDI device is connected to a MIDI interface that acts as a kind of patchbay. Software controls the routing of the MIDI signals to and from each MIDI device. (More information on setting up a hub-based MIDI network is presented in chapter 8.)

In its simplest form, a daisy chain MIDI network looks like figure 5.1. Here I show a rudimentary setup with a keyboard controller (Yamaha PSR-410) and a sound module (Roland JV-1010). The hardware connections are as follows:

■ **Fig. 5.1.**
A daisy chain configuration allows you to use multiple MIDI instruments with Digi 001's one-in/one-out MIDI interface.

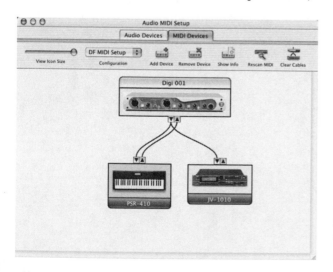

- PSR-410 MIDI out to 001 MIDI in

- 001 MIDI out to JV-1010 MIDI in

- JV1010 MIDI thru to PSR-410 MIDI in

With this setup I can utilize the sounds on the JV-1010 and PSR-410 (as long as each device is set up to receive MIDI messages on separate channels) while using the PSR-410 as the controller for both devices. Digi 002 has a one-in/two-out

You can silence stuck MIDI notes by choosing All Notes Off from the MIDI menu.

MIDI interface that allows you to hook up two sound modules to the interface and send MIDI data on 32 distinct channels. *Don't forget you need to connect the audio outs from your MIDI sound source to audio inputs on your Digi 002, 001, Mbox, Audiomedia III card, or third-party audio card to hear your MIDI sounds in Pro Tools.*

Once you've physically connected your MIDI network, you need to configure your computer to recognize your MIDI devices and route their signals properly. If using a Mac, open the Audio MIDI Setup application and click on the MIDI tab. The window shown in figure 5.1 will open. Add and connect MIDI devices in this window to create your MIDI setup. If using a PC, do the same except use your Sounds and Audio Devices Control Panel. For more detail on this part of the procedure, consult the manuals that came with your Digidesign software.

Setting Up Pro Tools for MIDI

To get MIDI happening in Pro Tools there are a few quick things you need to configure. First choose Input Devices from the MIDI menu. (You only need to do this if you use a Mac.) Make sure all of your MIDI controllers are enabled by checking the box for each device as in figure 5.2. My JV-1010 sound module is not a controller, therefore it's not on this list.

Second, make sure there's a check mark next to MIDI Thru in the MIDI menu; this allows you to monitor MIDI tracks while recording them. When using MIDI Thru, disable local control on your MIDI controller. Otherwise your controller might receive the same MIDI data twice, creating stuck notes or a phase-like effect. (Consult your controller's manual for information on local control settings.)

Third, if you'd like to hear the audio output of a MIDI device without having to create and record-enable a track, route your MIDI signal to the Default Thru Instrument. From the Setups menu choose Preferences and click on the MIDI tab. From the popup menu for Default Thru Instrument, choose the MIDI device and channel where you want to route your MIDI data. I recommend using a channel that you might not use on a regular basis (I use channel 16). To disable the Default Thru Instrument, select "none."

Finally, you can filter out any MIDI data you don't want recorded with your tracks by using the MIDI Input Filter. Open the MIDI Input Filter (shown in figure 5.3) from the MIDI menu and select what data you want to record.

Regarding the MIDI Input Filter window, Notes data refers to note on and off messages, including the velocity (how hard a note is played). Pitch Bend is self-explanatory, and Mono and Polyphonic Aftertouch are covered in the "Take Note" box in the margin. Program Changes do exactly what the name implies; they change the program (also called

Fig. 5.2.
Choose Input Devices from the MIDI menu to enable controllers for Pro Tools sequencing.

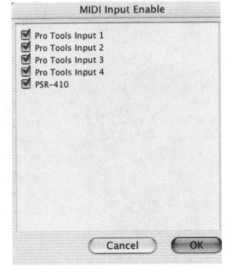

MIDI Input Enable

☑ Pro Tools Input 1
☑ Pro Tools Input 2
☑ Pro Tools Input 3
☑ Pro Tools Input 4
☑ PSR-410

Cancel   OK

Fig. 5.3.
The MIDI Input Filter gives you complete control over what data you want to record.

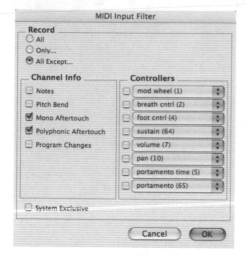

"patch," "sound," "timbre," or "voice," depending on the model and manufacturer).

Controllers refers to any other performance data that your MIDI controller sends; you can add to or subtract from this list by clicking on one of the controller parameter names. System Exclusive data refers to customized, device-specific MIDI data not part of standard MIDI messages. Consult your MIDI controller's manual for information on how to create and send "sys-ex" messages. Inserting and editing these types of MIDI data in Pro Tools is covered later in this chapter.

RECORDING MIDI AND YOUR MIDI INSTRUMENTS

Pro Tools includes a flexible MIDI sequencer that makes it easy to record and edit MIDI tracks right next to your audio parts. To record MIDI data on a track:

1. Create a MIDI track by selecting New Track from the File menu, or Shift + ⌘ + N (Mac) or Shift + Control + N (Win).

2. Select a MIDI controller (and a MIDI channel on that controller) as your input device (e.g., PSR-410, channel 1).

3. Choose the MIDI sound source and channel (e.g., JV-1010 sound module, channel 1) as the output.

4. Pick the sound you want from your MIDI sound source.

5. If you want to monitor the audio signal from your MIDI device without recording it, route the output of your MIDI sound source to an aux track: Create a new aux track (mono or stereo), select the audio output(s) from your MIDI sound source as the aux track input(s), and choose an output that feeds your speakers. *Don't forget you need to connect the audio outs from your MIDI sound source to audio inputs on your 002, 001, Mbox, Audiomedia III, or third-party audio card.*

6. If you want to record a MIDI track as audio, create a new audio track (mono or stereo), select the audio output(s) from your MIDI sound source as the audio track input(s), and choose an output that feeds your speakers. To hear MIDI-generated audio, record-enable the audio track.

7. Press Play and Record (or one of the keyboard shortcuts for recording audio listed in chapter 2).

There's an alternative way to record MIDI in Pro Tools. When you enable the Wait for Note button in the Transport window, Pro Tools

Aftertouch is a measurement of pressure put on a controller when it's played (e.g., the pressure on the keys, or single key, of a MIDI keyboard). Mono aftertouch refers to the pressure on one key, while polyphonic aftertouch refers to the strongest overall pressure on all the keys at any one time. My simple keyboard controller doesn't transmit aftertouch data, so it's pointless for Pro Tools to try to record it.

won't begin recording until it receives MIDI data. Use this function if you want the first MIDI event you play to be recorded at precisely the beginning of your specified record range. Figure 5.4 shows where to activate Wait for Note in the Transport window – the Record and Play buttons will flash until Pro Tools receives the first note.

Wait for Note button   MIDI Merge

Fig. 5.4.
The Wait for Note and MIDI Merge buttons in the Transport window.

You can record normally, punch in, or loop record using Wait for Note. If you want to use pre-roll, it will engage after the first MIDI event is received, then enter Record mode after the pre-roll time passes.

Overdubbing and Punching In Using MIDI Merge or Replace

When overdubbing or punching in MIDI data on a track, you can either completely replace the existing events or add to the new ones that are already there – the latter option is called MIDI Merge. You can engage MIDI Merge (the button is in the Transport window shown in figure 5.4) while playing or recording but it's not available in Loop record mode.

Input Quantize

I'm a drummer, and consider myself to have pretty good timing. However, when recording MIDI notes on a keyboard (like when I'm creating a drum loop), I sometimes have trouble getting the right feel. Input Quantize helps with this problem by automatically quantizing all incoming MIDI notes while you play them. **Quantizing** aligns MIDI notes to a rhythmic grid, helping/forcing them to be more in time or simulating a particular rhythmic feel. (More information on quantization is presented later in this chapter.)

To enable this function choose Input Quantize from the MIDI menu, then select the Enable Input Quantize box (figure 5.5).

Fig. 5.5.
Experiment with the Input Quantize function if you're having trouble getting the right "feel" when sequencing. Beware that quantizing on input can ruin a feel as easily as it helps, but it can be quite useful, especially for drum programming.

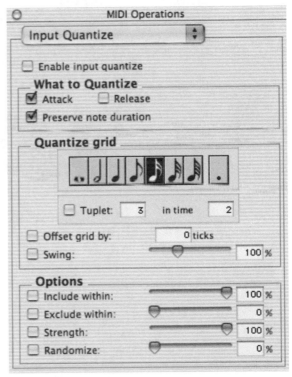

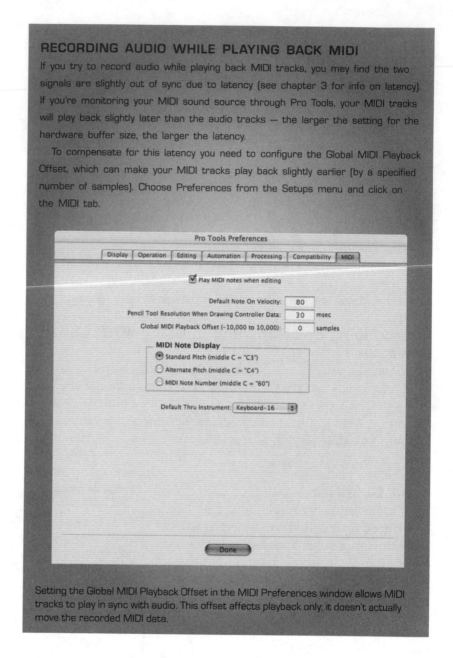

RECORDING AUDIO WHILE PLAYING BACK MIDI

If you try to record audio while playing back MIDI tracks, you may find the two signals are slightly out of sync due to latency (see chapter 3 for info on latency). If you're monitoring your MIDI sound source through Pro Tools, your MIDI tracks will play back slightly later than the audio tracks — the larger the setting for the hardware buffer size, the larger the latency.

To compensate for this latency you need to configure the Global MIDI Playback Offset, which can make your MIDI tracks play back slightly earlier (by a specified number of samples). Choose Preferences from the Setups menu and click on the MIDI tab.

Setting the Global MIDI Playback Offset in the MIDI Preferences window allows MIDI tracks to play in sync with audio. This offset affects playback only; it doesn't actually move the recorded MIDI data.

Similarities Between MIDI and Audio Record Functions

Just as in audio recording with Pro Tools, you can undo a MIDI recording, cancel a record take (before the transport has stopped), and record multiple MIDI tracks at once. The key commands for these functions are listed in figure 5.6.

Punch recording is essentially the same in MIDI as in audio, except that (a) you can use MIDI Merge if you want, (b) you can record-enable MIDI tracks on the fly at any time during playback, and (c) you can

Feature	Macintosh	Windows
Undo a MIDI recording	⌘ + Z	Control + Z
Cancel a record take	⌘ + Period	Control + Period
Record multiple MIDI tracks at once	Shift–Record Enable	Shift–Record Enable

■ Fig. 5.6.
Key commands for some common MIDI recording functions.

use normal Non-Destructive record mode instead of QuickPunch. To punch record a MIDI track, first start playback, then record-enable the MIDI track you want to record on and click the Record button in the Transport window (or press a footswitch connected to your 002/001); press Record or the footswitch again to punch out. Pro Tools continues to play after you exit Record mode, allowing you to perform additional punches at later points in the song.

There are two ways to utilize loop recording on MIDI tracks. The first is essentially the same as loop recording on audio tracks, and the second allows you to use MIDI Merge to create drum loops or other additive loop-style tracks — see the box "Creating a MIDI Drum Loop" for an example.

CREATING A MIDI DRUM LOOP

First put Pro Tools in Non-Destructive record mode and Loop Playback from the Operations menu [Loop *Playback* . . . not Loop Record]. Enable MIDI Merge in the Transport window. Create a new MIDI track, record-enable the track, and make sure the input, output, and sound source [drum machine, sound module with drum kits, etc.] are chosen correctly. Enable your MIDI click track [as described in chapter 2] and Input Quantize, if desired. Select the loop time range in the MIDI track [e.g., one measure], press Record and Play, and go at it!

Start with the kick and snare, or with the hi-hat, and build your beat. On each successive pass you can record additional MIDI data while the notes from previous passes play back. I like to use Input Quantize on the kick and snare but sometimes prefer turning it off for cymbal parts [hi-hat, ride, etc.], to give the loop more of a real feel.

EDITING MIDI TRACKS

Much of what you've learned about audio editing can be applied to MIDI. For example, just as you can draw audio automation and fix waveforms with the Pencil tool, you can also draw MIDI automation as well as insert MIDI notes with the Pencil tool. In fact, most aspects of a recorded MIDI note can be edited in the Edit window, including start and end points, duration, pitch, and velocity.

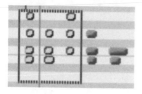

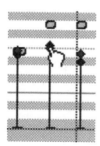

When editing MIDI data each editing tool assists in different functions. With the Grabber tool you can select MIDI notes, move the notes horizontally (in time) or vertically (in pitch), as well as edit velocity values. The Pencil tool allows you to insert, trim, and delete notes, as well as draw velocity curves for entire phrases. The Trimmer tool helps you change the start and end points of MIDI notes, and the Selector tool helps you select a range of notes.

Grabber Tool Editing Functions

Selecting notes with the Grabber tool can be achieved in three ways; you can click on a single note, Shift-click on multiple notes, or click and draw a rectangle around a group of notes with the cursor (as in figure 5.7). Note that any selection you make with the Grabber does not include underlying controller and automation data on that MIDI track.

By clicking on a single or selected group of notes, you can move them forward or back in time by dragging horizontally with the Grabber. You can also change the pitch of (transpose) the notes by dragging them vertically. To transpose a *copy* of a note, leaving the original note where it is, press Option (Mac) or Control (Win) while dragging — this is an easy way to make one-note riffs into chord progressions or add harmonies to melody lines.

With the Grabber you can also change any MIDI note's attack velocity. When a MIDI track's display format is set to Velocity (see figure 5.8), Pro Tools displays each MIDI note's velocity value as a "stalk" — the taller the stalk, the higher the value (from 0 to 127). When viewing the velocity of your MIDI track, simply drag the diamond at the top of a velocity stalk up or down to increase or decrease the value.

You'll notice in figure 5.9 that there are two diamonds on each of the stalks. That means there are two notes located at that same point on the track. In this case, select the note you want to edit with the grabber . . . the note's diamond will turn blue.

Pencil Tool Editing Functions

To insert new MIDI notes with the Pencil tool, set the MIDI track's display format to Notes, select the Free Hand setting of the Pencil tool, and click in the MIDI track at the desired pitch and location. If you want to insert particular types of notes (e.g., all eighth notes), set the edit mode to Grid and choose "1/8 note" in the Grid dropdown menu (upper-right-hand of the Edit window) as in figure 5.10. You can also use the Pencil tool to trim the duration of any MIDI note.

To hear the sound of notes as you insert them, check the Play MIDI Notes When Editing box in the MIDI Preferences window (Setups menu > Preferences > MIDI tab). While there you can also set the Default Note On Velocity, which determines the velocity for each note inserted with the Pencil tool.

To erase MIDI notes you can select them and clear or cut (standard Edit menu functions), or you can use the Pencil tool by pressing Option (Mac) or Alt (Win) and clicking on the notes. (To indicate this function the Pencil tool flips over so the eraser end points to the notes . . . clever, huh?) This is a cool feature to use when you insert a wrong note, since you can erase it immediately.

The Pencil tool is also useful for drawing automation on a MIDI track (the same as on audio tracks) as well as drawing velocity values. See chapters 4, 9, and 12 for more information on drawing automation with the Pencil tool, and the *Pro Tools Reference Guide* for additional info on inserting notes, deleting notes, and altering velocities.

Trimmer Tool Editing Functions

The Trimmer tool is mostly used for changing start and end points of MIDI notes. To do this, simply select what you want to trim then use the Trimmer to length or shorten the note. You can trim at a note's start or end point and apply the trimmed note(s) to Grid boundaries or Spot locations (if in Grid or Spot mode). In Slip and Shuffle modes the notes can be dragged freely. For additional uses of the Trimmer tool, consult the *Pro Tools Reference Guide.*

Inserting and Editing Continuous Controller Events

Continuous controllers that can be inserted and edited in Pro Tools include volume, pan, pitch bend, aftertouch (mono), and any other MIDI controllers (0–127). Polyphonic aftertouch can only be edited in the MIDI Event list.

Unlike all other continuous controller data, volume and pan are treated as automation data by Pro Tools and can be suspended (that is, not played back). All continuous controllers can be edited by dragging individual breakpoints with the Grabber, scaling breakpoints with the Trimmer, drawing new data with the Pencil tool, as well as copying, pasting, nudging, and shifting . . . just like audio regions.

Inserting and Editing Program Changes

You can insert a default program change on a track that's sent each time the track plays, as well as insert program changes at any point within the track. To set the default program change, first select the Program button on the MIDI track (which says "none" until you change it).

Click on the Program button (which opens the Program Change window) and select a program and bank (using controllers 0 and 32), if necessary. The program name or number will appear in the Program button and is saved with your Pro Tools session. You can also audition sounds while in the Program Change window by simply clicking on the program name or number and playing some notes, or you can have Pro Tools automatically audition them for you while the track is playing. For

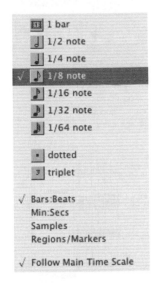

Fig. 5.10.
The Grid dropdown menu allows you to quantize manual note entry according to the selected value.

You can view single MIDI notes on a MIDI track by choosing "single note" from the track's Track View selector. This view is very handy for working with MIDI drum parts that are on their own individual MIDI tracks.

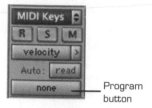

Fig. 5.11.
Use the Program button to set a default sound for your MIDI track.

Program button

Fig. 5.12.
With the display format set to Program Change you can see sound changes right in the track display.

It's a good idea to place your program changes in the track where there are no notes being played, as in figure 5.12. Program changes are notorious for interrupting playback when placed close to MIDI notes.

automatic auditioning, hit Play, open the Program Change window, click a starting program name or number, select the Increment Patch option, and specify the number of seconds between each program change.

To insert a program change within a track, first set the MIDI track's display format to Program Change and use the Pencil tool to click on the MIDI track where you want the change to occur. When you click on the track the Program Change window will open, and after you've chosen a program and clicked Done, the program change will appear in the MIDI track, as seen in figure 5.12. You can move the new program change with the Grabber and edit it by double-clicking.

I usually just make a new MIDI track for any new sound (program) instead of using program changes. For me, having one program per track makes the MIDI tracks easier to control because sometimes sounds have different volume levels and other settings that might make mixing a track more difficult if there are several changes throughout a song.

Inserting and Editing System Exclusive Data

System Exclusive ("sys-ex") data is MIDI data specific to an instrument or piece of hardware, allowing manufacturers to define MIDI messages that address parameters unique to a device (e.g., filter cutoff frequency). Sys-ex can be used to store patch and configuration data for a MIDI device and record realtime changes for non-standard parameters.

The most common reason for inserting sys-ex data in Pro Tools is to "dump" a module's patches onto the beginning of a MIDI track. This way, no matter how many changes you've made in the module since the last time you worked on a session, Pro Tools and your sound module will communicate so that the right sounds will be loaded back into your session every time.

To record the sys-ex data, first make sure System Exclusive is record-enabled in the MIDI Input Filter. While in normal Non-Destructive record mode choose the input device, record-enable your MIDI track, enable Wait for Note, then press Record. Pro Tools will wait until you initiate the sys-ex transfer from your MIDI device, then record as soon as it begins to receive the data. Click Stop when the sys-ex transfer is complete.

Once you've recorded sys-ex data on a MIDI track, it will be sent from Pro Tools to the MIDI device each time you play the track (from any point before the sys-ex data occurs). Just be sure that your MIDI device is set to receive sys-ex and that your Pro Tools MIDI track is properly assigned. Also keep in mind that sys-ex can take a few seconds (or longer) to transmit and be received – you may need to leave some blank measures at the beginning of your song to allow for this.

Sys-ex events appear in Pro Tools just like program changes: as small blocks. To view a block choose sys-ex as the display format on your MIDI track. Although you can't edit sys-ex messages directly in Pro Tools, you can move, nudge, copy, paste, and delete them. Use the Grabber to select and drag the sys-ex data left or right, or copy, paste, or delete it. Individual sys-ex event blocks can also be deleted by Option-clicking (Mac) or Alt-clicking (Win) them with the Pencil tool. (For more information on recording and editing continuous controller, program change, and system exclusive events, consult the *Pro Tools Reference Guide*.)

Editing from the MIDI Operations Window

Selections from the MIDI Operations window (figure 5.13) allow you to Quantize, Change Velocity, Change Duration, Transpose, Select Notes, Split Notes, and Input Quantize MIDI data; to alter the pitch, dynamics, timing, and phrasing of any MIDI performance. We've already covered Input Quantize, and most of the other functions are somewhat self-explanatory. I'll give brief explanations then focus on the most enigmatic of these operations: quantization.

The Select Notes function allows you to select notes based on pitch, whether it's a single note or a range — particularly useful for altering a single note for the entire length of a region or track. Slightly more advanced than the Select Notes function, Split Notes helps you divide notes into ranges. This is useful for splitting up parts that were played on a single track into multiple tracks, as you might like to do with a piano part.

The Change Velocity function adjusts attack and release velocities for selected MIDI notes — it's useful for creating dynamic changes that weren't recorded with original MIDI data. And the Change Duration function is good for making a MIDI track more staccato (short notes) or legato (smooth phrases).

The Transpose function moves selected notes up or down in pitch. This is what you use if you want to change the key of a song without re-recording the parts, or move a MIDI part up or down an octave to make it sound in a better range.

The Restore Performance function enables you to undo any edits you made using the MIDI editing functions in the MIDI Operations window. Thus, you can always get back to the original MIDI performance because these MIDI edits are non-destructive. Once you've finalized some or all of the edits on a MIDI track, you can open the Flatten Performance window and save the edits permanently. I recommend making a duplicate playlist of the edited MIDI track before flattening it.

■ **Fig. 5.13.**
In some ways the MIDI Operations window is the nerve center of MIDI editing in Pro Tools. It appears when any of the items in the second "block" of the MIDI menu is selected.

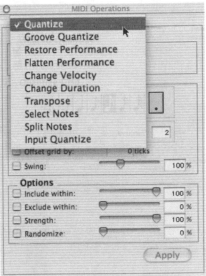

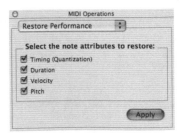

■ **Fig. 5.14.**
In the Restore Performance and Flatten Performance windows you can choose which specific attributes of the track to restore or flatten.

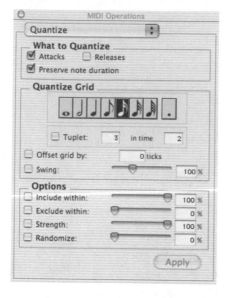

THE QUANTIZE FUNCTION

Quantizing aligns MIDI notes to a rhythmic grid to get them more in time, or to get a particular rhythmic feel. Some notes may be moved forward in time while others may be moved back, and some notes will be more drastically affected than others. A quantize "grid" determines the beat boundaries to which notes are aligned; note values from whole notes to 64th notes with any tuplet divisions can make up the grid.

You can quantize the attack (start point), release (end point), and/or the duration of MIDI notes to the quantization grid. Quantizing attacks means that the start point of each note will be moved so it aligns with the closest rhythmic grid value. Naturally, quantizing release times will move the end point of each note. With both the Attacks and Releases buttons checked, each note will be quantized to the beginning and end of the closest grid value, thus quantizing the note durations as well.

Regarding the Preserve note duration check box: When this box is deselected and the Attacks option is selected, note end points aren't moved – when it's deselected and the Releases option is selected, note start points aren't moved. If both Attacks and Releases are selected, the Preserve note duration option is ignored (and dimmed so it can't be checked).

TICK TALK

Pro Tools uses a quarter note as its reference point for timing and creating quantization grids. Each quarter note is divided into 480 subdivisions called **ticks**. The duration of a tick will vary according to tempo. For example the duration of a tick, if quarter notes equal 120 BPM, is 1.041ms. Faster tempos yield shorter tick values, while slower tempos have longer values. If you're the mathematical type, the formula for determining a tick's length is: One tick = 60,000 / tempo / 480 (where 60,000 refers to the number of milliseconds in a minute).

Once you've selected what you want to quantize and the quantization grid/note values, you can further alter the feel of MIDI performances in many ways. To give your MIDI track a pushed or laid-back feel, check the Offset Grid By box and enter a positive or negative tick value in the field. To add a swing feel to your MIDI track, check the Swing box and adjust the percentage. This shifts every other grid boundary, as selected in the Quantize Grid section (e.g., eighth notes), by the specified percentage.

Try these out for yourself! Create a straight eighth note hi-hat groove recorded to a click track, then adjust the Swing percentage and Offset Grid By commands to hear the effect on your track.

Press ⌘ (Mac) or Control (Win) while adjusting any sliders in the MIDI Operations window (such as Swing percentage) for finer resolution, or type an exact value into the slider input field.

Swing Percentage	Resulting Feel
0%	No swing
12%	Light swing
24%	Tighter swing groove
50–75%	"Triplet-like" swing
100%	Total triplet feel
300%	Every other grid boundary is moved to the next grid point, e.g., making eighth notes into quarter notes

Fig. 5.16.
You can automatically create just about any swing feel, from hokey to subtle and sublime.

Some other parameters for quantizing your MIDI data are Include Within, Exclude Within, Strength, and Randomize. Include Within quantizes attacks and releases located within a specified percentage of the quantize grid. That is, notes close to the grid will be quantized to the grid, but notes far from the grid will be left alone. A full 100% Include Within percentage includes all notes, while a 0% includes no notes. At 50%, the Include Within function includes 25% of the attacks and releases before a grid boundary and 25% after, for a total of 50%. The Exclude Within function works in the opposite way: When Exclude Within is selected, attacks and releases are *not* quantized if located within the specified percentage of the quantize grid.

The Strength function moves notes toward the quantize grid. Lower percentages preserve the original feel of the notes, while higher percentages align the notes more tightly to the grid. The Randomize function moves notes randomly forward or back in time after all other quantization occurs. For example, with the quantize grid set to quarter notes and Randomize set to 50%, notes are placed up to a sixteenth note before or after the beat boundary of the grid. Randomize affects attacks, releases, and durations, depending on what is selected in the What to Quantize section.

Parameter	
Include Within	Getting downbeats right on time while not affecting swung notes or notes far from the Quantize Grid
Exclude Within	Keeping the original feel of the notes close to the beat while cleaning up the notes that are far from the Quantize Grid
Strength	Tightening up a good performance or combining with other Quantize parameters to produce a better overall performance
Randomize	Humanizing a mechanical-sounding beat

Fig. 5.17.
Some parameters from the MIDI Operations Quantize window, and their uses.

Experimenting with Quantization

Through experience I've found that using low values on the Exclude Within parameter and high values for Strength give me good results when trying to preserve the original feel of a MIDI performance. But even with that and other basic knowledge of quantization, I find that quantizing a MIDI part requires experimentation. Because each recorded MIDI performance is different, you'll usually have to play with the parameters when you quantize.

Once you've quantized a track or part of a track, listen carefully to hear if you obtained the feel you were after. If not, undo the edit, adjust the parameters, and try again. If you can't seem to get the right feel using quantization, you may want to just rerecord the track and get a performance that has a better overall feel.

THE MIDI EVENT LIST

When you *really* want to fine tune your MIDI data, edit using the MIDI Event list. This powerful window allows you to precisely edit any parameters of a MIDI event as well as copy, paste, and delete individual parameters, events, or phrases. To open the MIDI Event list you can (a) choose Show MIDI Event List from the Windows menu, (b) Control + double-click (Mac) or Start + double-click (Win) a MIDI track name in the Edit or Mix window, or (c) press Option + = (Mac) or Alt + = (Win). You can also use this last command to toggle between the MIDI Event list and the Edit window.

Fig. 5.18.

The MIDI Event list gives you access to every detail of your MIDI performance. People have been known to obsess over MIDI event editing to the point where they're completely unable to finish a tune. Don't let this happen to you!

In the MIDI Event list in figure 5.18 you see the start time of the event, the type of event (e.g., the quarter-note symbols indicate note data), the note's pitch, the note's attack and release velocity, and length of the note (or other information such as an event's end time). Most of this data can be edited by double-clicking on the data you want to change.

From the menus at the top of the MIDI Event list you can insert events (figure 5.19) and perform many other functions (figure 5.20).

IMPORTING AND EXPORTING MIDI FILES

To import MIDI files from other MIDI applications (e.g., sequences from Logic Audio), the files must first be saved as Standard MIDI Files (SMFs). There are two types of SMFs — type 0 and type 1 — both of which are supported by Pro Tools.

Type 0 MIDI files store data for all MIDI channels on one track. When importing these files, Pro Tools separates the data by channel and places the channels in separate regions and tracks. Type 1 MIDI files,

MIDI Event List		
Options	Note	⌘N
Event	Pitch Bend	
15 –	Volume	
A3 48	Pan	
G3 48	Mono Aftertouch	
F3 50	Poly Aftertouch	⌘O
E3 50	Program Change	⌘P
F3 61	Controller	⌘L
E3 62		
G3 53	Another Note	⌘M

MIDI Event List	
Show Sub Counter	
Go To...	⌘G
Scroll To Edit Selection	⌘H
√ Page Scroll During Playback	
√ Scroll During Edit Selection	
√ Show Note Length	
Show Note End Time	
√ Insert At Edit Location	
Insert At Playback Location	
Insert At Playback Location With Grid	
View Filter...	⌘F

Fig. 5.19.
(Left) The Insert menu from the MIDI Event list.

Fig. 5.20.
(Right) The Options menu from the MIDI Event list.

If you choose Import Tempo From MIDI File, the tempo and meter events in your session will be overwritten by those of the imported MIDI file.

sometimes referred to as multitrack MIDI files, contain multiple tracks of MIDI data. When importing these files, each track's data is placed on its own new MIDI track in the Pro Tools session.

To import an SMF into Pro Tools, first select Import MIDI to Track from the File menu and choose the MIDI file you want to import. Then choose between importing the tempo and meter tracks or using the existing tempo in your Pro Tools session. Click Open to import the MIDI file.

If you need to export a MIDI file for use in another application, you can save it as an SMF (either type 0 or type 1). First unmute all MIDI tracks that you want to export. Then choose Export MIDI from the File menu, specify a destination for the file, select type 0 or type 1, and click Save.

The exported SMF includes notes, controller events, program changes, system exclusive data, tempo, meter, markers, and SMPTE start time information. Information not exported from Pro Tools on Standard MIDI Files includes muted regions and mute automation, device assignments, and playlist information.

HOW TO CREATE REALISTIC MIDI PARTS

If you do a lot of sequencing in your productions, there are some MIDI production concepts that can help you create more realistic parts – If that's what you're after, of course. For starters, if you're a piano player, be careful not to play other instruments as you would play a piano. Wind instruments (trumpet, flute, etc.) can only play one note at a time, so be careful not to inadvertently play chords. Also, wind instrument players need to take a breath every so often.

Try to write parts that real players could play . . . primarily, this means creating parts that stay within the instrument's range. (See appendix A for range charts for many instruments.) Using pitch bend, modulation, and differing velocities can also create more realistic sounds on these instruments. If you're trying to emulate an entire section of wind

General MIDI (GM) is a standardized set of sounds that many MIDI keyboards and sound modules have. Sometimes GM patches are the only sounds, and sometimes they're an extra set provided for compatibility, so that a sequence done on one manufacturer's GM instrument will sound similar on any manufacturer's GM instrument. Look for General MIDI, GM, GS (Roland), or XG (Yamaha) to find instruments that are GM-compatible.

instruments (e.g., a brass section), avoid dense voicings. That is, spread out the notes of the chord into at least two octaves instead of one. Doing this will make the chords sound more full and clear.

Sequencing guitar parts can be tricky, too. Guitarists often use the open strings of the guitar in their chord voicings. From lowest pitch to highest, the open strings on a guitar are E, A, D, G, B, and E. The pitch of the high E string is two octaves above the pitch of the low E string (which is two octaves below the E above middle C on a piano).

Because a guitar has six strings, don't play chords that have more than six notes in them! And if you're playing a guitar part on a keyboard, you should try rolling the chords to simulate the strumming motion of a guitarist. Finally, you might consider adding fret noise (a General MIDI patch) between chords to make the part sound more realistic.

Sequencing string parts is a popular thing to do because not very many people can afford to hire an orchestra or even a small group of string players. However, be careful with string pad sounds. They can add thickness that easily makes your songs sound "washy." Single countermelodies that come and go might be more effective, and keeping the melodies simple and low in the mix will add depth but won't distract the listener from the main melody of the song.

Almost everyone sequences drums these days — I'm a drummer and I sequence them all the time! Sequenced drums will never replace the feel of a real drummer, but there are some techniques you can use to make your drum parts sound more real. Blanket quantization is usually a bad idea: Completely quantized drum parts sound rigid and have no groove. To combat this, play any piece of a drum part that you can on your own. For example, create a basic quantized kick and snare part and then play the hi-hat part in real time. In most cases, this will add instant groove to the track. If this is difficult for you or doesn't sound good, try quantizing the hi-hat and playing the kick and snare parts in real time.

If all else fails you can quantize everything (using the functions mentioned previously in this chapter) and then go back and alter the parts individually. To make an even more realistic sound, randomize the velocities of hi-hat attacks, giving stronger velocities to downbeats. Surprisingly, this can make all the difference between a rigid computerized drum beat and a killer get-up-and-dance groove.

Using MIDI can be helpful all the way through the production process. In preproduction, you can use MIDI tracks to sketch out basic song ideas — from drum loops to chord progressions. In production, you can turn these ideas into full-blown tracks and fine-tune them with all of the MIDI features in Pro Tools. In postproduction, you can use MIDI in your mixes, by automating outboard MIDI effects processors or utilizing a MIDI control surface. Being able to effectively use the MIDI functions in Pro Tools will not only make you a better engineer, it will also open your productions to new sounds that could take them to a whole new level. ▐▌

PRO TOOLS HANDS-ON

Set Up Your Computer for Recording MIDI

Follow the instructions in this chapter and the Digidesign manuals to hook up your MIDI gear correctly. Launch Pro Tools and create several MIDI and audio tracks in a new session to test your studio's signal routing. Route the signals so you can hear the audio outputs from your MIDI instruments and sound modules when you record-enable the tracks. Follow the signal path through each gain stage in your MIDI setup to ensure you are getting good audio recording levels into Pro Tools from your MIDI instruments and sound modules.

Most times you can record directly from the line outs of your sound module right into your Digidesign hardware. If you can't get good levels out of your sound module, you should probably use a direct box (DI) to change the low line-level out of the sound module into mic-level. Then you can route the DI signal into a mic preamp and boost the signal there.

Either way, whether you use line-level signals or mic-level signals, be sure to get good recording levels without clipping. This will ensure that you've recorded your MIDI tracks with the best possible signal-to-noise ratio and that you utilized the entire bit depth. (Remember those audio terms from chapter 3?)

Create, Record, and Experiment with MIDI

Record some MIDI tracks. Try all of the record modes including MIDI Merge and recording while in Loop Playback mode. Experiment with the edit modes and edit tools to explore the similarities and differences of editing MIDI and audio. Try all the Track Views, especially the "single note" view. Get comfortable with maneuvering MIDI notes and tracks in the Edit window.

Create and Edit a MIDI Drum Loop

One of the most powerful functions MIDI serves in music production is for creating drum loops. Many folks who record at home are not trained drummers and also do not own drum sets and percussion instruments. MIDI makes it easy to create a drum loop as a foundation for your musical ideas. Even if you want to use real drums (and a real drummer) for your final recordings of a song, creating a MIDI drum part for the demo of the song is a great idea. It can greatly improve the effectiveness of getting your demo ideas across to other people, as well as establish a "feel" to the song. Even if you don't want to use loops in your production, creating a MIDI drum loop is an essential skill for preproduction.

First, open a new Pro Tools session and create several new MIDI tracks for each individual percussion instrument that you want in your loop. Then create the audio tracks you need to monitor your MIDI instruments/sound modules. Make a drum loop by inserting MIDI notes with the Pencil Tool while in Grid mode. Use the Grabber Tool to edit the velocities of the notes to give the loop a more human (less mechanical) feel. Experiment with the tempo, note velocities, feel, sounds, etc.

For a more challenging assignment, try to mimic one of the drum patterns from the Naked Drums demo session using MIDI. Open the Naked Drums demo session, then choose Save Session As from the file menu and choose a new name for your soon-to-be altered session. Try to capture all of the performance nuances and elements of the groove using the MIDI editing techniques you've learned. If you can, record the MIDI data by playing it yourself instead of using the Pencil tool to add notes. You may need to quantize your MIDI performance data…

Quantize a MIDI Performance

Quantizing adjusts inaccurate rhythmic performances by aligning notes individually to a grid. Just as easily, quantization can also be used to change the rhythmic feel of a performance.

It's very simple to quantize a MIDI performance so that each note lines up perfectly with the beat. This creates a mechanical-sounding MIDI part. In some cases, the music may call for this. However, most times you'll want your MIDI parts to have some life… that is, some inconsistencies, some imperfections, some humanistic elements. The real trick is using quantization to turn a halfway decent performance into a tight yet slightly imperfect performance with a great feel.

Before quantizing any tracks, you should figure out and describe the rhythmic feel that you want the song (or the specific track) to have. People describe rhythmic feels in a variety of ways, usually using nontechnical adjectives like "driving" or "chilled." Often, feels are expressed as being "ahead of the beat" for a pushed, excited, or driving song, "behind the beat" for a laid-back, relaxed, or even dragging song, or "right on the beat" for a steady song that's "in the pocket."

How do you apply quantization to create a particular rhythmic feel that is either ahead of, behind, or right on the beat? Pro Tools enables you to move the start point (attack) and/or the end point (release) of any MIDI note in a variety of ways to create different feels using the MIDI Operations Quantize window (figure 5.15).

1. Choose the Quantize Grid value; that is, the rhythmic value that you want to align your MIDI notes with. It's often a

good idea to use the most common subdivision of the main beat in the song when selecting the grid value. Here are a few generalized examples: You can probably use eighth notes for many pop or rock songs, and sixteenth notes for funk, disco, and fast samba tunes. For swing or shuffle songs, select eighth-note triplets by choosing an eighth-note grid value, checking the Tuplet box, and entering "3" in the time of "2." Obviously, use your own best judgment, as each song in any style may require a different quantization grid value.

2. Choose whether you want to align the attacks and/or releases of the notes. Aligning the attacks to the grid ensures that your rhythms are lined up with the beat (or subdivision of the beat). Aligning the releases to the grid means your notes will be held out to the end of the beat (or subdivision of the beat).

   In many cases, I align the attacks and check off the Don't Change Durations check box. This keeps all of my MIDI performance data intact, but lines up the attacks better with the quantization grid. This is particularly useful for piano tracks, or any other tracks where you want to preserve the player's style while simply improving the timing of the performance. Or, you can turn a staccato part into a more legato part by aligning the release times to ensure each note gets its full duration. Each new musical part you record may require a different application of quantization.

3. Decide if you want to change the overall rhythmic feel using the "Offset Grid By" and "Swing" parameters. The Offset Grid By parameter enables you to move the overall MIDI performance data ahead or behind the beat by fractions of the beat, called ticks. The Swing parameter actually alters the Quantize Grid to help you create a "swung" part from a performance that lacks a triplet-like swing or shuffle feel. The higher the percentage you choose, the more swing is added to the performance, as shown in figure 5.16.

4. Adjust the Include Within, Exclude Within, Strength, and Randomize parameters. Include Within and Exclude Within, often collectively called "Sensitivity" in other sequencers, determine which MIDI notes are to be quantized. In most performances, the notes between the beats (or between the quantize grid) give the performance its style and sometimes even its rhythmic feel. You can use these parameters in Pro Tools to quantize the notes closest to the grid and leave the notes in between alone. Include Within and Exclude Within

are based on percentages. To quantize the notes that are 10% away from the grid (on either side), choose 20% as the Include Within value. If you want to include all notes, choose 100%. Exclude Within works in the same way, except with the opposite results.

Like a magnet, the Strength parameter determines how close MIDI notes are pulled to the quantization grid. 100% strength means every note will be pulled all the way to the closest grid value, while a 50% strength value only draws the notes halfway towards the grid. Strength should be used on almost every sequenced part that needs to be quantized. This parameter may be the most important one for transforming halfway decent tracks into tight musical performances.

5. Use the Randomize function. It's funny that Randomize is a quantization parameter, because it essentially mucks up the work that all the previous quantization parameters performed on a MIDI performance. A value of 100% randomize will move some notes up to 50% away from the quantization grid (on either side). Usually, this will sound terrible! The rhythms will be way off. However, small percentage values are useful for adding a human element to an otherwise mechanical-sounding track. Use this parameter with care.

Now try it. Using the drum loop you created in the previous section, adjust the swing percentage and Grid Offset By commands to hear the effect on your track. Then, adjust the Include Within, Exclude Within, Strength, and Randomize percentages to hear the effect on your track. Experiment with all the quantization parameters and try to create a tight, yet slightly imperfect performance with a great feel.

Record MIDI as Audio

Once you've created and edited some MIDI tracks, record the MIDI tracks as audio so that you can mix them with other audio tracks and apply plug-ins and outboard effects to them. Unless you're hurting for track space, it's usually a good idea to record each MIDI track individually to its own audio track. This even includes drums...a track for the kick drum, one for the snare, one for the hi-hat, etc. That way you have more control when you mix. (Note: If you have all of your MIDI drum parts on one MIDI track, use the Split Notes function in the MIDI Operations window to split up the parts into different tracks.)

Try it. Record some MIDI tracks (e.g., the drum loop you made) as audio. Watch your recording levels.

Create a MIDI Session Template

Once you've ironed out your MIDI setup after successfully recording some MIDI tracks, create a session template for recording MIDI. Create separate tracks (MIDI and audio) for each MIDI instrument and sound module/sampler so you can be instantly ready to record when a new MIDI idea strikes you.

Further into Preproduction — Adding MIDI Tracks to the Song Demos

MIDI provides an excellent way to explore preproduction ideas. With MIDI data controlling sound modules and samplers, you can simulate almost any sound or come up with your own new sounds. Open up the sessions "Chap5Electronica" and "Chap5Hiphop" to see the accompanying MIDI data for some of the preproduction/ songwriting ideas I came up with for that song. Then, move on to section 2 to get deeper into the process of preproduction.

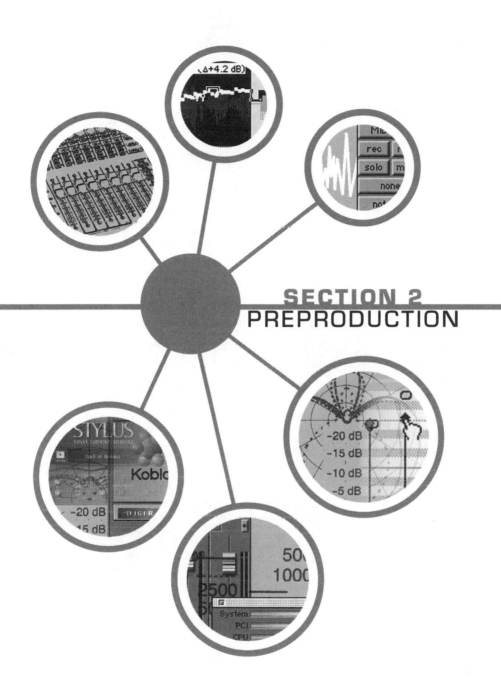

SECTION 2
PREPRODUCTION

The Producer's Role in Preproduction

In this chapter:

- **Working with artists**

- **Planning and budgeting your project**

- **Songwriting and arranging concepts**

- **Hiring help and scheduling sessions**

- **The importance of rehearsals**

> *"Three primary elements predict whether a producer will help create a successful project: organization, preparation, and documentation."*
> — Terry Becker (Berklee faculty member, professional producer, and engineer for artists such as Bonnie Raitt and Taj Mahal)

Now that you've got a firm grasp of many of the functions and features of Pro Tools and have learned some production techniques, it's time to take a step back and look at the big picture of music production. Let's start with the producer's role in preproduction.

As you read in the introduction, preproduction consists of all the activities that take place before a recording session, and is probably the most important step in the production process. Getting songs ready to record can take much more time than actually recording and mixing them, but the time is well spent.

Whether you're working on your own music or someone else's, these ten elements are the foundations of preproduction:

1. Meeting the artist

2. Listening to the artist's material

3. Considering the artist's identity

4. Choosing the best material to record

5. Planning the project: time and money

6. Writing, rewriting, and arranging

7. Hiring help

8. Scheduling rehearsal, recording, and mixing sessions

9. Rehearsing

10. Getting ready for the recording sessions

Below I explain how to implement these steps in your productions, enhancing the descriptions from the introduction. Remember, for our purposes the term "artist" can refer to a single person or a group. Here we go....

1. MEETING THE ARTIST

Obviously, if you're producing your own music you're familiar with your material and work ethic. However, if you're producing someone else's music you have to develop an **artist/producer relationship**. In the first meeting, this involves listening to the artist's ideas, asking questions about the project, and sharing experiences. A few funny stories help, too. Whatever you do, the goal is to connect with the artist and make them feel comfortable with you.

You need their trust. They'll be spilling their guts to you in the form of songs, and that can make them feel vulnerable. But getting to that point where the artist allows the deepest part of their heart, mind, and soul to be exposed is right where you want to be — it's when the best music is created. Developing this kind of relationship with an artist takes time, but the foundation for it is set in the first meeting.

Defining the Scope of the Project and Your Role

At the beginning of every project, define its scope. This usually happens when you first meet the artist, or when you decide you're going to record something serious for yourself. The scope of a project may be recording one song, a three-song demo, or a full-length album. It might require you to be the engineer only or it may also include the duties of engineer and producer (as well as artist and songwriter). If you're producing someone else's music you might be asked to act only as an opinion-giver or you might take part in every aspect of the song's development (writing, rewriting, arranging, etc.). Understanding your role in the recording process is imperative and will influence every action you take during a project.

Further, if you're producing an artist you should create a contract to outline the scope of your duties. This should include a schedule and a budget (see Planning the Project: Time and Money later in this chapter), as well as royalty agreements and other clauses to be mutually approved. Read other books on the music business for details on contracts and, as much as you might not want to, consult a lawyer to make sure the contract you're signing is good. (I'm sure you've heard of people unknowingly signing severely binding contracts, so be careful!)

2. LISTENING TO THE ARTIST'S MATERIAL

Even if you're producing your own music you should consider playing through all your material (new and old song ideas). You may stumble across a song (or even a song fragment) you haven't heard for a while and discover that it's really good. Or you may see that your best material is your latest material. In any case, try to evaluate your ideas objectively; that is, try to listen like it's the first time you've ever heard the song. Also play your stuff for other people — their feedback can be quite valuable.

If you're working with a new client and you're not familiar with their music, you should listen to everything they have available — previous CDs, live shows, old demos, tapes of random guitar licks, etc. This will give you an idea about (a) the style of music they want to make, (b) the direction their most recent music is going, and (c) the sound they want to have. It will also help you decide what you think is their best material. Sometimes artists get bored with their older material...if they only bring you recent music they might bypass great tunes for the project.

3. CONSIDERING THE ARTIST'S IDENTITY

Defining an artist's identity, purpose, sound, and image helps focus your efforts. There are several important questions you should ask about any project you produce:

1. What's the purpose of the recording? For fun, a demo to get gigs, a demo to shop to record labels, a full-length CD to sell....

2. What do you want this recording to sound like? A style similar to a known artist, a conglomeration of styles, something completely different....

3. Who will want to listen to the recording? Your family and friends, most people who like the genre, pop radio listeners....

These questions appear easy to answer. However, if the ultimate goal is to sell the music you're producing, then a lot of effort should go into

When I engineer and/or produce music for friends, I sometimes rely on a handshake as a contract, but only with close friends. Having a lawyer draft a contract for a project — or using a boilerplate from a music business book — may save you a lot of headaches (and money) if things don't turn out as all parties expect.

dealing with the issues above. You need to help artists (especially if the artist is you) find their current identity, and figure out if it matches their vision of the project. If it doesn't, you need to help them change either their identity or their expectations.

Demographics

Finding detailed answers to the three questions above will help artists define themselves and create a vision for the final recording. And this vision should align with the demographics of the audience you want to buy the music. **Demographics** are statistical data of a population, used to market a product. Common music-related demographic data includes age, ethnicity, gender, income, geographic location, tastes, buying habits, and education.

For example, these days some of the biggest pop acts sell their music primarily to a pre-teen and teen white female population who use their parents' income to buy the recordings. They're located all over the country (within reach of Top-40 radio) and their tastes, buying habits, and level of education are fairly homogeneous. You wouldn't try to sell an avant-garde jazz album to this population, just as you wouldn't try to sell teen pop music to an avant-garde crowd. This is obvious. However, there are overlaps among audiences — okay, maybe not between the two I mentioned, but there's overlap between other audiences (e.g., people who like blues and jazz, rock and country, hip-hop and reggae, metal and techno). Many people like a variety of music, and finding the overlap or niche where you or the artist you're producing fits in – now, that's the tricky part. Therefore, defining the artist's identity, purpose, sound, and image, as well as the target demographic for the music, is well worth your time.

4. CHOOSING THE BEST MATERIAL TO RECORD

This is probably your most important duty as a producer. If you're choosing songs for your own recording, be honest with yourself. Combine your own "objective-as-you-can-be" opinions, feedback from others, and analysis of your identity and potential marketing demographic. Sometimes this can be difficult; sometimes it's quite easy. You don't want to delay the decision, but if it's difficult to choose among several songs, you might record all of them and then decide which one turned out best, or most "on target." Naturally, not everyone has the time and money to take this approach.

If you're producing an artist, helping them choose the songs on their record is a big responsibility. However, they came to you so you could help them decide. If you've developed a close relationship with the artist, they look to you for honesty and will respect your opinions. Remember, they're your client: You're working for them and they want you to do your job. That said, there will be situations where you have to speak with great tact.

Tact and Diplomacy

What if you and the artist disagree about which songs to record? There will probably be times when your opinions differ from the artist's, and in the music business, differences of opinion can be more intense than usual because you're not just quibbling over business decisions. You're dealing with people who have exposed their souls to you and shared their heartfelt creations. Egos are easily hurt with stray negative comments. Therefore, if you need to disagree with an artist you must be *diplomatic*. It's a true skill to deal with sensitive matters without hurting people . . . while keeping them motivated.

How do you put this into practice? You need to state your opinions in honest, yet non-offensive and non-confrontational words. It's best to say something positive first, then follow that with a tactful opinion. For example, instead of saying "Song 3 stinks! Song 4 is better," say something like "I like Song 3 . . . it's got a strong chorus, but Song 4 really gets me. Its lyrics grab me, its melody is so catchy. . . ," and so on. With comments like these, you get your point across but keep the artist motivated to do great work.

Also notice that my comments personified the song. By personifying the song you discuss it as its own entity, which allows you to be critical of the song without being critical of the writer. This is a useful strategy because people tend to be less defensive if you point at an object instead of at them. You can also personify the entire recording by saying something like, "This demo only needs one love ballad, not two." By personifying the songs or the record, you create a working environment focused on the music, not the people.

As a producer, you need to be especially tactful when suggesting changes to existing songs. It can be tricky to tell someone that the chorus of their song needs work, but you can handle it using the same method as above. Instead of saying "The chorus sucks, write a new one," try "The current chorus is good, but it's not grabbing me like the verse does. Can we try some other ideas just to see what they might sound like?" This technique works better with sensitive artists (who are numerous). Some other artists might prefer a more direct (or "tough love") approach, but they'll respect your tact if you use it without sounding too flattering or wishy-washy.

Without learning tact and diplomacy as a producer, you'll have difficulty getting your opinions accepted. That said, I should mention that all producers have different personalities and use different tactics in their discussions with artists.

I HAVE A THEORY

If you're working with musicians who have some knowledge of music theory, you can make your comments more pointed by "talking shop." For example, you might suggest to the artist that the chord resolution in the chorus might sound stronger with a V-I instead of a IV-I progression. However, making comments like these to musicians without music theory chops will not only be ineffectual; it may also intimidate them or disconnect you from them.

So, after listening to *all* of the artist's material (even if the artist is you) and considering the artist's identity and marketing demographic, the producer and artist together should choose which songs to record. Some songs may be completely ready to record and others may need extensive work. Still others might just be ideas that haven't been fully realized. Even after the songs have been chosen, there should be some amount of flexibility because you (or the artist) might write a completely new tune during the project that's better than any you've chosen so far. However, choosing the material to record early in the process is beneficial because it gives you an idea of how much work needs to be done, and helps estimate the time and money needed to complete the project.

5. PLANNING THE PROJECT: TIME AND MONEY

Time and money are constraints on almost any project you'll be producing. Understanding how much of each you have to work with is imperative to a successful recording . . . and running out of time or money can obviously have a detrimental effect. Therefore, you should create a schedule and budget for each project: Schedules and budgets not only provide organization and documentation and are also tools that help focus your energy.

It may be more difficult to create a schedule if you're producing your own music. When working on my material, I tend to set aside specific times but I also work on it in my spare time — this practice doesn't lend itself to a strict schedule. However, having a date when you want the project done is probably the best motivating factor. I usually pick a date that has some significance, for instance, to meet a festival submission deadline, or a friend's birthday. Otherwise — because it's your music and you're probably somewhat of a perfectionist — you might work on it forever.

Depending on your financial status, creating a budget may also be very important. There are many expenses to take into account: What materials will you need? CDs, DATs, copies, additional equipment? Will you rent, buy, or borrow the equipment? Do you need to hire additional musicians, an arranger, an orchestrator, a lyricist, an engineer, etc.? Do you need to rent a rehearsal space to practice? Will someone else be mixing or mastering the project?

Working with friends, playing most of the parts yourself, practicing at home, borrowing equipment you need, and engineering, mixing, and mastering the project yourself will save tons of money. However, you

I've included a PDF file on the CD-ROM called "Project Budget." Use it as a template for creating a budget for your project: include materials, equipment, people, studio time, and any other expenses on it to create a reasonable estimate of the project's total cost.

PROJECT BUDGET | EXPENSES

Date	9/1/2002		
Artist	Flat Five Blues Band	Project Title	Three-Song Demo
Producer(s)	Andrew Stern/David Franz	Engineer(s)	David Franz

MATERIALS/EQUIPMENT (CDs, copies, food, strings, drum heads, new and rental gear, etc.)

Item	Cost	Number Needed	Total Cost
CD-Rs	$1	20	$20
Food & Drink			$50
		SUBTOTAL	$70

REHEARSAL SPACE AND STUDIO TIME

Item	Cost/hour	Hours Needed	Total Cost
Studio Time	$20	18	$360
		SUBTOTAL	$360

MUSICIANS (rehearsals and recording sessions, including AFM and AFTRA payments, if applicable)

Name	Instrument	Session #	Hours	Rate	Other Expenses	Total Cost
Andrew	Guitar	All				—
Eric	Drums	All				—
Ilona	Vocals	All				—
Noah	Bass	All				—
					SUBTOTAL	

PRODUCER/ENGINEER (recording, mix, remix, and mastering – fee or hourly rate)

Engineer	Cost/hour	Hours Needed	Total Cost
David Franz – recording	$20	18	included
David Franz – mixing	$20	10	$200
David Franz – mastering	$20	3	$60
		SUBTOTAL	$260

OTHER EXPENSES

Item	Cost	Number Needed	Total Cost
		SUBTOTAL	

PRODUCER'S SIGNATURE   GRAND TOTAL $690

Fig. 6.1.
A sample project budget. The old carpenter axiom "measure twice, cut once" definitely applies here. Plan your budget carefully, as running out of time or money can put a damper your dreams of becoming famous . . . much less finishing your album.

may not have the time or skills to do this. It might be worth it to spend some money where it either (a) improves the recording, (b) allows you to keep your head in a creative space, or (c) saves you time. I recommend figuring out what your budget can handle early on, because it can save you a lot of grief later.

If you're producing (or just recording) an artist or band, it's *imperative* to set a schedule and budget at the beginning of the project. That way you'll know what they expect of you and what you can expect from them. You can charge an hourly rate or set a flat fee for your services.

Engineers often work on hourly rates whereas producers usually work for a fee. Charge what you feel you (and your studio) are worth. Adding the other expenses mentioned above (i.e., materials, equipment, musicians, etc.) to your rate or fee will give you an estimated recording budget. Creating a budget before the project begins will prepare you and

If you're producing a band that sells a lot of their recordings, you may want to ask for a percentage of sales. Big-name producers working with big-name acts usually get 3%, and up to 5% on rare occasions. However, this may be difficult to keep track of if the artist isn't affiliated with a record label or some other sort of accounting service.

I've included a PDF file on the CD-ROM called "Project Schedule." Use it as a template for creating a schedule for your project: include dates, times, descriptions of the sessions, and any other scheduling notes on it. Make copies and give them to any other people involved in the project . . . so you're all on the same page, so to speak.

■ Fig. 6.2.
 A possible schedule for a three-song demo; notice the events are primarily in the evening. Besides the fact that people have day jobs, remember that musicians tend to shy away from morning gigs.

the artist for what to expect — if the artist you're working with has been signed by a record label, the label will invariably ask for one.

As you know, a budget is an estimate. Coming in under budget at the end of a project is always welcome, but being over budget isn't good. Many times the amount over budget is paid by the producer, so consider yourself warned. Because of this, its usually a good idea to include some sort of "slush fund" to cover any unexpected costs. (I'll let you figure out how to incorporate the "slush fund" into your budget.)

Creating a schedule can help a project *stay* on budget. Not only that, it will help organize the work and focus the artist's and your energy. Here's a sample schedule for a band you might produce or engineer. The band wants to record a three-song demo.

If you're engineering but not producing the project, then you might only need to be present for the last six or seven events on the schedule in figure 6.2. If you're working on a project that requires writing new

PROJECT SCHEDULE

Artist	Flat Five Blues Band		Project Title	Three Song Demo
Producer(s)	Andrew Stern/David Franz		Engineer(s)	David Franz

DATE	TIME	EVENT	NOTES
8/1	6 pm	Band meeting	discuss songs to record
8/3	7 pm	Rehearsal	play thru all potential songs to record
8/6	6 pm	Band meeting	choose best songs to record
8/8	7 pm	Rehearsal	play thru chosen songs
8/10	7 pm	Meeting/Rehearsal	work out a new chorus for song #2
8/13	7 pm	Rehearsal	tighten up the arrangements
8/15	2 pm	Recording session	tracking the basics (drums, bass, guitar, scratch vocal)
8/17	7 pm	Overdub session #1	record guitar solos, other overdubs
8/20	7 pm	Overdub session #2	record vocals
8/24	8 pm	Mix session #1	
8/27	8 pm	Mix session #2	
8/30	8 pm	Mastering session	

material, rewriting old material, and arranging and/or orchestrating the material, you should also create a schedule for working on those activities. I know . . . scheduling time to write a new song might sound strange, contradictory to your artistic/creative flow, or even impossible. As a good friend of mine once said, "There is no timetable on inspiration." However, you'll find that once you do sit down with a handful of ideas, you just might be able to create new songs on a schedule – this is actually a skill that develops with practice. I'm not suggesting you try to force creativity, I'm simply saying that focused work toward a specific goal usually pays off.

AFTRA AND AFM

Many producers hire professional musicians and singers to record on their projects. These professional musicians are often part of a union and are paid at pre-determined session rates. Producers fill out contracts with the unions and hire the musicians through the unions. The two main unions you might deal with if you want to hire professional musicians are AFTRA and AFM.

AFTRA: The American Federation of Television and Radio Artists (AFTRA) is a national labor union affiliated with the AFL-CIO. Its headquarters are in New York City and there are 36 local offices throughout the country. AFTRA represents its members in four major areas: 1) news and broadcasting, 2) entertainment programming, 3) the recording business, and 4) commercials and non-broadcast, industrial, and educational media. AFTRA's 80,000 members are seen or heard on television, radio, and sound recordings and include actors, announcers, news broadcasters, singers (including royalty artists and background singers), dancers, sportscasters, disc jockeys, talk show hosts, and others. According to the AFTRA Web site (www.aftra.org), talent payments under AFTRA contract are over $1 billion a year.

AFM: The American Federation of Musicians (AFM) is the largest entertainment labor organization in the world and is also affiliated with the AFL-CIO. AFM represents professional musicians similarly to the way in which AFTRA represents its members. AFM has over 120,000 members throughout the United States and Canada.

Producers deal with AFTRA for hiring vocal talent and AFM for hiring musicians. The national AFTRA organization determines the payment rates for singers; the information can be found on their Web site. In contrast, local chapters of AFM set their own rates for paying musicians. For example, AFM Chapter #47 sets rates for recording in the Los Angeles area (see their Web site at http://promusic47.org). But if current AFM rates aren't posted on a Web site for your area, you'll have to call the local chapter.

6. WRITING, REWRITING, AND ARRANGING

I mentioned earlier that choosing the best material to record is probably a producer's most important duty. As such, writing, rewriting, and arranging that material may be the most important step in the entire production process. This is when you transfer your (or your artist's) musical identity, purpose, and image into sound. This is when you iron out most of the details in each song by making important decisions about the effect of the music on the intended listener. This is when new material is written, older material is rewritten, and all material is arranged. This is when you can really use Pro Tools as an instrument for writing, recording, editing, and experimenting with new ideas.

Your primary job as a producer during this step of preproduction is to rework each song (if the song needs alterations) by adjusting the music, lyrics, and arrangement. Here are some general questions to ask yourself about the content of the songs.

Music: Does the music match the mood of the lyrics? Does that matter? Do the dynamic changes (loud vs. soft parts) work? Are the feel and tempo right? Do all the parts fit together well? Is the music too busy or not busy enough? If it's a pop song, do you make the listener wait too long for the chorus? Are you working in the best key for (a) the tune itself, and (b) your vocalists or instrumentalists? Or, is the music too difficult for the players/singers you have access to?

Lyrics: Do the lyrics make sense? Are they supposed to make sense? Do they flow? Do they capture the emotion, image, or event in the song? Are they easy to sing? Do they have a good rhythm? Are they too hokey? Does it matter if they are?

Arrangement: Does the current instrumentation work or does the song need additional (or fewer) instrumental parts? Does the song's form match its emotion? Does the form need to be rearranged to create a better flow? Is the attitude of the song being captured by the arrangement? Overall, does it feel like anything is missing from the song? Do you have access to the musicians or gear to really carry this arrangement off?

If you're working on your own music, try to remain objective. Often we get tied to our original ideas so much so that we can't look past them . . . we can't see things that could be changed to make the overall song better. On the other hand, over-thinking and reworking a song too much can do more harm than good. The real emotion or spirit of the original idea may be processed too much and ultimately lost. It's a fine line that producers have to walk everyday. The bottom line is that your job as a producer is to help the artist craft the best songs they are capable of creating.

Craftsmanship

What does it mean to craft a song? It means creating a story or mood in which every piece of the song fits together somehow in the way you want the story told or the mood experienced. Each part, from the lead vocal to the bass drum, should be right for the song. This comes from a collaboration of the artist's and producer's creativity in music and lyric writing, arrangement, and production planning, and from a unified idea of how the song should sound when it's complete.

To achieve this, the producer must specifically analyze all aspects of the song including key, tempo, length, lyrics, arrangement (instrumentation, song form, and attitude), and its overall meaning and intent.

Key: The key is the principle tonality found in the song or the scale on which the song is based (e.g., the key of C major). It can help set the mood for the song because certain keys have particular sounds (e.g., Spinal Tap's usage of the sad sound of the key of D minor). It's also very important to choose a key in which the singer (or lead instrument) can perform well. Choosing a key that's out of range (too high or too low) for the vocalist (or lead instrument) can ruin a recording. If you don't want to change the key, you should probably change the melody to accommodate the vocalist's range or choose another vocalist/lead instrument to perform the part.

Tempo: Choosing the right tempo (or speed of the song) is also very important. A song that's recorded when the tempo is too slow will drag on and bore the listener. A song recorded at a tempo that's too fast will lose its groove and often sound rushed. Use a metronome to evaluate the tempo at which your song sounds best. You can have a range ($\downarrow$ = 118– 120 BPM) or you can get very specific ($\downarrow$ = 84.5 BPM). You'd be surprised how a small change in tempo (sometimes even just a fraction of a beat per minute) can make all the difference in the feel of a song.

CREATING TEMPO AND METER CHANGES

The acronym BPM stands for "beats per minute" and is usually written as: $\downarrow$ = 120.

The Tempo/Meter Change window makes it easy to create even complex "conductor" tracks.

This means a quarter note gets one beat at a tempo of 120 beats per minute. You can have other note values or resolutions (e.g. half notes) as the basis for your tempo, but the quarter note is the most frequently used. In Pro Tools you can create a simple click track to test different tempos (see chapter 3 for more information on click tracks). You can also create a "conductor" track if the song has multiple tempo changes by defining changes in the Tempo ruler. Simply click the quarter note on the Tempo ruler box and enter changes into the Tempo/Meter Change window. If you need to change the meter of your song, the Meter ruler works the same way. If you don't see these rulers in your Pro Tools session, choose Ruler View Shows from the Display menu and select Tempo and/or Meter.

Length: When considering the length of the song you should consider the song's purpose. If you and the artist want the song to be "radio-friendly," you should think about what radio stations will play it and how long their songs usually are. It seems most major pop radio stations play three- to four-minute tunes these days, with five minutes being the maximum. You can record a longer version of the song for the album version, but edit it in Pro Tools to comply with other radio material. Of course, if you're not worried about radio airplay, a song can be any length you want — just try to keep the overall meaning and intent in mind.

Music: You can analyze the music by simply listening and getting in touch with how it makes you feel. Does the music express the intended emotion of the song? Do the harmony and melody interact well? Is the music itself catchy? Does the melody have a hook — something that you sing to yourself even after the song is over?

Lyrics: As a producer, you should know all the lyrics to every song you produce. You should also be able to sing them, even if you're not a good singer; this will give you increased understanding of their "singability." You'll learn the spots where the singer might struggle with the melody, syllables, or overall rhythm of the vocal part. When you sing the lyrics, you'll also become more involved with the song emotionally as you absorb its meaning.

You should have a copy of the lyrics with you at all times so you can refer to them when discussing the song. Have the artist give you a copy early on during preproduction or write/type them out yourself. Also, having a lyric sheet is imperative when recording the vocal tracks. (See chapter 10 for more information on vocal production.)

Arrangement

The producer and artist must create the best arrangements of the songs together. In my view, a great song arrangement consists of three main components: instrumentation, song form, and attitude. Instrumentation refers to what instruments are played on the song and what their parts are, including vocal parts. Song form refers to the structure and sections of the song (e.g., how many verses and choruses there should be and where they'll be placed). Attitude refers to the emotion, feel, and point of view that the song should portray. The attitude of the song will greatly influence what instruments should be used and what the song form should be. In fact, all three of the components of song arrangement affect each other, so if one is altered, the producer should consider the effects on the other two components.

Instrumentation: Like any facet of songwriting, arranging is a skill that's honed with practice. Part of a producer's job when arranging is adding any vocal or instrumental parts to augment the song. When arranging these parts you should be mindful of leaving space for everything. For example, most times you don't want an intricate horn

Musicians often refer to arrangements as "charts" (e.g., the horn chart). There are professional arrangers who specialize in writing charts for all types of instrumental groupings (e.g., horns, strings, percussion sections, etc.).

line to interfere with the lead vocal. Likewise, multiple guitar tracks can really fill out a song, but if they're all playing something different at the same time the song can sound cluttered. Placing each part in the right place in a song is an important production duty.

To do this you should listen to the basic tracks (e.g., guitar/vocal or piano/bass/drums/vocal, etc.) to determine (a) where you might want more or less instrumental support, (b) where the open spaces in the song are, and (c) *if* you want to fill the open spaces. (Just because there's an open space doesn't mean it needs to be filled!) Discuss your ideas with the artist and get feedback. Sketch out the ideas and play them along with the basic tracks.

If you're going to create parts for instruments you don't usually write for, be aware of each instrument's range. I've included range charts for many instruments in appendix A; refer to them when you're coming up with the parts, whether you're going to be recording real instruments or synthesized/sampled versions. That way your parts will actually be playable by real musicians or at least sound more realistic when played by your MIDI instruments. You should also consider hiring someone else to do the parts for the arrangement if you have little time or experience writing for particular instruments.

Song form: The song form establishes a structure that helps guide the listener through the song. Skillful arrangement of the pieces of a song (verses, choruses, bridge, etc.) creates a natural musical flow. The song form can help establish imagery, story line, prosody (explained in the next section), and repetition. There are no rules for the form of a song, but some forms are fairly common in music today. For more on this topic, consult one or more of the songwriting books listed in appendix E.

It's easy to try different song forms using Pro Tools; you can order sections any way you want. As a matter of fact, by cutting and pasting different sections together you can test basic arrangements without actually recording new tracks.

Attitude: There are no rules for this aspect of arranging, either. You should simply consider whether the emotion and feel of each individual instrument fits with all the others and solidifies the meaning and intent of the song. The point of view should be consistent, unless you *purposefully* change it.

Songwriting Concepts

As a producer and a songwriter, you know there are many ways to write songs. You might start with a great lyric, a strong melody idea, a cool chord progression, or a tasty drum beat. Building that one idea into an entire song is a challenge for both the songwriter and the producer. Even though there are no rules on how to do this, there are some principles that hold true in a great majority of songs. Understanding and applying these principles during your creative process may improve your songwriting, and considering them in your role as producer is imperative. The relative importance of each of these principles varies from genre to genre, but much of the music being created today possesses all of them in some form.

Imagery: Many songs evoke images in the listener's mind. Imagery can be created verbally and sonically through descriptive lyrics and expressive music. They help connect the listener to the song in a way that allows them to imagine the setting for the music. The stronger the development of the image, the deeper the listener can connect with the meaning of the song.

Story line: Songs with stories also help connect the listener to the music. Depending on the genre, the words in a story are the most important part of a song. But just as there are many ways to write a song, there are many ways to tell a story. Most stories have some sort of character introduction, plot development, and then build to a climax, resolution, or surprise. When crafting a story with music, you should consider how the story unfolds as the song progresses and try to match the story line with the emotion of the music. This leads to prosody. . . .

Prosody: Prosody occurs when the mood of the music (expressed primarily in the harmony and rhythm) matches the mood of the lyrics and melody of the song. Basically this means that every part of a song fits together. Being entirely subjective, prosody is impossible to measure but you'll know it when you hear it. For example, if the tune "Happy Birthday" were played in a minor key, the melody wouldn't fit the celebratory mood of the lyrics and thus would lack prosody. You may strive to produce music with prosody or you may purposely avoid it, but you should always consider it before the recording is complete.

Hook: A hook is a small piece of a song that's considered catchy and [hopefully] makes the listener want to hear the song again. Usually repeated several times, a hook can be a unique lyric, melody, chord progression, sound effect, or rhythmic figure, to name the most common examples. As a producer and songwriter, you should consider the frequency and placement of hooks in the music.

Repetition: Another device to help listeners follow your songs is repetition. Repetition is found mainly in song form (Verse > Chorus > Verse > Chorus), harmony (recurring chord progressions), and lyric structure (repeated words or phrases). Repetition helps the listener remember the song and creates a sense of predictability that makes them feel more comfortable.

Creating Lead Sheets

People learn songs by several different methods. They can listen to a recording of a song and play along. Someone else can show them how to play it. Or they can read it from a musical chart, score, or lead sheet. The quickest way to learn a song is to use a combination of these methods.

At some point in your musical lives, you'll have a recording session and will need to organize players who don't already know the song.

A great way to get those players up to speed beforehand is to provide them with a demo tape and lead sheet. The demo tape can be a simple recording of just the chords and melody. The lead sheet can also be rather simple.

In its most basic form, a lead sheet shows the song's structure, key, tempo, time signature, and chord progression. More detailed lead sheets show the melody, lyrics, and rhythmic hits.

Fig. 6.3.
A section from a typical lead sheet.

Besides helping musicians learn the songs, there are additional benefits to creating lead sheets. Once the song is down on paper you (the producer) can analyze it from a different perspective — especially helpful if a song doesn't seem quite right but you can't figure out why. For example, you might notice that a chord progression doesn't resolve, or that a melody doesn't have enough tonal variety. Among other things, you can also tell if a rhythm is off or if the melody is too high or low for a vocalist's or instrumentalist's range. Additionally, a producer (and engineer) can use the lead sheet as a road map of the song when recording and mixing. While looking at the lead sheet in a recording session, a producer might say to the artist, "That whole guitar take was great . . . we just need to punch in bars 3 and 4 of the bridge." Besides providing organization and documentation, a lead sheet helps a producer offer explicit comments and keep the energy focused.

Writing out lead sheets on staff paper can be convenient, but it can also be time consuming. Learning how to use a music notation program like Finale (MakeMusic!) or Sibelius (Sibelius) can be a real asset to your musical career. (There are freeware music notation programs as well.) The software programs print out neater parts than handwritten ones, and will play your music so you can hear if there are any mistakes.

As a songwriter, lead sheets can help you resolve problematic areas in your songs. As a producer, creating lead sheets early in the preproduction phase can eliminate many problems, and will ultimately lead to improved efficiency in later phases.

Producer's Perspective — Interacting with an Artist

At any time during the preproduction process, if you find that any part of a song has to be reworked, you need to be articulate about what needs to be changed and why. If you're working with a sensitive musician, you've got to use tact and diplomacy, as discussed earlier. You'll also need to gain trust and respect from artists. First and foremost, artists need to feel comfortable around you. You need to gain their confidence as a counselor and a confidant. To do this you need to cultivate an open relationship by not being judgmental and by allowing them to be themselves. You should be open-minded and flexible. In an environment like that, special things happen.

Most artists are afraid other people won't like their music. Fear prevents people from doing a lot of things — it certainly prevents artists from opening up and exposing their souls. You need to use all of your power as a producer to quell this fear.

You should also try to be a catalyst for ideas, a stimulus for creativity. Build on their ideas and provide encouragement. A producer should provide a different point of view...artists are looking for that different view from you. You're also expected to have a tremendous amount of patience. You need to mediate and moderate any tricky situations and protect the democratic process when dealing with a group of artists or a band.

The artist wants to create the best recording of their life with you. Thus you must support their music, provide translations of their musical visions, and offer camaraderie. You need to develop your psychology skills to deal with the many moods, egos, and personalities of artists. And develop your management chops to help focus the artist's attention while following the budget and schedule, without making them feel pressured.

Every producer must figure out how to do all of these things for their artists. But every artist is different, so you'll have to alter your techniques. When working on your own music, allow the producer in you (as best you can) to be a non-judgmental, flexible, and open-minded objective source. That way the artist in you can truly express itself.

Artist's Perspective — Interacting with a Producer

Collaborating with a producer can be a tricky thing for an artist. It may be difficult to completely open up to someone new. If you (the artist) want to have a close relationship with a producer, you've got to spend time breaking down any barriers the two of you might have. And you've got to be as articulate as you can when describing your musical ideas and overall vision.

Ideally you and your producer will create a relationship based on honesty, trust, and respect. Both of your opinions on where the music should go should be relatively mutual. However, there will be times when you disagree. Maybe the producer wants to change a lyric or a chord progression. Maybe the producer wants to change a song of yours more drastically than you'd like. Comments about changes, if worded poorly, can sound like criticisms of your musical ideas. However, the producer is only giving his opinion. You should try to keep an open mind because ultimately he's only trying to help improve your songs. Listening to and validating the producer's ideas will connect the two of you in a collaborative way, even if you decide that you disagree.

There's something to be said for uncompromising artistic expression, but you (the artist) need to be clear with the producer about why you don't want to change part of the song. For example, if you feel a producer's change would lose what you're trying to state as an artist, then you should stand up for your original idea. In doing so, however, you might also want to suggest a smaller or similar change that addresses the producer's concerns but stays true to your intent. That way you'll satisfy the producer and maintain your artistic expression at the same time.

There's also something to be said for connecting with your audience. If these two concerns (artist expression and audience connection) clash, it's the producer's job to inform you. Just try not to shoot the messenger — you hired the producer for his or her honest opinion and guidance. That said, the artist usually has the final say on any musical decision.

The relationship you create with your producer will determine how well your musical vision comes across in the final product. If you spend time cultivating a solid relationship based on trust and honesty you'll usually get much in return.

7. HIRING HELP

In many regards a producer acts as a project manager. Like project managers, producers create budgets and schedules and generally make sure things are moving ahead as planned. Good managers also delegate duties in order to get things done more effectively. Hiring good help is a form of skillful delegation: If you (or the artist) can't or don't know how to do something you feel is needed for your project, you should consider bringing in outside talent.

As the producer, one of your primary jobs is to create a certain sound for the recording. Hiring someone for their specific vocal or instrumental ability is a very common practice in the music business. The same goes for arrangers, orchestrators, programmers, recording engineers, mix engineers, and mastering engineers. Most producers aren't capable of competently performing all of these functions by themselves, so they hire experts.

Obviously, the more skills you have in these areas (e.g., instrumental abilities, arranging, etc.), the more you'll be able to get done on your own, which will make you more desirable to artists looking for a well-rounded producer. And some things you may want to try yourself even if you've never tried them before. For example, maybe you've never written a horn chart but you'd really like some horn stabs in a song. Because this is a small assignment it might be a good time to try learning about writing for brass. Starting small and working your way up to more involved projects is the way to go.

However, if you bite off more than you can chew it might come back to hurt you in several ways. First, it might take your focus away from your other duties as a producer. Second, it might take you too long to do what you thought you could do, pushing your project off schedule. Third, what you do might not turn out very well because you didn't take the time to really learn the skill. Fourth, you may overextend yourself causing a number of side effects (stress, tiredness, irritability, etc.) that could negatively impact the project. Any of these reasons provide additional justification to hire some help for your project.

Choosing the right people can be complicated. Who should you hire? Do they have the necessary skills? Do they feel comfortable with the musical style? Have they done projects like this before? Are they easy to work with? When choosing players and singers, you should also consider their range and if they can read music.

Where can you find help? Through friends, friends of friends, the *Yellow Pages*, the Internet, and local chapters of the professional unions (AFTRA and AFM). Mostly I try to use my friends or other acquaintances. I also meet people in the Digidesign Production Network (DigiProNet). Sometimes I just search the 'Net for musicians, arrangers, or other artists to use on projects. The 'Net is also useful for finding bandmates, used gear or instruments, and musical services. Better yet, some Web sites list their entries by geographical location, making it easier to find people close by. A non-exhaustive list of Web sites I've found to be helpful is located in appendix B.

If you're thinking of working with someone you've never worked with before, I recommend getting demos. If they have a good demo you should meet them to see what they're like personally. Also, playing demos of *your* project will give them an idea of where you're heading and allow you to get a feel for what they think of the music. It always helps to hire folks who will enjoy the music they'll be making.

8. SCHEDULING REHEARSAL, RECORDING, AND MIXING SESSIONS

At some point you might need to book time in a professional studio. Maybe you need to record a full drum set but your neighbors or roommates aren't cool with hearing death metal grooves for hours. Or maybe you're going all-out and recording a full orchestra! Whatever your needs, you should try to book your time early and at a reputable studio. Call around to compare rates and available times. You should also visit potential studios to meet the people you'd be working with and see their equipment and recording room.

Also, the recording studio has to have a Pro Tools setup. Most professional studios have Pro Tools HD or Mix systems with the full-blown professional version of Pro Tools LE. The beautiful thing is that any session you record in Pro Tools LE and Free can be brought into Pro Tools HD/Mix and vice versa (I've done it many times and it works flawlessly). In fact, sessions can even be shared between Windows and Macintosh systems if saved properly (see chapter 3). However, Pro Tools LE and Free sessions can only have a certain number of tracks and mix busses. HD and Mix systems allow up to 128 audio tracks and up to 64 mix busses, whereas LE systems are limited to 32 audio tracks and 16 mix busses, and Free is limited to eight audio tracks. If you bring an HD/Mix session into LE or Free that exceeds their limits, that additional information will be inactive in the transfer. Also, any plug-ins from the original system (HD, Mix, LE, or Free) that don't have equivalents in the new system will be inactive.

Finally, as a producer you're responsible for everyone showing up to rehearsals, recording sessions, and mixing sessions. When scheduling the dates and times for these events, be sure to verify that those who need to be there *can* be there before you set the date in stone. This seems obvious, but you'll never need to be reminded again after the first time you have to make 25 calls to reschedule a session because you wrongly assumed the drummer could make it.

9. REHEARSING

It is a given that rehearsing songs before the sessions will improve the recordings. If practice makes permanent (as one of my drum teachers told me), rehearsals serve to solidify the song's arrangement (feel, form, and attitude) in the artist's memory. The better the artist knows the song, the easier it is to record. However, too much time spent rehearsing a song can kill its freshness and energy. To capture the best recordings, you must find the balance between rehearsing too little and too much.

I recommend recording all rehearsals, even if only on cassette. By doing this you can separate yourself from the energy of the rehearsal and listen carefully, without being influenced by the live performance. You can gain a lot of information by listening back to these recordings before the actual session. It may also be useful to play rehearsal tapes for other people (friends, family, other musicians, etc.) to get their feedback. Why record rehearsals?

- You can figure out if the agreed upon arrangements are working. For example, maybe you'll hear that the four extra bars you added after the bridge interrupt the flow of the song.

Even in free-form jazz recordings — where spontaneity and improvisation are fundamental elements of the music — it's beneficial for the musicians to play together before the recording sessions to get a feel for the energy of the song and create synergy within the group.

- You can analyze the parts individually. For example, maybe you'll find that the bass line is too busy.

- You can identify areas where "ear candy" can be added. For example, maybe you'll hear a small section of the song that needs an additional guitar lick to fill a space. Or maybe you'll imagine a sound effect panning back and forth through the stereo field during a particular section. This kind of work can be the most exciting and satisfying part of being a producer.

- Or . . . you may find you're happy with the work you did prior to the rehearsal and are satisfied with everything. This means you are ready to record!

If you're rehearsing in your studio, it's a good idea to record directly into Pro Tools. Sometimes rehearsals have the best energy because everyone's relaxed and not worried about performing perfectly like they might have to for a recording session. The performances are often quite good, and if you mic everything well but keep the pressure of recording to a minimum, you might capture a performance you can keep. Even if you grab just a small section of "keeper" material (like a cool drum loop or guitar lick), it's still valuable given the composing and arranging functions offered by digital editing in Pro Tools.

10.   GETTING READY FOR THE RECORDING SESSIONS

As I've stated many times before, the producer is responsible for *everything* in a project, and as producer, you have several main concerns in the final days before a recording session. Your first is connecting with everyone who's a part of the session: This means calling, e-mailing, paging, faxing, writing a message in the sky . . . anything it takes to make contact with the participants, remind them of the session, and confirm that they'll be there. Musicians — maybe even more so than other people — forget things. They lose messages, phone numbers, and directions. They get distracted and lose track of time. If you haven't experienced this, then consider yourself lucky. . . . I've worked with several fantastic musicians who don't wear a watch or carry a planner or Palm Pilot. Multiple calls to these types of folks are a necessity. When you're working with a close-knit bunch of musicians this may not be as much of an issue because they'll talk to each other often. However, if you're working with folks who spread themselves pretty thin (like most talented people) communication about scheduled events is imperative.

Your second main concern in the final days is discussing the upcoming session with the recording engineer. If you're not engineering the session you need to discuss three main items: studio setup, equipment setup, and track assignments. Talking about these topics beforehand will greatly improve the efficiency of the session because

Mitch Benoff (Berklee faculty member and producer) includes a funny yet poignant multiple choice question on one of his production class tests. It reads something like: If an instrumentalist doesn't show up for a recording session, who's fault/ responsibility is it? (a) The producer's, (b) the producer's, or (c) the producer's?

the engineer can prepare everything before you arrive. (Chapter 7 outlines what to discuss with the engineer.) If you're the producer and engineer for the session then discussion may not necessary (unless you like talking to yourself) – but planning is still a must.

Your third concern as producer is creating a plan of action for the recording session. This plan begins with the three items you discussed with the engineer (see previous paragraph and chapter 7). It also includes creating a rough timetable for what you'd like to get done and how you'd like to do it. For example:

6:00   Set up instruments and mics.
7:00   Begin to get sounds into Pro Tools.
7:30   Run through Song 1 to warm up.
8:00   Have first take of Song 1 . . . and so on.

Obviously, this plan should be as flexible as possible, given any time constraints you may have. Flexibility allows for new ideas and mistakes – both common occurrences in a fertile and imperfect recording environment.

If you do all of the preproduction steps suggested above, you'll definitely be prepared for a great recording session using Pro Tools. ∎

PRO TOOLS HANDS-ON

Evaluate Song Demo Ideas

The four demos now have all of the basic song elements in their Pro Tools sessions...rough melodies are taking shape, lyrics are coming together, grooves are starting to gel, possible arrangements are in place, etc. From a producer's perspective, evaluate the song ideas in the four demo sessions. What do you think of the key, tempo, lyrics, music, instrumentation, song form, and attitude/mood for each song? Is there prosody? Are the songs coming together, or do they need serious work? What needs to be rewritten or arranged differently?

Maybe the rock song needs a new chorus – both melody and harmony. Maybe the hip-hop song needs a better beat and a tighter hook. Perhaps the jazz tune could use an altered melody and a change of rhythm in one section. The electronica song might need another section with a hook. What do you think? As a producer, what would you do to these song demos? The beauty of art is that we all will do something different.

Time Compress/Expand a Region

During preproduction, you may decide that the original tempo of your song demo isn't quite right. But what if your song is dependent on an audio sample you really like (e.g., a killer drum loop, an unbelievable bass line, a wacked-out horn melody, etc.)? Fortunately, it's easy to change the sample's tempo to fit the song. Use the Time Trimmer tool. As you read in chapter 4, the Time Trimmer expands or compresses a region without changing the pitch using Digidesign's Time Compression/Expansion (TC/E) AudioSuite plug-in. I used the Time Trimmer tool with Serato's Pitch 'n Time plug-in to lengthen the acoustic bass loop in the hip-hop session.

Serato's Pitch 'n Time, Wave Mechanics' SPEED, or SynchroArts' Time Mod plug-in, you can use either one of those as the default plug-in (instead of Digi's TC/E) with the Time Trimmer tool. To change the default plug-in:

1. Select Preferences from the Setups menu

2. Click on the Processing tab

3. Choose the plug-in from the Default TC/E Setting pop-up menu

Normalizing the region before using the Time Trimmer can improve the quality of the processed region.

To normalize a region:

1. Select the region

2. Choose Normalize from the AudioSuite menu

3. Set the parameters for the Normalize plug-in

4. Click Process

Try it. Use the Time Trimmer to alter the length of an audio region. Expand and compress the region to find out how much you can alter the length without degrading the quality of the sound. Experiment on different types of sounds. Does this process work better on some sounds than others? How much can you change the BPM on a drum loop without noticeably affecting the sound quality? Try using the Normalize plug-in to improve the sound quality of your compressed/expanded regions.

Change the Key of a MIDI-Driven Song

Making the vocalist sound the best he/she can is one of the most important duties you have as a producer. Because of this, many songs written in one key end up in a different key during preproduction to better suit the singer's range. Changing the key (transposing) in MIDI-based songs is quite easy. (I changed the key down a whole step to better fit the vocalist's range in the Electronica song.)

Try it. First, triple-click with the Selector tool on a track you want to transpose. Press Shift and triple-click on any other tracks you want to transpose to select multiple tracks at once. Be careful not to select drum tracks to transpose. Choose Transpose from the MIDI menu and the Transpose MIDI Operations window will open, as in the figure at right.

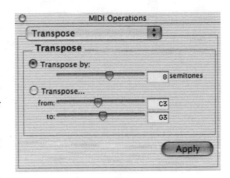

Use the sliders in the Tranpose by Semitones or Tranpose From/To area of the Transpose window to move the key of the song up or down. There are 12 semitones in an octave. To move the key up a perfect fifth interval, use 8 semi-tones or "From C4" and "To G4." To move the key down a minor third interval, use –4 semi-tones, or "From C4" and "To A3." Click "Apply" when you're finished.

Create a Budget and Schedule

Print out the Project Budget and Project Schedule PDFs from the CD. Use them to plan out a project that you've recently started. Preproduction is the phase where the planning must happen so the project stays focused, within the budget, and on schedule.

The Engineer's Role in Preproduction

In this chapter:

- **Studio and equipment setup**

- **Microphone basics and phase cancellation**

- **Other equipment to set up**

- **Making track assignments**

- **Additional duties**

Now that you know what goes into preproduction from a producer's standpoint, let's look at things from a more tangible and technical perspective — as an engineer.

Like a producer, an engineer has many responsibilities during preproduction, all of which revolve around the upcoming recording session. There are three main topics to consider: studio setup, equipment setup, and track assignments.

Studio setup involves decisions about where instruments will be placed and where the players will be situated in your recording space. **Equipment setup** includes choosing microphones, amps, headphones, effects, etc. and checking to see if the equipment is in good working order. **Track assignments** refers to how many tracks you're going to record and how you want to record them. The number of tracks may be limited by the number of mics you have, the number of physical inputs, or the number of tracks in Pro Tools you want to use. You may also need to consider setting up separate headphone mixes for individual musicians (explained in chapter 11).

STUDIO SETUP

The first step when preparing for a recording session is to plan how you'll use your studio space. Some questions to ask yourself include: What is the instrumentation of the session? Do I need sound separation, isolation, or baffling of some sort? Do the musicians need to see each other? Where can the musicians stand or sit comfortably? Does the studio need some special acoustical treatment for the session?

While you're considering these questions you might try sketching diagrams of possible setups to help you visualize how the studio will look with everyone in it. I've included a sketch (figure 7.1) of a session

■ Fig. 7.1.
The studio setup at Chéz Dave. As you can see I put the guitar amp in the closet, the bass out in the hallway, the drums in the corner, and the keys/vocals in the adjacent corner. This setup facilitated eye contact among members of the band and provided enough sound separation to record great tracks.

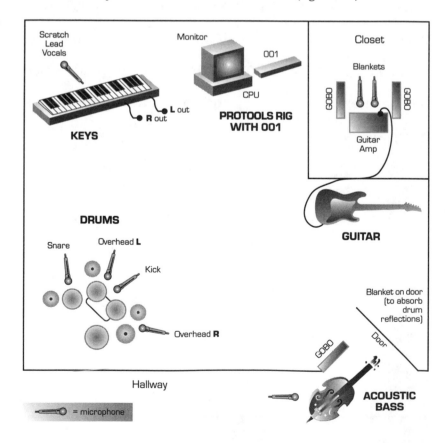

I engineered once in a small apartment...we recorded drums, electric guitar, acoustic bass, keyboards, and scratch vocals all at once in my home studio (a.k.a. Dave's Bedroom).

SOUND SEPARATION

When doing multitrack recording we usually try to isolate sounds as best we can to have more control over the mix. That is, if the guitar is isolated from the drums we can put different effects on each track. But if there's a lot of leakage from the drums into the guitar track, then *however* we effect the guitar you'll also hear that effect on the drums to some degree. There are several techniques engineers use to achieve sound separation, often utilized in combination.

The first technique is microphone placement — aiming mics at only one source is the key. For example, if you're recording a drum kit, pointing the hi-hat mic away from the snare drum will decrease the amount of snare leakage on the hi-hat track.

The second technique is physical separation of the instruments from each other, which provides greater isolation for their tracks. For example, as you see in figure 7.1, I put the guitar amp in my closet. This physically separated the loud amp so its mics picked up far less of the other instruments and vice versa.

Engineers also use various devices to achieve sound separation and isolation. Gobos are essentially movable walls, usually smooth on one side and carpeted on the other. The smooth side provides reflections, while the carpeted side absorbs sound. You can make your own gobos using common items: I often use the front and back covers from my equipment rack and some large pieces of wood, and sometimes even my mattress! Plexiglas shields/walls are also used but they can cause a lot of reflections — on the plus side, people can see through them since they're transparent. Blankets can be used to cover reflective surfaces as well as isolate instruments from others. They're good for absorbing sound and I often use them on pianos and around guitar amps.

Ideally, multitrack recording captures the best sound of instruments playing together while keeping those great sounds (tracks) separate from each other.

Along with the sketch you should consider how many mic/line cables, microphones, mic stands, headphones, and headphone extension cables you'll need for the session. But your access to these items may influence the setup you're planning. For those of us on tight budgets, creative setups are the only way we'll be able to maximize our equipment while minimizing expenses. Regardless, when it comes right down to it you may have to buy some extra equipment to make sure sessions go smoothly and sound good.

Even with planning, there are still many last-minute contingencies you should be ready for with a flexible setup. Inevitably, the musical lineup will change and you'll have to record different instruments than you expected. Or the band may have a particular requirement.... For example, the bass player and the drummer may ask to be next to each other, even though it would work better for you if they were across the room. To help accommodate sudden changes like these, you might want to sketch several scenarios ahead of time instead of just one.

If you're only recording yourself, one instrument at a time, then you won't need to worry about these situations at all. However, once you start recording multiple instruments at one time in the same room, studio setups and mic placement become important.

EQUIPMENT SETUP: MICROPHONES

Once you've considered your studio setup you need to think about what equipment you'll use during the session — many engineers start with microphones. If you have a limited number of mics your choices might be out of necessity, or you may have mics you always use for specific applications (for example, a Shure SM57 on the guitar amp). Either way, the more mics you have, the more interesting and creative the decision-making process becomes.

Microphone Basics

When choosing a mic you need to consider its polar pickup pattern(s), frequency response, if it has a pad or rolloff, the mic type, and if it needs phantom power. And some mics are better suited (i.e., commonly used) for certain applications. Knowing this information will help you choose wisely. Ultimately it will help you record good sounds into Pro Tools.

Microphone **polar patterns** range from omni-directional to super-cardioid (very uni-directional). The patterns (shown in figure 7.2) indicate from what direction the mic receives audio signals.

■ Fig. 7.2.

Microphone pickup patterns. Keep these in mind when you're deciding how to mic different instruments and whether you want more of a "clean" source sound or more room ambience or bleed from other musicians.

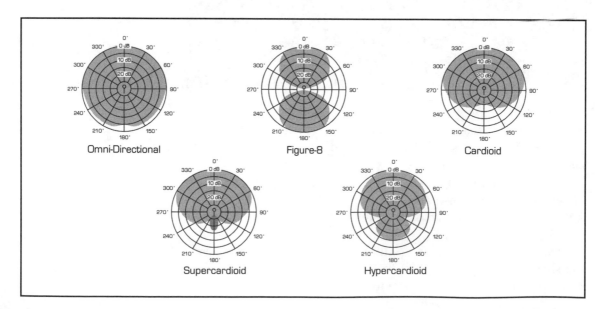

An omni-directional mic receives audio signals from all directions, whereas cardioid microphones (including hyper-cardioid and super-cardioid) receive the majority of their signal from one direction only. Bi-directional (or figure-8) mics pick up audio signal from the front and back of the mic while rejecting sounds from the side. In addition, if you look at the specifications of any mic you own you'll notice that the polar pattern is slightly altered at different frequencies. For example, most cardioid and omni-directional mics tend to become more directional when picking up high frequencies (see example in figure 7.3). Consult your microphone's user guide for more information about its polar pattern.

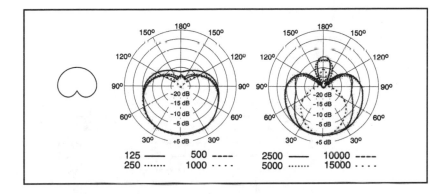

Fig. 7.3.
The cardioid polar pattern at different frequencies for Shure's KSM44. This microphone also has settings for omni-directional and figure-8 patterns.

The directionality of a microphone can help determine its use in a recording session. Typically, directional mics are used to pick up one sound source at a time whereas omni-directional mics are often used as room mics — to pick up everything. Most mics have only one pattern, however some allow you to switch between several.

Condenser, dynamic, ribbon, and electret are the most common types of mics. And of those, you'll use condenser and dynamic mics for most applications. Condenser mics require phantom power and are fragile, whereas dynamic mics are more rugged and don't need phantom power. **Phantom power** is a 48V current that powers condenser mics, but it won't hurt dynamic mics. Ribbon mics — which use ribbons to pick up acoustic audio signals — are the most fragile and can be destroyed if given phantom power, so be careful! The Digi 002, Digi 001, and Mbox can provide phantom power to their microphone inputs when needed by pressing the 48V switch. Otherwise, phantom power can be supplied by a mixer or, in few cases, by a battery pack that comes with the microphone.

Knowing the frequency response of a mic will help you choose the right application for it, as well. In this case, **frequency response** refers to a microphone's ability to pick up a certain frequency range. Some mics are designed to primarily pick up bass frequencies (20Hz to 800Hz), while others are better for middle frequencies (800Hz to 8kHz) or high frequencies (8kHz to 20kHz). For example, the Shure Beta 52 is specifically designed to capture bass frequencies while the Shure SM57 has a boost in its mid range. So you see, it's no coincidence that professional engineers use the Beta 52 on kick drums and the SM57 on snare — the frequencies those drums produce align with the best areas of response for those mics. Condenser mics usually have flat response curves, whereas dynamic mics have some peaks and valleys. For example, check out the frequency response curves for the KSM44 (condenser) and the SM57 (dynamic).

COURTESY OF SHURE INCORPORATED. USED BY PERMISSION

Fig. 7.4.
KSM44 and SM57 frequency response curves.

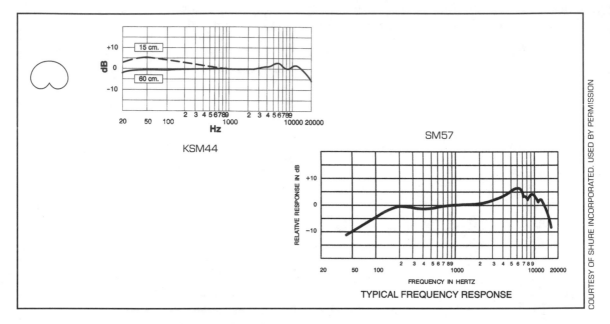

Some mics have bass rolloff and pad switches. A bass rolloff switch is a low-frequency filter that can help reduce unwanted background noise (such as the low hum of an air conditioner) or counteract proximity effect (see box). For example, the KSM44 has a three-position bass rolloff switch: You can choose flat response (no rolloff), low-frequency cutoff (which provides an 18dB-per-octave cutoff at 80Hz), or low-frequency rolloff (which provides a 6dB-per-octave rolloff filter at 115Hz) See figure 7.5.

Fig. 7.5.
The KSM44 offers three bass rolloff settings.

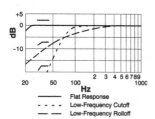

PROXIMITY EFFECT: PLEASE STAND TOO CLOSE TO ME

As a sound source moves closer to a directional microphone, the bass response of the mic increases. This phenomenon is called **proximity effect**. To hear this, set up a mic and talk into it — move your mouth very close and notice the sound is more bass heavy than when you're off the mic a bit. Sometimes the increased bass response is desired, however, a mic's bass rolloff switch can help reduce the proximity effect if you don't want it. Another way to get rid of proximity effect is to lower the EQ gain at around 200Hz.

A **pad** switch attenuates the incoming signal, preventing extremely high signals from overloading and damaging the microphone. For example, the KSM44's pad is –15dB. This reduces signal level at the mic by 15dB without altering frequency response.

The Digi 001 also has a –26dB pad to attenuate "hot" mics or to use line-level signals through the front mic preamps. Most mixers also have pads for when incoming signals overload the preamp. Digi 002 and Mbox have buttons enabling you to switch between mic, line, and instrument (DI) inputs. Being able to switch between input types eliminates the need for a pad.

-26dB Pad

■ **Fig. 7.6.**
The Digi 001's pad switches come in handy if you're getting extra "hot" signal or using line-level instruments.

Acoustical Phase Cancellation

Microphone frequency response can depend on the mic's surroundings and its relationship with a closely positioned mic. When two or more sound waves of the same frequency arrive at a mic at the same time, an effect called **phase cancellation** can occur. If the sound waves are out of phase some frequencies will be cut or even completely lost. How does this happen?

Acoustical phase refers to the time relationship between two or more sound waves and where those waves are in their wavelength cycles. This means that when two sound waves of the same frequency come together at the exact same time, the amplitudes of the waves will add to each other. Depending on the phase of each wave, you will hear either a boost or a cut in the frequency. Figures 7.7 and 7.8 show the results of two sine waves added together that are in phase and out of phase.

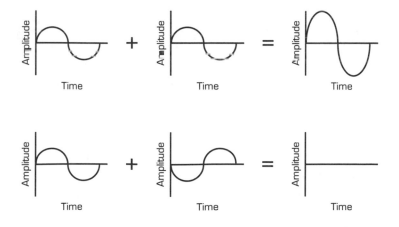

■ **Fig. 7.7.**
(Top) When two sound waves are in phase, the amplitude (or sound output) is boosted. If they're perfectly in phase, the amplitude will be doubled. This is very rarely a problem.

■ **Fig. 7.8.**
(Bottom) Phase cancellation occurs when a particular frequency arrives at a mic at the same time as the out-of-phase version of the same frequency. Here we see that the sound wave has been completely destroyed.

Fortunately, most sound waves are much more complex than sine waves and thus aren't as easy to eliminate. However, partial phase cancellation does occur more often than complete phase cancellation and is more difficult to hear. To detect phase cancellation on an input, listen for unequal low- and low-mid frequency response or an unstable or washy quality to the sound.

Phase cancellation can also occur when using one mic in a reverberant environment. The mic will pick up the original signal plus a quick reflection of the signal from the wall, floor, or ceiling. If you find a mic is picking up less low-end than expected, cover the reverberant surface with some sort of absorptive material (blanket, carpet, etc.).

However, phase cancellation happens more often between two microphones. To rectify this situation be sure to follow the Three-to-One (3:1) rule: That is, microphones should be placed no closer together than three times the distance between one of them and the sound source. For example, if a mic is one foot from a sound source, another mic shouldn't be placed within three feet of the first microphone. A common usage of the 3:1 rule is shown in figure 7.9 for a pair of overhead mics used on cymbals.

Fig. 7.9.
Follow the 3:1 rule to avoid phase cancellation between two mics.

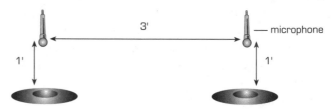

Phase cancellation can also be an issue when miking the top and bottom head of a drum. I often use top and bottom mic on snare drums and find that, depending on their positioning, I usually need to flip the phase of the bottom mic. Flipping the phase inverts the amplitude of the sound wave as seen in figure 7.10.

Fig. 7.10.
Flipping the phase. This can be done using a Pro Tools DigiRack EQ or delay plug-in by pressing the Phase Invert button (inset).

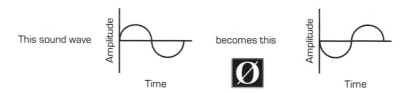

You may also find phase cancellation due to improper wiring in the microphone itself or in the mic cable. In this case, you can also flip the phase using a Pro Tools plug-in. (More information on this topic can be found in the *DigiRack Plug-Ins Guide*.)

Regardless of mic specifications, you should experiment with your microphones. Try using them in different positions, on different instruments, and with different effects and EQ settings. You'll learn much more about the nuances of each mic and how unique it sounds, as well as develop some new techniques that will become part of your "sound." Visit appendix D for more information on Shure microphones and links to some very useful and pertinent mic usage information on their Web site.

EQUIPMENT SETUP: OTHER GEAR

Besides mics you'll need to choose which amplifiers, outboard effects units, compressors, and other tools you want to use in the session. This might be easy if you don't have any of this gear, but if you do have choices, plan it out just as you would with microphones and the rest of your studio setup.

You'll need the right cables, and you'll want to be clear on the routing of the audio signals. I recommend labeling everything – put tape labels on all cables, effects units, etc., and on your inputs and outputs. Then if you have to change something midway through a session it will be much faster to find what you're looking for.

You should also create a list of everything you'll need for the session. This includes mics, mic stands, mic cables, pop filters, instrument cables, headphones, headphone extension cables, and instrument stands and music stands. Also included are any instruments and instrument supplies (e.g., guitar strings, drum sticks, etc.) as well as other hardware you'll need such as amplifiers, monitors, and outboard effects processors. The artist, producer, and engineer need to work together on the list so that everyone has what they need.

TRACK ASSIGNMENTS

When recording using a finite number of inputs and tracks, you and the producer need to think about how you're going to allocate these to the instruments. For example, if you're recording into the Audiomedia III card you've got a maximum of four inputs. If you want to record an entire drum set on those four tracks, how do you do it? One track for the kick, one for the snare, and two for the overheads (including cymbals and toms)? What if you also want to record an electric guitar and bass at the same time? You might create a submix of the drums on your mixer, then use one track for the guitar, one for the bass, and two tracks (panned left and right) for the drums.

Recording using Digi 002/001 gives you many more inputs, but you're still limited to 32 tracks in Pro Tools LE. This seems like a lot of tracks when you start recording a song, but the "real estate" gets eaten up fast if you're not careful. I recommend creating a track sheet that lists all the tracks you intend to record on the song (see figure 7.11).

Pro Tools makes track assignments and management really simple. You can assign any input for any track and move tracks around easily (by dragging them to new locations). You can name every

Phase cancellation may not be apparent when listening in stereo. Listening in mono sums the stereo sound waves and helps identify the problem. See chapter 13 for more information on this topic.

I've included several worksheets on the CD-ROM that might be useful as you set up for a recording session. They cover input and output connection diagrams of Digi 002, 001, Mbox, Audiomedia cards, a standard 16-channel mixer, and other equipment. You can quickly draw out your connections as you're setting up and then refer to them during a session. My hope is that — amidst the numerous cables and jacks — they'll help you follow the signal flow in your studio.

Fig. 7.11.
A track sheet for "Come 'n' Get It." The CD-ROM has a template for track assignments.

I've included a worksheet in PDF format on the CD-ROM called "Equipment Needed List" to help you coordinate your equipment requirements for upcoming recording sessions.

TRACK ASSIGNMENTS

Song Title: Come N' Get It   Artist: The Cool Grape Goodness
Producer: David Franz   Engineer: Simon Hessler

Track Name	#	Intro	Verse 1	Chorus 1	V2	C2	Bridge	B2	C3	C4	Outro	#
Kick	1	Kick →										1
Snare Top	2	Snare Top →										2
Snare Bot	3	Snare Bot →										3
Hihat	4	Hihat →										4
Hi Tom	5	Hi Tom →										5
Mid Tom	6	Mid Tom →										6
Lo Tom	7	Lo Tom →										7
Overhead L	8	Overhead L →										8
Overhead R	9	Overhead R →										9
Room L	10	Room L →										10
Room R	11	Room R →										11
Bass	12	Bass →										12
B-3 L	13	B-3 L →										13
B-3 R	14	B-3 R →										14
Guitar L	15	Guitar L →										15
Guitar R	16	Guitar R →										16
Gtr Riff	17	Intro Riff								Main Riff	Outro Lick	17
Grt Solo	18	Lead Vox →								Riff harm.	Gtr Solo	18
Lead Vox	19											19
Back Vox	20			Back Vox		Back Vox				Yeahs		20
Rap	21						Rap			Yells		21
Rap Backs	22						Rap Backs			Yells		22
DJ L	23	sample Loop	sample	Loop	sample							23
DJ R	24	sample Loop	sample	Loop	sample							24

track and make remarks in the comments section of the Edit and Mix windows. You can also use playlists to keep multiple takes of tracks stored on top of each other, without using up other tracks (though you still need to document them all). Also, each file you record is saved with a unique identification number to differentiate it from other files and make it easier for Pro Tools to find and manage files for you. (For example, if you don't label your tracks before you record, you might end up with 15 "Audio 1" files on your hard drive, but Pro Tools can tell them apart because of their unique IDs.) However, just because Pro Tools knows which files go with what sessions, you might not know. Try to name your tracks before you start recording, that way the files will automatically be easier to find and work with.

Also, if you think you might come close to filling 32 tracks you should consider submixing and bouncing logical instrument groupings to free up tracks for additional overdubs. This subject is fully explained in chapters 9 and 11.

ADDITIONAL ENGINEERING DUTIES

There are several other duties an engineer should perform in preparation for a recording session. If you're recording material that's unfamiliar to you, consider going to a rehearsal or live show — that way you'll understand what the music sounds like before you mic it. Also consider recording the rehearsal or show as a reference. (If you're rehearsing in your studio it's especially good to record. You might get lucky and be

I've included a worksheet in PDF format on the CD-ROM called "Track Sheet" to help you manage track assignments for upcoming recording sessions.

able to keep a great take.) If you can't do any of this try to get your hands on previous recordings of the music or other material from the artist.

There are also some clerical things to take care of before engineering a session. You should make sure you have adequate hard drive space for the project. If you don't, there are several things you can do:

1. Defragment your hard drive. Using Norton Utilities or comparable software, defragment your hard drive to eliminate holes in its storage. To me, defragmenting is like compacting trash: All of your files are pushed together making room for more. Consult the software manuals for instructions on how to do this and understand any risks to your files.

2. Eliminate unneeded files from your hard drive. Instead of trashing them outright, you should probably write them onto another storage medium (CD-R, CD-RW, DVD RAM, DAT, JAZ cartridge, tape backup systems, etc.), especially if you haven't made backup copies. Consult chapter 9 for more information on saving hard drive space.

3. If the two options above aren't available, you can either use fewer tracks than you intended or purchase another hard drive. This isn't desirable if you're on a budget, but it may be necessary to get the job done (and external hard drives are increasingly affordable).

As you're getting your computer ready for the recording session you should consider making a Pro Tools template (as mentioned in chapter 3). Create and label the tracks, set the inputs and outputs, etc. Doing this will save a great deal of time during the actual session. And if you need to synchronize equipment you should make sure you know how to do it beforehand (more information on syncing in chapter 8).

Finally, you should know whom to contact if you have problems with your system. Consult the *Pro Tools Reference Guide* for troubleshooting information, and the first page of that same manual for Digidesign contact information (also located in your "Product Registration and Customer Services Information" packet that came with your equipment). Technical support info is also located in appendix C of this book. In addition, Digidesign has an elaborate support section, answer base, and user group on their Web site (www.digidesign.com). Just choose Support under the Digidesign logo on their main page.

If all else fails, call Digi's technical support staff. But before you call be ready with information regarding your computer, Digidesign hardware and software, external hard drives, and other hardware and software. Having this info accessible when calling will help the support person help you quickly and effectively.

You might also seek out people with systems similar to yours, ask questions of each other, and if necessary, get immediate help in times of need (like when you're "on the clock" during a session). Some people find it rewarding to start local user groups.

Always make backups! Computers crash and hard drives die. Make backups of everything. As the engineer, this is your responsibility. Clients and musicians aren't especially fond of "the dog ate my files" argument, nor do they care if it's not your fault that the latest version of your OS is buggy, or there was a freak electrical storm in your studio during the session. If the files are lost, it's your fault. (Sorry, I'll get off my soapbox now.)

If you plan your studio setup, equipment setup, track assignments, and perform additional engineering duties before the recording session, you'll be prepared for a smooth experience with Pro Tools. And your producer (or the producer in you) will be very pleased . . . it never hurts to impress the boss! ▐▐

PRO TOOLS HANDS-ON

Experiment with Mic Placements and Mic Choices

Probably the best way to learn how to capture great sounds is experiment with different microphones and where they are placed. Experiment with mic placement on several different instruments. Try putting mics close to the sound source, then move them away. Record into Pro Tools and note the differences in sound. Angle the mics differently and point them at different parts of the instrument. Try combinations of mics on a sound source. Use the different polar patterns, pads, and bass rolloff settings on your mics, if they have them. Try putting mics in strange places, away from the sound source, even behind a barrier or inside of a box. The better you know your mics, the more you'll know how to capture good sounds with them, and the better your recordings will sound.

Flip the Phase

Open the "Phaseflip" session in the BookProjects folder. Listen to the Direct Input (DI) bass track and the amped bass track individually (by muting each one) and then listen to them together. Flip the phase on the DI bass track using the DigiRack plug-in to hear the sonic outcome. How is acoustical phase cancellation affecting the combined bass sound? Amazing, isn't it? Zoom in on the waveforms to check out how out of phase they really are.

Check out the next example, which demonstrates vocals and an acoustic guitar recorded simultaneously with one mic for each sound source. Flip the phase on the vocal track to hear a different phase relationship between the two tracks. Would you choose to flip the phase, or re-record this track with different mic placement?

Now try flipping the phase on acoustic guitar mic tracks instead of the vocal mic. What gives you the best sound? As always, let your ears be the judge.

I/O Connections, Equipment Needed List, and Track Sheets

Print out the I/O Connections, Equipment Needed List, and Track Sheet PDFs from the CD. Use these documents when getting ready for a recording session. Organization is one of the most important parts of preproduction. These PDFs can help you stay organized and help you remember the mundane details so you can keep your ears open and be attentive to more important and interesting aspects of production.

In this chapter:

- **Optical and S/PDIF inputs**

- **External effects and dynamics processors**

- **Configuring additional MIDI gear**

- **Setting up software synths, additional plug-ins, and samplers**

- **Control surfaces, external hard drives, and CD burners**

If you're anything like me you look forward to getting gear for your home studio. Whether you buy it new or used — or even if you rent or borrow it from a friend — it's exciting to integrate new tools into your setup.

I've been fortunate to purchase and borrow some cool equipment while writing this book. My studio has grown to include a PreSonus Digimax preamp, Emagic's Unitor8 MkII MIDI interface, Glyph FireWire hard drives, a Glyph FireWire CD-RW, Spectrasonics' Stylus and Atmosphere virtual sound module, plug-ins from Waves, Antares, IK Multimedia, GRM Tools, and Serato Naked Drums drum samples from MultiLoops, PACE Anti-Piracy's iLok USB key, CM Lab's Motor Mix, and Digidesign/Focusrite's Control|24. This new stuff, when added to my existing gear, turns my setup into a pretty powerful home studio! (Additional information about these products and their manufacturers is included in appendix D.) Let's take a look at how the types of gear above can be connected.

ADDITIONAL INPUTS

Optical (lightpipe): If you want to use your 002/001 to do any recording that involves numerous microphones — more than four (for Digi 002) or two (for Digi 001) — you'll need additional mic preamps. And though your mixer probably has additional preamps to use, you'd still be limited to eight total analog inputs on Digi 002/001. However, there are several other ways to get more inputs into Pro Tools: The first is through the optical (lightpipe) connection. Originally designed to help link Alesis ADATs to other equipment, the optical connection on the Digi 002 and 001 PCI card also allows dedicated mic preamps with lightpipe outputs (like the PreSonus Digimax) that provide up to eight additional inputs. Connecting an ADAT or mic pre with lightpipe outputs can double the number of inputs you get in Pro Tools at one time.

The connection couldn't be easier. Simply plug the lightpipe output of your device (optical out) to the optical input of the Digi 002/001 using the special optical cable that came with your Digi 002/001.

Note: Your Digi 002/001 came with covers over these optical ports. You need to remove the cover on a port in order to insert the lightpipe cable. Also, you'll notice the optical out port has a red light coming from it (that's the output signal), while the optical in does not. This helps you tell which port is which: output = red light, input = no light.

Once you've connected the lightpipe, you need to make Pro Tools aware of the device and make sure everything's in sync. When we talk about sync it can mean many things. In this case it means that Pro Tools and your optical device are always sampling at the exact same time. So you need to make sure the sample rate of your Pro Tools session (e.g., 44.1kHz) is the same as the sample rate of your optical device.

The optical device must be the sync master, which allows Pro Tools to adjust and exactly match the sample rate and start time. If you don't set it up this way you'll hear little clicks and pops every few seconds, indicating that Pro Tools isn't in sync. The crackles are obvious and annoying, and will be recorded on your tracks if you don't make things right.

Fig. 8.1.
Digi 001's optical (lightpipe) connections are on the PCI card, not the main rack unit.

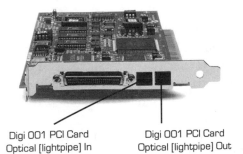

Digi 001 PCI Card
Optical [lightpipe] In

Digi 001 PCI Card
Optical [lightpipe] Out

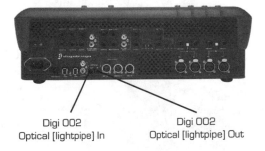

Digi 002
Optical [lightpipe] In

Digi 002
Optical [lightpipe] Out

To switch the sync mode, select Show Session Setup from the Windows menu and choose Optical from the Clock Source list (figure 8.2). The inputs from your optical device will appear in the track input/output area of your Pro Tools session. Then you can choose whichever optical track you want as an input, the same as you would choose from Digi 002/001's analog inputs (figure 8.3). You now have access to eight more inputs!

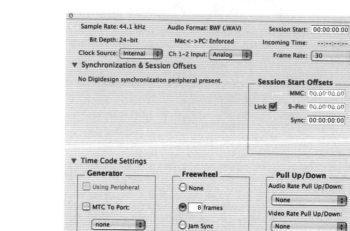

■ Fig. 8.2.
The Show Session Setup window allows you to set important parameters for making sure Pro Tools "plays nice" with the other gear in your studio.

■ Fig. 8.3.
Renaming your inputs in the I/O setup helps to clarify your signal path.

S/PDIF: Another way to get audio signals into any piece of Digidesign home studio hardware is through the coaxial S/PDIF connection (coaxial, or "co-ax," is just another name for what you'd normally think of as an RCA connection). An S/PDIF cable carries two channels of digital audio (usually a stereo pair), but you may need two cables: one to bring the digital audio in and one to send it out of your Digi hardware. However, unless you're recording through the S/PDIF input and simultaneously listening to the S/PDIF output, you'll need only one cable.

As with the optical connections, Pro Tools must be in sync with any devices connected to it via S/PDIF. Select Show Session Setup from the Windows menu and choose S/PDIF from the Clock Source list.

The *Getting Started* guide you got with your Digi hardware also explains the use of the S/PDIF connection and an important Pro Tools LE feature called S/PDIF Mirroring (select Hardware under the Setups menu then click on Other Options). In a nutshell, if S/PDIF Mirroring is enabled, the S/PDIF output carries the same signal as the output of analog channels 1–2. This is useful if you want to simultaneously record the signal to a digital device and monitor it through your main outputs.

DAT recorders often use S/PDIF connections, as do some CD players, digital mixers, and digital effects processors. In my home studio I can connect my Line 6 Guitar and Bass Pod Pros to the S/PDIF input for Pro

To change the labels of your inputs, outputs, inserts, and/or busses, choose I/O Setup from the Setups menu. Rename the inputs, then press Set Default (if using Pro Tools Free) or Export Settings (if using Pro Tools LE).

Tools. For the Bass Pod Pro, the S/PDIF connection allows me to bring in the uneffected direct signal on one track (S/PDIF left) and the amp model signal on another track (S/PDIF right) using only one cable. For the guitar Pod Pro, the S/PDIF connection allows me to bring in a stereo guitar track using only one cable. This produces a pure 24-bit digital input. The S/PDIF connection opens up my home studio to allow a total of 18 inputs at once (in combination with Digi 002/001's eight analog inputs and the PreSonus Digimax's eight lightpipe inputs).

S/PDIF IN [white]
S/PDIF OUT [red]

■ Fig. 8.4.
The S/PDIF input and output are found on the back of the Digi 001 rack unit, as well as on the 002, Mbox, and Audiomedia III card. Each connection carries a stereo signal.

USING ALL 18 INPUTS AT ONCE ON DIGI 002/001

To use all 18 inputs of your Digi 002/001 at once, you need the digital audio from all inputs to be recorded at the same sample rate and synced to the same sample start time. First be sure all of your input devices are set to the same sample rate as your Pro Tools session (e.g., 44.1kHz). Then, to sync all of the input devices to the same sample start time, you need them all working from the same word clock. **Word clock** provides the timing to sync all of the devices together.

Figure 8.2 shows how to sync Pro Tools to either an optical or S/PDIF input. To use all three at once, however, you need to connect your optical and S/PDIF devices together using a word clock (BNC) cable. This word clock cable is a coaxial cable (similar to but not the same as a VCR cable), and it has BNC connectors on each end.

In my home studio I connect the word clock out from my Digimax to the external digital clock in on my Line 6 Guitar or Bass Pod Pro. I then select Optical sync mode from the Session Setup window in Pro Tools. The word clock is sent from the Digimax to both Pro Tools and the Line 6 S/PDIF device. This allows me to record using the eight inputs of Digi 002/001, the eight optical inputs from the Digimax, and the two S/PDIF inputs from my Line 6 device — all 18 at once!

The lightpipe port can also function as an optical S/PDIF connection (used by some devices such as MiniDisc players). However, you can only use one S/PDIF port at a time: either the co-ax connection or the optical connection. To use the optical connection as a S/PDIF port, choose S/PDIF as the optical format in the Playback Engine window (Setups menu).

A standard BNC connector/ word clock cable.

S/PDIF stands for Sony/ Philips Digital Interface Format, and is usually pronounced "es pee dif," though some people say "spi-dif." Despite what some high-end cable manufacturers would have you believe, it's usually fine to use standard RCA cables (as you'd use with your home stereo) for S/PDIF connections.

CONFIGURING ADDITIONAL MIDI GEAR

Once your studio grows to include several MIDI devices you'll probably have to get a MIDI interface/patchbay. These devices route MIDI signals to and from your MIDI devices and Pro Tools. Regardless of the manufacturer, they all work basically the same way.

Essentially, all you need to do is install and configure any software that came with your interface, plug in the device, and then configure your Mac or PC to be aware of the presence of each piece of MIDI gear attached to it. This enables Pro Tools to route the MIDI data to the right places. Mac users should open Audio MIDI setup, click on MIDI devices, and configure their MIDI connections there. Windows users should do the same except in the Sounds and Audio Devices Control Panel.

After getting MIDI configured correctly on your computer, it's a good idea to set up a new Pro Tools session template that utilizes your MIDI gear so it's easy to sit down and quickly record any musical ideas that come to you.

Fig. 8.5.
In Mac OS X, set up your MIDI interface using the Audio MIDI Setup window.

Your MIDI interface may have additional features that allow synchronization using time code (e.g., SMPTE, VITC, LTC, etc.). See the PDF document entitled "Does Pro Tools LE Support Time Code?" included on the CD-ROM if you're interested in syncing Pro Tools LE with an analog tape machine, video deck, or QuickTime movie. It should answer all of your questions on how to perform these activities using your Digi gear with Pro Tools LE.

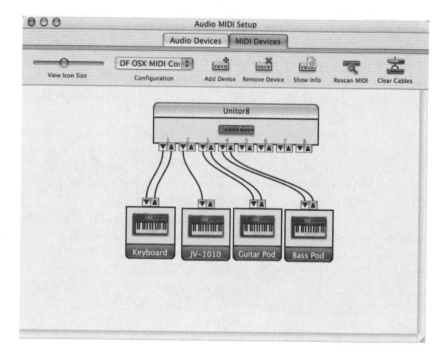

EXTERNAL EFFECTS AND DYNAMICS PROCESSORS

If you have any external (outboard) processors you can connect them to your Digidesign hardware to use as an insert or send. For example, you might like to run your bass track through a tube compressor or a guitar track through a stereo delay connected as shown in figure 8.6.

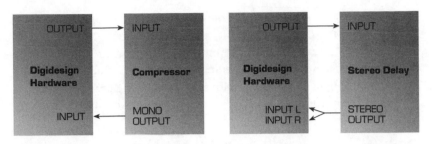

Fig. 8.6.
Connecting external effects
and dynamics processors to
Pro Tools allows you
to keep your favorite hardware
processing "in the loop."

Be sure to check whether the inputs and outputs of the processor are mono or stereo. If your processor has stereo outputs and you'd like to take advantage of that, you'll need to use two inputs on your Digi hardware.

Connecting a digital processor is very similar, but there are two additional things to consider: sync mode and S/PDIF Mirroring. In most cases here you'll want Pro Tools to be the sync master (because the signal feeding the processor will be coming from Pro Tools), so choose Internal as the sync mode in the Session Setup window (see figure 8.2). You should also make sure S/PDIF Mirroring is turned off. This procedure is the same for all Digi home studio systems. Note: There is some delay incurred when routing signals out and then back into your Digi gear. If using outboard gear while mixing, be sure to keep your tracks in phase with each other. Nudge audio files as needed to account for this delay. See chapters 4 and 12 for more information on nudging and keeping tracks in phase with each other.

ADDITIONAL PLUG-INS

Besides outboard gear and the DigiRack plug-ins that came as part of your Pro Tools software CD, many additional RTAS and AudioSuite plug-ins are available from Digidesign and other manufacturers. More and more plug-in manufacturers are becoming Digidesign development partners (check Digi's Web site for the latest info on plug-in development). Visit the plug-in manufacturers' Web sites to download demo versions of their plug-ins.

Plug-ins are as easy to install as any other piece of software, though be aware that most software companies use a "challenge/response" procedure for authorizing plug-ins. This means that once you install the software you'll have to contact the manufacturer to give them your authorization challenge. (An authorization challenge is usually a string of short words, such as BLAB MOTH JUST PICK SLOT CAN REST, that you'll be given the next time you start up Pro Tools.) Your plug-in software should work for a short amount of time (typically 10–14 days) during the authorization process. After receiving your challenge the manufacturer will send an authorization response (a different string of short words) that allows you to continue to use the software. In most cases the fastest way to get your software authorized is by using e-mail to send the challenge and receive the response. If you don't use e-mail, you can often fax or mail the info to the manufacturer.

Many plug-in developers are now supporting PACE Anti-Piracy's iLok key for storing software authorizations. The iLok is a USB device that can hold up to 120 authorizations, making it safe and easy to move authorizations from one computer to another. Read more about this product in appendix D.

CONNECTING SOFTWARE SYNTHS AND VIRTUAL SOUND MODULES TO PRO TOOLS

▶ Via RTAS

Similar to using plug-ins, one way to use software synths (or virtual sound modules) in Pro Tools is to simply instantiate them as RTAS plug-ins on a track. A cool example of this type of instrument is Stylus by Spectrasonics. (For more information on Spectrasonics, look in appendix D).

Fig. 8.7.
You can use your mouse to control Stylus, but a MIDI controller enables inspiring real-time performances.

Fig. 8.8.
With this setup, you can simultaneously record MIDI and audio signals from an RTAS instrument.

To use Stylus or any other RTAS instrument, create a stereo audio track (or aux track) and instantiate the RTAS plug-in on that track. Then create a MIDI track and choose the RTAS instrument name as that track's output. Finally route the signal from the track with the RTAS plug-in on it through a stereo bus to a record-enabled audio track, as in figure 8.8.

▶ Via DirectConnect

You can also stream the output of your favorite software synthesizer or sampler directly into Pro Tools with DirectConnect. DirectConnect provides a 24-bit digital path from compatible standalone audio applications into the Pro Tools mixing environment. Up to 32 separate audio channel outputs can be independently routed, recorded, mixed, and processed, just like any other audio signal. DirectConnect is a DigiRack plug-in bundled free with most Pro Tools systems.

SOFTWARE SAMPLERS

Samplers are great for adding realistic sounds or cool loops to your productions. Using a MIDI controller you can trigger and record the sampler directly into Pro Tools (just like your other MIDI sound modules). You can also edit, trim, loop, and add effects to the samples either through the sampler or, in many cases, in Pro Tools itself.

Software samplers like Native Instrument's "Kontakt" are very convenient to use with Pro Tools. Because they are entirely software based, there are no cables to attach . . . you can simply integrate them into a Pro Tools session using Direct Connect. This enables up to 32 separate audio channel outputs from the sampler to be independently routed, recorded, processed, and mixed within the Pro Tools environment. And, because these samplers support many types of files, you can use samples created for a wide variety of sample libraries or even samples that you've recorded yourself in Pro Tools.

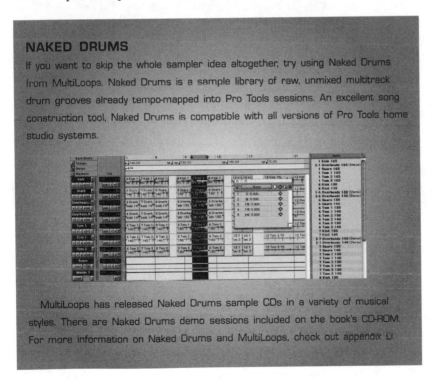

NAKED DRUMS

If you want to skip the whole sampler idea altogether, try using Naked Drums from MultiLoops. Naked Drums is a sample library of raw, unmixed multitrack drum grooves already tempo-mapped into Pro Tools sessions. An excellent song construction tool, Naked Drums is compatible with all versions of Pro Tools home studio systems.

MultiLoops has released Naked Drums sample CDs in a variety of musical styles. There are Naked Drums demo sessions included on the book's CD-ROM. For more information on Naked Drums and MultiLoops, check out appendix D.

CONTROL SURFACES — MOTOR MIX AND CONTROL|24

Control surfaces add instant control to Pro Tools functions. If 001/Mbox/ AMIII users prefer to adjust onscreen faders, knobs, transport controls, scrubs, etc. with their hands instead of a mouse, a control surface can act as a hands-on mixer. Pro Tools LE supports the following products:

- Digidesign/Focusrite Control|24

- CM Lab's Motor Mix

- Peavey PC 1600

- JL Cooper MCS-Panner and CS-10 series

- Mackie Design's HUI control surface

- Penny and Giles MM16 and DC16

All of the devices (except the Control|24) use MIDI to communicate with Pro Tools. Getting these devices set up and ready to use is fairly easy. The two essential steps are:

1. Connect and configure your MIDI interface and computer so that they recognize the device.

2. Configure Pro Tools to recognize and interact with the control surface. Detailed explanations of the setup procedures for the MIDI control surfaces supported by Pro Tools can be found in the *MIDI Control Surfaces Guide* pdf document that came with your Pro Tools software. Note: You can download the latest version of this document from the Technical Document Library on Digidesign's Web site. You can find the instructions for connecting the Control|24 to Pro Tools LE on the Digi site as well.

Fig. 8.9.
CM Lab's Motor Mix offers real-time, hands-on control for Pro Tools software.

THE CONTROL|24: HOW COOL IS THIS?

Pro Tools LE now supports the Control|24, an ergonomic control surface and analog front end for Pro Tools systems. Designed to enhance the speed of working with Pro Tools, Control|24 transforms even the most complex sequence of functions into a series of intuitive movements.

With 24 touch-sensitive motorized faders, illuminated switching for dozens of functions — including Mute, Solo, Record Arm, Channel Selects, and Automation Mode, as well as dedicated EQ and Dynamics switches on every channel — Control|24 offers hands-on access to nearly every recording, routing, mixing, and editing function in Pro Tools.

EXTERNAL HARD DRIVES AND CD BURNERS

These days the most common ways to connect external hard drives and CD burners to your system are SCSI, USB, and FireWire. USB and FireWire are plug-and-play connections, that is, in many cases all you need to do is install some software specific to the device (usually included) or download a driver from the manufacturer of your computer. Then you simply plug in the device to a USB or FireWire port and it's ready to go without any hardware installation. To burn CDs, USB and FireWire CD burners also need the right software drivers to interact with different CD burning software (e.g., Toast FireWire support). These software drivers usually come with the burner or can be downloaded from the Web.

USB hard drives are slower than FireWire hard drives and should only be used as backup devices, not as drives for recording to or mixing from. FireWire drives should have the Oxford 911 FireWire bridge chipset or something comparable to enable audio recording and playback capabilities.

With SCSI, there are additional procedures you might need to perform to connect your device:

- To use an Ultra Wide SCSI hard drive you'll need to install an Ultra Wide SCSI card (or "SCSI accelerator" card) in your computer. SCSI CD burners are often connected to the regular SCSI ports (not Ultra Wide) on your computer.

- SCSI devices can be used in a daisy chain setup. That is, up to 16 SCSI devices can be connected to each other in a row (depending on the type of SCSI connection). You should connect a SCSI terminator to the last SCSI device in your chain, and none of the other devices should have a terminator. If you only have one SCSI device, connect the terminator to that device. (Just to clarify: USB and FireWire devices can easily be used in daisy chain fashion, but I mention SCSI chains here because they're much more finicky.)

- Finally, you need to choose a unique identification number (0–15) for each SCSI device in your system. You choose this number by dialing it in on the SCSI ID switch. Be sure none of your SCSI devices share the same ID or your computer won't be able to communicate with them accurately. Also, you must turn off the power to both your computer and the SCSI device when switching the SCSI ID number. Only after restarting your computer will the device be recognized. (USB and FireWire devices can be connected and disconnected with everything turned on. This is why they're called "hot-swappable.")

Digidesign offers their own line of SCSI and FireWire hard drives called DigiDrives. Check out their Web site for more information on these high performance drives.

This chapter covers many types of gear you might add to your Pro Tools home studio. If you experience any problems when connecting things, don't hesitate to contact the specific equipment manufacturers and Digidesign for up-to-date information. And most important, try not to get frustrated if things don't work like they should right away. Believe me, *everybody* — from rank beginners to top pros — runs into stumbling blocks when trying to set up and operate their studios. ▌▌

PRO TOOLS HANDS-ON

Create New Session Templates

As you add more gear to your studio, it's a good idea to create session templates that reflect your current setup. In the templates, include tracks for your new MIDI devices (including samplers, software synths, and virtual sound modules) as well as labeled routing for any outboard gear that you've connected as an insert. Creating session templates will save you tons of time that you'll appreciate particularly when you've got a brilliant but fleeting musical idea that you need to record immediately.

Design Your Own Sound

Sound design is an important part of the creative process when writing music, whether it's for your band, a movie/TV score, a multimedia presentation, a video game, or anything else. Coming up with your own sounds can differentiate your music from everyone else's. With Pro Tools, there are no limits to the sounds you can make from sampling wacky audio to tweaking MIDI patches to using plug-ins for mangling "normal" sounds.

One plug-in manufacturer that has a particular fondness for sound "manglement" is GRM Tools. Open the session "Soundesign" to hear some mangled sounds that I created with their plug-ins. Listen to the original tracks first, then to the twisted versions. See if you can spot the mangled sounds in the later stages of the production process. For these examples, I used the Freqwarp and Contrast plug-ins from GRM Tools.

To get more involved, go to the GRM Tools Web site (**www.grmtools.org**) and download demo versions of their plug-ins. Then, open the "Soundesign" session again and check out how I used the parameters on their plug-ins to create the mangled sounds.

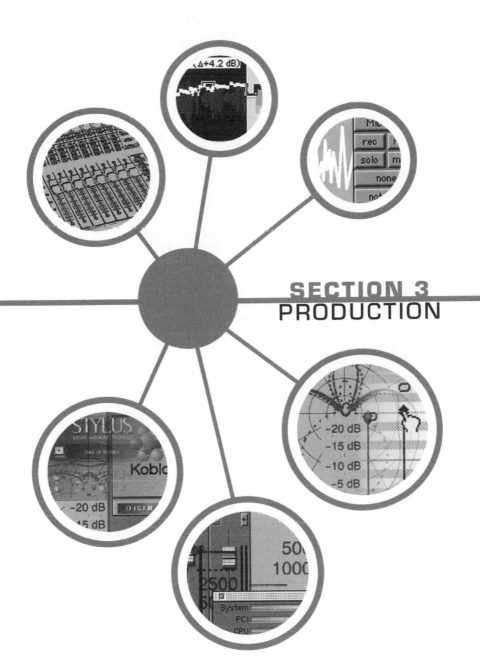

SECTION 3
PRODUCTION

Improving System Performance and Efficiency

In this chapter:

- **Understanding and improving system performance**

- **Getting the most from your plug-ins**

- **Operating systems, tips for Mac and Windows**

- **Hard drives and saving hard drive space**

- **Six features to improve your efficiency**

Before jumping into the nuts and bolts of producing and engineering a recording session, you should understand several key concepts and techniques about your equipment and Pro Tools. The better you know your studio equipment and Pro Tools software, the more efficiently you can record and mix your music. This chapter shows you how to get the most out of your Pro Tools–driven computer and how to use several features that can improve your effectiveness in the studio.

UNDERSTANDING SYSTEM PERFORMANCE

Once you start creating Pro Tools sessions with high track counts and plug-ins, you may reach the limits of your computer's power. However, there are many techniques to handle large sessions.

Before we dive in you should understand the meaning of several terms that have to do with the performance of your computer.

CPU power: Your computer's central processing unit (CPU) determines how many tracks can be played or recorded at once, how many plug-ins can be instantiated (turned on) at one time, and how much edit and automation data can be handled. As a matter of fact, it's the main determinant of your entire system's performance. The processing power when using Pro Tools not only depends on the speed of your computer (e.g., 500 MHz), but also the CPU usage limit (e.g., 75%) and the hardware buffer size (e.g., 256 samples) assigned to Pro Tools.

CPU usage limit: The CPU usage limit is the amount of your computer's total processing power assigned to Pro Tools. For example, if you assign 75% of your computer's power to Pro Tools, 25% is left for other applications (including your operating system). You can assign up to 85% to Pro Tools for single-processor computers. Beyond that would seriously slow down your user interface or even prevent your operating system from running. On multiprocessor computers, you can choose 99% CPU usage limit, which dedicates one entire processor to Pro Tools.

Hardware buffer size: The hardware buffer size is the amount of audio data (in samples) that the CPU grabs and processes at one time before it spits it back out for monitoring or recording. Large buffer sizes give your computer more time to process audio data, but also increase the amount of latency and cause slower user-interface responsiveness. Small buffer sizes decrease latency, but don't allow the use of as many plug-ins. Small hardware buffer sizes are more useful for recording sessions (less latency, less plug-ins) and large buffer sizes are more useful for mixing sessions (more latency, but more plug-ins).

DAE playback buffer: This is based on the amount of RAM used to buffer your computer's hard drive. The RAM temporarily stores audio data coming from and to the drive. The buffer refers to the time between when the input signal is received at the PCI card (or USB/Firewire port) and when the hard drive records it. The higher the buffer setting, the longer the time between when the signal is received and recorded. Consider a portable CD player. If you bump the player and the CD skips, you may not hear the skip because a few seconds of the music is held in the CD player's RAM buffer. Fragmented (and FireWire) hard drives benefit most from higher DAE playback buffer settings.

Pro Tools RAM: Like any other program, allocating more RAM to the Pro Tools application increases the efficiency of the application. Windows does this automatically but you must manually change the RAM allocation on a Macintosh. One direct benefit of increasing the RAM allocation to Pro Tools is that it will cache more waveform overviews. That is, the additional RAM helps the computer display the most current waveform overviews with all of the proper edits, automation, etc.

THE TRADE-OFFS OF HOST-BASED SYSTEMS

There are processing power trade-offs in host-based systems such as Pro Tools LE and Pro Tools Free. That is, there are finite processing resources available at any given moment, and these can be allocated for different tasks at different times. Basically if the computer needs more of one thing, it will take resources from another. For example, a computer might play back 32 tracks at once with no problem, but only allow a few plug-ins. In contrast, if you delete some of the tracks, you might be able to add more plug-ins. Being aware of the trade-offs will help you understand how to allocate your computer's resources to achieve the best performance for each situation.

IMPROVING SYSTEM PERFORMANCE

CPU usage limit: Within a Pro Tools session there are several actions you can take to improve your computer's performance. One of the first things to do is increase the CPU Usage Limit percentage. To do this choose Hardware from the Setups menu. Click on the CPU Usage Limit percentage and a list of values will appear. If you want the most CPU power, choose 85% as shown in figure 9.1.

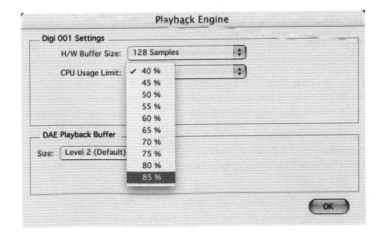

Fig. 9.1.
The CPU Usage limit box decides how much of your computer's processing power is allocated to Pro Tools. Choosing 99% on multiprocessor computers dedicates an entire processor to Pro Tools.

Fig. 9.2.
Fig. 9.2.
Show System Usage from the
Windows menu allows you to
see how hard your computer is
working to run Pro Tools.

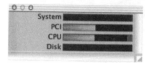

Whenever you want to view your system performance simply select Show System Usage under the Windows menu (figure 9.2) If you get an error message saying that you're running out of CPU power, watch the CPU load at the time when the track stops playing/recording and gives you the error. At that spot, reduce the edit or automation density. Techniques for doing this are discussed later in the chapter.

Hardware buffer size: The Hardware Buffer Size setting determines the amount of monitoring latency you experience when playing back or recording tracks. When recording you'll usually want a lower setting (128 or 256 samples) to keep latency to a minimum. However, during a mix session you may want to increase the buffer to 512 or 1024 samples when latency isn't a factor and you want to max out the track count and use more plug-ins. I've found that 256 samples is a good all-purpose setting, but I definitely switch between buffer sizes depending on the circumstances. See chapter 3 for more information on hardware buffer size settings and latency amounts.

Fig. 9.3.
Setting the Hardware Buffer
Size. Lower numbers are good
for recording; higher numbers
are best for mixing.

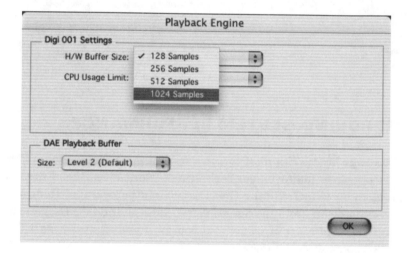

DAE playback buffer: As explained earlier, the DAE playback buffer size determines the amount of memory allocated within DAE to manage disk buffers. A smaller buffer size might improve the speed of playback/record initiation if you're experiencing lag time when you press Record or Play, but it might also make it more difficult for slow hard drives to play or record tracks reliably. A larger buffer size might improve the performance of a session with a great number of edits, however, large buffer sizes tend to increase the time lag before playback or record initiates. Digidesign recommends a value of 2 and this seems to work fine for me in most cases. To change the DAE Playback Buffer setting, choose Playback Engine from the Setups window.

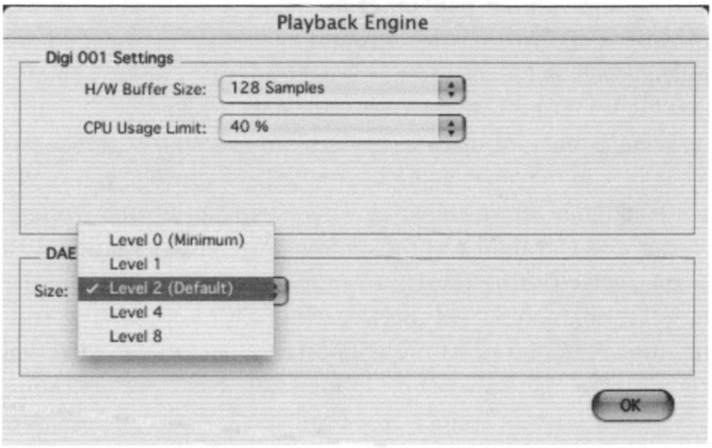

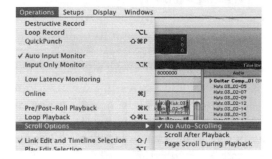

Fig. 9.4.
The DAE Playback Buffer setting can affect the responsiveness of the Pro Tools user interface.

Page scroll during playback: Disabling page scrolling saves processing power that would have been allocated for redrawing the computer screen to show your track displays advancing in real time. Each screen redraw takes up power that could be used for something else, like higher track counts and more plug-ins. To turn off page scrolling, select either No Auto-Scrolling (as the least processing-intensive option) or Scroll After Playback under Scroll Options from the Operations menu (figure 9.5).

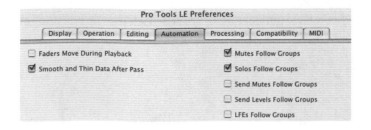

Fig. 9.5.
Selecting No Auto-Scrolling might allow you to squeeze more tracks or plug-ins into your session.

Faders moving during playback: Turning off moving faders can improve your system's performance, especially if you have a lot of automation written — as above, the screen redraws for the faders eat up power. (Don't worry, the automation still plays even if you've told the faders not to move.) Choose Preferences from the Setups menu. Click on the Automation tab and the dialog box shown in figure 9.6 will appear. Uncheck the "Faders Move During Playback" button.

Fig. 9.6.
Turning off moving faders may give you less to look at, but it's a small price to pay for more processing "oomph."

Smoothing and thinning automation data: All automation takes up processing power. Pro Tools records automation moves from continuous controllers (such as faders and pan pots) as a series of very small steps, often creating staircase patterns with many data breakpoints. Thinning this data to remove some of the breakpoints can make processing easier for your computer. In the same dialog box shown in figure 9.6, you can choose to smooth and thin your automation data automatically after writing it.

You can also highlight certain sections of your automation data and thin them yourself using the Thin Automation command from the Edit menu – this command uses the Degree of Thinning setting from the Automation Preferences window. Figure 9.7 shows the difference in breakpoints before and after some automation data has been thinned.

■ **Fig. 9.7.**
(a) Before thinning automation data. (b) Degree of Thinning set to Some. (c) Degree of Thinning set to Most.

(a)   (b)   (c)

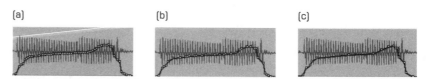

Be careful, though. When using high amounts of thinning the resulting automation may differ noticeably from the original, creating uneven or choppy level and pan adjustments. Listen to the tracks after thinning them . . . you can undo any thinning you don't like, or thin certain areas of a track more than others. Also note that thinning applies only to audio tracks – it does not affect MIDI tracks.

Consolidating regions: Similar to thinning automation data, reducing the number of edits on an audio track can save processing power as well. To turn multiple edited regions into a single region, simply select the regions you want to consolidate with the Grabber or Selector tool (or triple-click somewhere in the track to select all regions in that track) and choose Consolidate Selection from the Edit menu. This will create a new audio file that contains all of the selected range, including any blank space. For more information on this, see chapter 11.

Turning off sends view meters and moving faders: Just as turning off moving faders during playback conserves CPU power, turning off the sends view meters reduces CPU load as well. Figure 9.8 shows a sends view with meters, a sends view with no meters, and send assignments only. By displaying only the assignments, you can save even more CPU power if you have automation on your send faders or pan control.

■ **Fig. 9.8.**
(a) Sends view with meters.
(b) Sends view without meters.
(c) Sends view, assignments only.

(a)   (b)   (c)

To remove the faders from your sends view, choose Preferences from the Setups menu. Click on the Display tab and uncheck Show Meters in Sends View. To show only send assignments, select Sends View Shows from the Display menu and choose Assignments.

Making items inactive: In Pro Tools LE you can make sends, side-chain inputs, plug-ins, hardware inserts, paths, and track inputs and outputs inactive. Inactive items are silent and consume no system resources, but their settings are still saved with the session. When items are inactive their names appear in italics, and their background becomes dark grey. Figure 9.9 shows a channel strip with an inactive plug-in, send, input, and output.

Be aware of the difference in function and appearance of plug-ins that are inactive and plug-ins that are hypassed (figure 9.10). Bypassed plug-ins still consume system resources but inactive plug-ins do not. When you click on an inactive plug-in, the window shown in figure 9.10 will appear.

To make an item inactive, ⌘ + Control + click (Mac) or Control + Start + click (Win) the item. To make an entire track inactive, select the track and choose "Make Selected Tracks Inactive" from the File menu, or ⌘ + Control + click (Mac) or Control + Start + click (Win) the Track Type indicator in the Mix window.

Fig. 9.9.
A channel strip with an inactive plug-in, send, input, and output.

(a)  (b)

Fig. 9.10.
(a) Bypassed plug-in. (b) Inactive plug-in window.

Reducing the levels of undo: Pro Tools keeps track of undoable editing operations (e.g., cutting, pasting, etc.) in a queue that's temporarily stored in your computer's RAM. This queue can be memory-intensive, so reducing the levels of undo will help free up RAM for other needs. The maximum number of levels is 16; this is also the default value. To change this choose Preferences from the Setup menu and click Editing. Click in the Levels of Undo field, enter a value from 1–16, and click Done.

Certain Pro Tools operations are not undoable, such as saving. Also, several operations clear the Undo queue, including deleting a track, or clearing a region from the Audio or MIDI Regions List.

Fig. 9.11.
Reducing the number of available undos can free up more RAM . . . and I've found that I've never needed to go back further than eight steps to undo a mistake.

Deleting unused or unwanted tracks: All tracks use up some processing power, whether they have data in them or not. I've found that deleting unused and/or unwanted tracks can drastically improve my computer's performance. To delete a track first select it, then choose Delete Selected Tracks from the File menu.

EFFICIENT USE OF PLUG-INS

The number of plug-ins that can be used in a session is largely determined by your CPU speed. Plug-in count varies from computer to computer, but in general the faster the processor, the more RTAS plug-ins, real-time automation, and track edits you'll be able to apply. Because Pro Tools LE and Free are host-based processing systems, the software is reliant on the CPU for all necessary calculations – it doesn't receive any additional support from external hardware (as in Pro Tools|HD and Mix systems). When you've finally exceeded the limits of your CPU, an error message will appear stating, "You're running out of CPU power. Take out some plug-ins to free up CPU power (-9128)." Don't ask me what "-9128" has to do with anything, but the end result is you'll have to un-instantiate (deselect and turn off) one or more of the plug-ins to achieve playback.

To squeeze the highest RTAS plug-in count out of your system you must manage your CPU resources wisely. Besides the ones mentioned in the previous section, here are a few more recommendations for optimizing your CPU usage.

Using AudioSuite instead of RTAS plug-ins: RTAS (Real-time AudioSuite) plug-ins rely on CPU power for real-time processing (i.e., to be able to hear and change effects while the track is playing), whereas AudioSuite plug-ins apply processing to a track while the track isn't playing.

Fortunately, most RTAS plug-ins have AudioSuite counterparts. Once you've found the plug-in settings you like for a track using the RTAS version, save the settings and take that RTAS plug-in off the insert of the track. In the Edit window select the track (using the Selector or Grabber tool) and choose the same plug-in from the AudioSuite menu, then choose your saved setting.

Select Preview if you'd like to double-check the settings, then hit Process to apply the plug-in. Processing with an AudioSuite plug-in creates an entirely new audio file – the original isn't erased – so you can always go back if you decide later that you don't like the newer version. Figure 9.12 shows the selection of an EQ setting called "Gilday's Bass comp" on a DigiRack Compressor II AudioSuite plug-in.

Using AudioSuite instead of RTAS can really free up a good amount of processing power to use for other plug-ins. For example, a common practice of mine is finding EQ and compression settings that I like

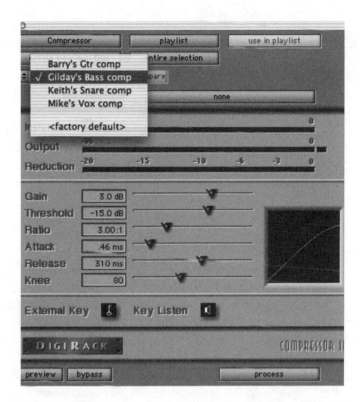

Fig. 9.12.
Applying an AudioSuite plug-in instead of an RTAS plug-in can free up system resources.

using RTAS plug-ins. Then once I've got a basic mix going I'll save those settings, take the RTAS plug-ins out one by one, and process the individual tracks using the AudioSuite version.

Also, be mindful of the order in which you process your tracks; that is, if you're going to use multiple AudioSuite plug-ins make sure you process them in the order you've been listening to them using the RTAS versions. Process insert 1 (top of inserts list) first, followed by the remaining plug-ins in descending order. If you don't follow the RTAS order your track will invariably sound different. For example, processing a track with EQ then compression will sound different than processing the track with compression first. Figure 9.13 shows the inserts list of a track with a compressor plug-in followed by an EQ plug-in. The order of inserts on tracks will be discussed further in chapter 12.

Fig. 9.13.
Be aware of the order of your inserts, especially when trying to recreate an RTAS effects chain using AudioSuite plug-ins.

In fact, I recommend making a new playlist for each processed file. Using the example in figure 9.13, I would create a new playlist (titled something like "Track compress") for the AudioSuite compressed file, then a new playlist for the compressed and EQ'd file. That way, I can always compare the sounds of each processed track with the original and change them at any step along the way if needed.

Using sends, busses, and auxiliary tracks: What if you want the same reverb plug-in on four different instrument tracks? Instead of instantiating the same plug-in on each track and using gobs of CPU power, assign the tracks to the same bus using sends and create one

■ **Fig. 9.14.**
A classic effects send/return
setup in Pro Tools.

auxiliary track with the reverb plug-in. You can then adjust the amount of each track sent to the reverb aux track using the track's send level fader. You can also adjust the send panning and mutes, and all of these can be automated. (Refer back to the explanation and example given in chapter 3 about sends, busses, and aux tracks. Also check out the CD-ROM session entitled "Basic Effects Send.")

Let me explain further: You can send a copy of each track's signal on up to five sends (labeled "a–e"). You assign each send to route its signal on a bus (a signal path in Pro Tools), which takes the signal to another track (usually an aux track). In order to receive the signal, the aux track must have the bus as its input.

For example, figure 9.14 shows the "Vox" track being sent (send "a") on stereo bus 1–2 to the Reverb Aux (an auxiliary track). The Reverb Aux track has bus 1–2 as its input and the main stereo out as its output. Because both of these tracks are assigned to the same main stereo output, you'll hear both tracks at once. You control how much of Vox's signal goes to the Reverb Aux by using the send level fader on Vox send "a." Notice the plug-in on the Reverb Aux track: You control the amount of signal from bus 1-2 that goes to those plug-ins using the Reverb Aux's fader.

If you don't want the volume fader on Vox to affect the send level, choose Pre (the little "p" in the Send display). That way you can move Vox's fader (or even mute the track) and the track will still be sent on the bus to the aux track to be effected. If you choose to send the signal post-fader (not selecting the "p" as shown in figure 9.14), the volume fader on Vox will also affect the send level — the level that goes to the plug-ins. For even more information on using sends and busses, consult chapter 12.

Using less CPU-intensive plug-ins: Another solution to improving your system's performance is to use less CPU-intensive plug-ins. There's no obvious way to tell which plug-ins are power hogs, but some generalities can be made about the DigiRack plug-ins:

1. Mod delays (slap echo, chorusing, flanging) and reverbs tend to consume a lot of CPU power.

2. Single-band EQs take up little CPU power but multiband EQs use as much as a single-band EQ multiplied by the number of bands.

3. Gates, compressors, limiters, expanders, and dither are not very CPU-intensive.

You can check your CPU load by clicking on Show System Usage from the Windows menu. The display (shown in figure 9.2) indicates the load on your system, PCI card, and CPU. High PCI and CPU usage can cause system errors, while high system loads can cause Pro Tools to miss playback of automation data during particularly dense periods of activity, such as while using the Bounce to Disk command.

OPERATING SYSTEM

There are several actions you can take regarding your operating system to make your computer run more efficiently with Pro Tools. First turn off or remove unnecessary applications running in the background (e.g., calendars, virus protection, file savers, etc.). Also turn off any power management features of your system and remove all screensaver software. All of these can either take CPU resources or get in the way of normal Pro Tools functioning. Additionally, deactivating performance-enhancing extensions or control panels for CD-ROM and other removable media, and disabling networking cards or connections (unless you're using them for the exchange of audio data), can improve the system's performance.

MAKING THE MOST OF HARD DRIVES

Disk speed: Your hard drives should operate at a spin speed of at least 7200 rpm, an average seek speed of less than ten milliseconds, and with a sustained data transfer rate of at least 3MB per second. If your drives can't achieve these specifications you should consider buying new ones — hard drive speed is very important for accurate playback and recording multiple tracks. Firewire drives should have the Oxford 911 Firewire bridge chipset or something comparable. Additionally, if you're using a SCSI hard drive you should use a SCSI accelerator card to increase the speed of the connection (the data transfer rate). Look on Digidesign's Web site for more information about SCSI accelerators and approved SCSI and Firewire drives.

Disk allocation: Another way to maximize your computer's performance is to record tracks to different drives, or record to one drive while playing back from another. The idea behind this is to distribute audio files so that individual hard drives don't have to work as hard. However, **do not** spread audio files across different types of hard drives. For example, if your session has audio on a FireWire drive, you shouldn't also have audio for that session on a SCSI drive or an internal drive. Spreading audio across different types of drives can cause errors.

Note: Digidesign warns against recording to your "system volume." Although it's true you shouldn't record to the same drive your system software is on, you can partition that drive to separate your audio files. I've found that the partition for audio on my internal hard drive works flawlessly. Partitioning is explained in chapter 1, but you should consult your computer manual for directions on how to do this with your particular system.

Saving Hard Drive Space

Removing unused regions and compacting audio files: As you well know, audio files take up a great deal of hard drive space. Once you've finished editing a Pro Tools session and have no further use for the audio (and MIDI) regions that aren't used, you can remove or delete them. Simply removing regions will eliminate them from the session, but the files will still reside on your hard drive. Or you can choose to delete the unused regions completely using the Clear Audio command.

To do this first choose Unused Regions, Unused Regions Except Whole Files, or Offline Regions from the Select submenu in the Audio Regions popup menu (see figure 9.15) – Unused Regions is usually your best option. For MIDI, choose Select Unused from the MIDI Regions popup menu.

Fig. 9.15.
Selecting Unused Regions from the Audio Regions popup menu. Unless you're an audio pack rat this is a great way to reclaim hard drive space after you've completely finished a tune.

Deleting regions or audio files using the Clear Audio or Compact Selected commands cannot be undone!

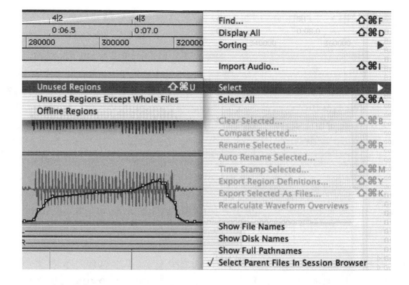

Then choose Clear Selected (also in the Audio or MIDI Regions popup) and the window in figure 9.16 will appear. Choose Remove to take the regions out of the session or Delete to permanently delete them from your hard drive.

Fig. 9.16.
The Clear Audio dialog box.

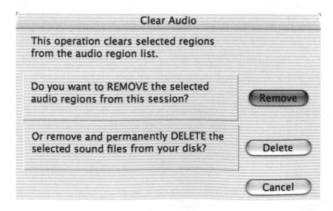

You can also remove unused files by compacting. Choosing Compact Selected from the Audio Regions popup deletes audio if there are no regions in your session that reference the data. However, only use this command when you're completely finished editing and sure that you have no need for the files — compacting permanently deletes audio data! I recommend waiting until a project is totally complete and being reproduced to use this function.

While there's some danger in deleting files, the benefits can be substantial. After compacting some of my sessions I've opened up literally gigabytes of hard drive space.

Undo Record and canceling a take: In Pro Tools LE you can remove files that were just recorded by choosing Undo Audio Record (or Undo MIDI Recording) from the Edit menu — or by pressing ⌘ + Z (Mac) or Control + Z (Win). Instead of keeping all your takes you can make a judgment on whether to keep each one just after recording it. This command removes the audio files from your hard drive and deletes the region from the track's playlist.

You can also discard the current take while recording it — simply press ⌘ + period (Mac) or Control + period (Win) while recording. This command also removes the audio files from your hard drive and deletes the region from the track's playlist.

Creating submixes: To save hard drive space as well as open up some additional tracks in your session, create a submix. A submix can be as simple as combining two tracks into one track or multiple tracks into a stereo track (or two mono tracks). For example, say you want to submix a drum kit from eight tracks to stereo. There are three ways to do this: using sends to record to tracks within your session, recording directly using inputs and outputs, or bouncing to disk and importing the files back into your session. Consult chapter 11 for more information on using sends to submix. Once you've created a submix you're happy with (or even before you do it), you can backup the original files to CD-R, DVD, or some other storage medium and erase the files from your hard drive(s). This can save a lot of space!

Backing up finished projects and erasing them from your hard drive: Once you're done with a project, it's wise to save your files on at least two different storage mediums if possible. Free up space on your main audio drives by backing up to dedicated storage drives, CD-Rs, DVDs, or other storage media. I back up all my projects to at least one, if not two, hard drives and burn the files onto CD-Rs if the sessions aren't huge.

Recording using smaller bit depths and sampling rates: As discussed in chapter 3, bit depths and sampling rates are the determinants of audio file sizes. Recording at 16-bit and 44.1kHz (CD-quality) instead of 24-bit and 48kHz reduces the size of your audio files by 40%. Higher sampling rates consume even more space.

Recording destructively: Another way to save space is to record destructively. That is, you can record over existing regions, permanently replacing the original audio with new files. I don't recommend doing this . . . ever. You can easily lose important files this way, and with hard drives getting cheaper each day you can buy additional space if none of the other options presented above work for you.

Fig. 9.17.

You can save up to five horizontal zoom presets in Pro Tools.

I've included several useful Pro Tools session templates on the CD-ROM. Copy the Session Templates folder from the CD-ROM to your desktop. When starting a new session, simply click on the most appropriate template and begin working from there. The templates are a starting point to get you and Pro Tools set up and recording quickly. If you want, alter the templates or create new ones to fit your needs.

EIGHT FEATURES THAT CAN IMPROVE YOUR EFFICIENCY

Maximizing your system's power is great, but Pro Tools works even better when *you're* operating at peak efficiency. Here are some features that can help you fly....

1. Zoom Presets

You can save five horizontal zoom presets in Pro Tools (1–5 in figure 9.17). These presets make it easy to zoom out and see the big picture of the session or zoom in close for fine editing. To save a zoom preset, navigate to the zoom level you want using any of the Zoom buttons or the Zoomer tool (magnifying glass).

While pressing ⌘ (Mac) or Control (Win), click one of the five Zoom Preset buttons. The button will flash as it's being assigned. To recall a zoom preset you can (a) click on the Zoom Preset button or (b) press Control (Mac) or Start (Win) and type the preset number on the alpha keyboard (not the numeric keypad). Zoom presets can also be stored with memory locations.

2. Half-Speed Recording and Playback

If you have a difficult part to record, half-speed recording can really help you to achieve the performance you want, whether you're recording audio or MIDI. If you record audio at half-speed it will play back an octave higher at normal speed than where you originally recorded it – in other words, you'll have to play one octave lower than where you want the pitch played back. You don't need to worry about this when using MIDI, as MIDI tracks recorded at half-speed will play back at normal speed in the same octave in which they were recorded.

To record at half-speed press ⌘ + Shift + Spacebar (Mac) or Control + Shift + Spacebar (Win). To play at half-speed press Shift + Spacebar. (Half-speed playback is also very useful when learning or transcribing difficult musical passages.)

3. I/O Settings and Session Templates

Creating I/O setting documents as well as session templates for particular project types can save a great deal of time when starting a project. In fact, session templates store I/O settings as well as a host of other information about a setup. Chapters 1 and 3 discuss the procedures for creating and using these items.

4. Managing Region Names Using Auto Naming

Sessions can easily get flooded with audio and MIDI regions. One quick way to stay on top of all the region names during recording and editing is to specify auto naming parameters. To do this select an audio or MIDI region from the Regions list and choose Auto Rename Selected from the Regions list popup menu. A Rename Regions dialog box (figure 9.18) will appear. Enter the root name for the auto created regions (Name), a starting point for the sequential numbering (Number), the number of zeros that occur before the auto numbers (Zeros), and the text to append to the regions' names (Suffix), then click OK.

5. Drawing and Trimming Automation

Drawing automation data using the Pencil tool can save time over using the mouse to move faders and pan pots in real time. Open the automation data you want to edit by selecting it from the Track View selector in the Edit window (figure 9.19 shows that Volume automation is selected). Choose the Pencil tool and alter the volume curve as desired. A pencil-drawn fade out is shown in figure 9.20.

Be careful! Although it's easy to use, this process can become addictive, causing you to spend too much time perfecting automation moves.

Trimming automation data is one of the best and most useful features of Pro Tools. Say you've recorded some automation (e.g., a volume ride on a lead vocal). Then you realize the vocal ride itself is good but the overall vocal level in comparison to the rest of the track *isn't* good during the first half of the song. Using the Trim tool you can bring the overall vocal level up or down while keeping all of the relative level automation. Figure 9.21 shows the vocal track volume automation being increased by 4.2dB to a level of +1.4dB at its highest point.

Notice how the ends of the selected area are placed on automation breakpoints. If you don't select a region with end points, Pro Tools will create *new* end points before and after the selected area. If you want to suppress the creation of these breakpoints press Option (Mac) or Alt (Win) while using the Trimmer.

Fig. 9.18.
Making use of the Rename Regions dialog box can help you keep track of regions during a session without having to manually assign names after each take.

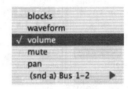

Fig. 9.19.
Choosing Volume automation from the Track View selector.

Fig. 9.20.
You can use the Pencil tool to draw volume automation for the perfect fade-out.

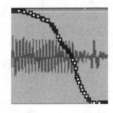

Fig. 9.21.
Trimming volume automation. Use the Trim tool to change the overall level of automation while maintaining the relative ups and downs.

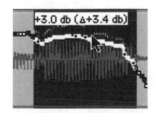

A ride refers to moving a fader to increase or decrease the volume of a track, as in "riding a fader." For instance, in the case of a vocal ride you may want certain words or phrases louder or softer during playback. You can record volume rides as volume automation.

6. Key Commands and Shortcuts

Print out the file titled *Keyboard Shortcuts* that was installed with your Pro Tools software and begin to learn the key commands on it. They are big time savers. The more you work with Pro Tools, the more you'll become aware of the many useful ways you can use your keyboard instead of constantly clicking with the mouse. Ideally you should get to the point where you're using both your mouse and keyboard concurrently.

7. Command Focus Mode

In addition to the regular key commands, Pro Tools LE now supports Command Focus Mode. With this mode activated, you can use yor computer keyboard to access a wide range of single-key shortcuts for playing and editing track material. The Command Focus Mode shortcuts are also listed on the Keyboard Shortcuts document.

■ Fig. 9.22.
To activate the Command Focus Mode, press the a...z button shown here. **a...z**

8. DigiBase and Task Manager

When working on several projects at once while using multiple hard drives, it's hard to keep track of all the files you need for each Pro Tools session. DigiBase is a file management utility (like Mac's Finder and Windows' Explorer) that you can use to view complete file information, including duration, timestamps, waveform thumbnails, and two user comments fields. While using DigiBase, you can audition files before importing them into a session, regardless of their sample rate or file format. Then, you can drag and drop the files into your session and Pro Tools will automatically convert them so they're compatible with the current session.

■ Fig. 9.23.
You can customize the DigiBase windows (Workspace, Volume, and Project Browsers) to display only the information you need to see.

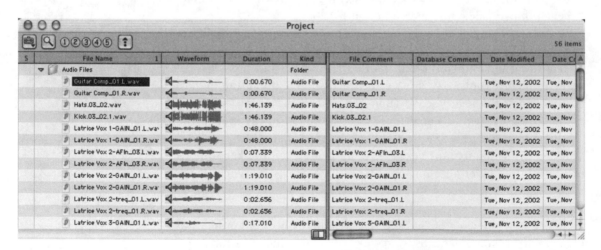

Pro Tools now handles many tasks such as copying, file conversion, and fade creation in the background without interrupting your workflow. Open the Task Manager window to monitor and manage any processes that are taking place in the background.

		Tasks		
				3!
S	File Name	Status	Progress	
↻	▷ Rendering Fade jCh#wGrE6PRk		▨▨▨▨▨ 1 Fades	
	▷ Rendering Fade DFh#wGrE6PRk			
	▷ Rendering Fade Wlh#wGrE6PRk			
	▷ Rendering Fade KJh#wGrE6PRk			
Paused tasks:				4:
	▽ Create Fades		▤▤▤ 75/179 Con	
	▽ Rendering Fades		▤▤▤ 75/179 Fad	
	▷ Rendering Fade ONf#wCr		▨▨▨▨ 1 Fades	
	▷ Rendering Fade PQf#wCr		▨▨▨▨ 1 Fades	
	▷ Rendering Fade IRf#wCrE		▨▨▨▨ 1 Fades	

Fig. 9.24.
With certain processes working in the background, your efficiency while using Pro Tools can increase dramatically.

By understanding the concepts and practicing the techniques presented in this chapter, you'll be on your way to maximizing your system's performance and working more efficiently and effectively with Pro Tools. ▮▮

PRO TOOLS HANDS-ON

Optimize Your Pro Tools System

Tweak your system so that it's running on all cylinders. Use all of the information in this chapter to optimize the performance of your Pro Tools system. Specifically, adjust the CPU Usage Limit, Hardware Buffer Size, and DAE Playback Buffer to best suit your system. Try these actions:

1. Turn off "Page scroll during playback"

2. Turn off "Faders moving during playback"

3. Smooth and thin automation data

4. Consolidate regions

5. Turn off sends view meters and moving faders

6. Make items inactive

7. Reduce the levels of undo

8. Delete unused or unwanted tracks

9. Use AudioSuite plug-ins instead of RTAS plug-ins

10. Use sends, busses, and aux tracks instead of multiple copies of the same plug-in

11. Use less CPU-intensive plug-ins

12. Optimize your computer's operating system for Pro Tools

Practice the file management techniques for saving hard drive space, including:

1. Removing unused regions and compacting audio files

2. Undoing and canceling record takes

3. Creating submixes

4. Backing up finished projects and erasing them from your hard drive

5. Recording using smaller bit depths and sampling rates

Finally, experiment with some of the features that improve your Pro Tools efficiency, like:

1. Zoom presets

2. Half-speed recording and playback

3. I/O settings and session templates

4. Auto-naming of regions

5. Automation drawing and trimming

6. Key commands and shortcuts

7. Command Focus Mode

8. DigiBase and Task Manager

Once your system is optimized, you and your Pro Tools system will be primed for the more advanced stages of production.

The Producer's Role in Production

In this chapter:

- **Types of recording sessions**

- **The ins and outs of producing**

- **Interacting with the artist and the engineer**

- **Vocal production**

Now that you have some tips for getting the best performance from your computer (chapter 9), we need to discuss ways of getting the best performances from yourself or your artist. I'm assuming that by this time you've done any preproduction that's needed for your project and are ready to record the songs. But before you start recording there are several steps that ensure a smooth session.

RIGHT BEFORE THE RECORDING SESSION

Preparation is a key element of any successful recording session, even if you're recording only yourself. First you should make sure you have all the equipment you need. You and the engineer (probably one and the same) should have already filled out the "Equipment Needed List" on the CD-ROM. Double-check that you have the right number of mic stands, mic cables, pop filters, instrument cables, headphones, headphone extension cables, and instrument and music stands. Also check for mic selections and any instruments and instrument supplies (e.g., guitar strings, drum sticks, etc.) as well as other hardware you'll need, such as amplifiers, monitors, and outboard effects processors. Don't forget to check the space available on your hard drive(s), and to defragment the drives if necessary. Also, be sure you have enough CD-Rs, DATs, cassettes, etc. to make rough mixes for the artist after the session.

Check the studio diagram you made to see where each player and piece of equipment should be set up, and always be aware of the line-of-sight between players and sound separation between instruments. Arrange the studio as best you can before the artist/players arrive.

It is also beneficial to have copies of the music and lyrics handy during a session. That way you can look at the chart or lyrics and direct your comments to specific parts of a song — a lyric sheet is essential in a vocal tracking session (see the section on vocal production later in this chapter).

Studio Ambience

There are many attributes of your studio to consider other than its sound characteristics and placement of people and equipment. Consider your studio environment: Is it clean? Is it conducive to creativity and an emotional performance? Will it make the artist comfortable? Does it make you feel relaxed? How is the temperature? How's the lighting? And consider your light sources: direct, indirect, candles, fluorescent, halogen, etc. If you're working with an artist they might prefer a different environment than you'd think, so check with them. Ask at the beginning of the session about the temperature, lighting, placement of equipment, instruments, etc. Do everything you can to make the environment favorable to musical expression.

Preparation can greatly improve the mental state of the artist by helping them feel comfortable — little things can pay big dividends in the long run. This also includes having food and beverages available, preferably items and brands the artist likes.

My studio is in my bedroom . . . my *small* bedroom. The room is roughly 12' by 12', including a closet. And I have a bunch of stuff crammed in even without additional musicians and their gear. I feel like I've packed ten pounds of stuff into a five-pound bag! However,

I've recorded several five-piece bands in this room with excellent results because it has an inviting vibe.

I always prepare the room before any musicians arrive. I do anything I can to make the environment better for encouraging and capturing great performances. For me, this includes flipping my mattress and box spring up against the wall (which actually helps the room acoustics), moving items from my room to the hall or another room, rearranging some equipment, and adjusting the lighting and temperature. I also buy food and drinks that the artist likes. All I can do is work with the space I have and make it comfortable, for both me and the artist I'm recording or producing.

It's the producer's job to make the artist feel comfortable, and if you're not comfortable in your own studio then no one else will be either. Make your studio a place where you enjoy creating music.

Types of Recording Sessions

Typically, several recording sessions are needed to capture all of the tracks for a song. The first tracking session (often called the "basics session") is commonly used to record rhythm section instruments like drums, bass, and guitar. This creates a rhythmic and harmonic foundation on which to build and keeps the groove element of recording live musicians together. The other instruments (including voice) might play or sing along with the rhythm section, but they're usually recorded later. Loop-based music often follows this convention as well, building songs from drum loops and bass grooves first, then adding other tracks (e.g., lead vocals, instrumental solos, etc.) in overdub sessions. Often, overdubs are recorded one at a time and can take as long or longer than the basic tracks, especially if you're recording vocals.

Once the overdubs are finished, "sweetening" tracks are recorded to fill out the song or add a special sound. Horns, strings, and backing vocals are examples of sweetening and are called this because they're not the main instrumental or vocal parts. Sweetening tracks shouldn't interfere with the main tracks — especially the lead vocal or instrument — but can augment them in a number of ways.

Of course, you don't need to record your projects in this order. Sometimes I build my songs around an acoustic guitar played to a click track, then overdub drums and bass. I've even built tracks starting with just an *a cappella* vocal. Pro Tools enables you to build songs track by track or in any order that works for you and the song, but whatever you do, try to think like a producer and plan your sessions.

When working with union musicians, producers have to fill out AFM and AFTRA paperwork at the end of every recording session. Consult the AFM and AFTRA Web sites (as listed in chapter 6) for more details on this procedure.

PRODUCING A RECORDING SESSION

If there was an exact procedure for running a recording session as a producer I'd include it here. However, there's no specific "right" way so you're going to have to plan it out as you see fit. I can tell you that the usual flow is:

1. Setting up the studio (mics, environment, etc.)

2. Getting sounds (making sure the mics work, that they're placed well, and that Pro Tools is getting good recording levels)

3. Doing a warmup/practice take (which you should record anyway)

4. Recording as many takes as necessary (with breaks in between, when needed)

5. Tearing down the equipment, making a rough mix of what you recorded, saving and backing up the files

This process is fairly obvious so I'll move on to what it takes to run a successful session. But first let me clarify something: I can't tell you how to become a good producer; I can only tell you about some of the things that successful producers do. Producing a recording session is an art, learned from experience. The more sessions you work on, the better producer you'll become.

A Producer's Style and Energy

All producers have their own style. Some are very hands-on — they get up and dance around, feeding on the energy of performers and bouncing energy back at them. Some stay somewhat detached, letting the artist simply do their thing. The really good producers can do *both* of these things when called for. They do whatever it takes to get the best performances from their artists.

The ability to figure out what an artist needs to evoke their best effort is one of the most (if not *the* most) important skills a producer can have. It requires the producer to really understand the artist. (And if you're producing yourself, you need to figure what motivates you to draw out your best performances.) All of the work you did building a relationship with the artist during preproduction pays off in the production phase.

Another important concept to remember is that the energy you display in each recording session is important . . . other people will feed off of your enthusiasm (or negativity). Often the producer must act as "the inspirer" when artists are down, tired, nervous, etc. A producer's energy has a huge effect on not only the performances in the sessions, but on the entire project.

What an Artist Wants from a Producer

Artists want a number of things from their producers.... They want someone who supports their music, who provides camaraderie, and who can translate (or at least interpret) their musical vision. They want a creative ally who will help them make the best music of their lives. To provide all of this for the artist you need to do many things, including:

- Making them feel comfortable enough to be really open and expressive

- Focusing their attention on the work that must be done

- Helping to spur their creativity . . . being a catalyst for new ideas

- Keeping an open mind and being flexible about new ideas

- Knowing when to offer opinions and when to keep your mouth shut

- Providing a different point of view

- Being prepared to accommodate anything they need

- Mediating and protecting the democratic process (when dealing with a group)

- Knowing when the democratic process isn't working, and making a decision

- Creating an atmosphere where special musical moments can happen

This list is very "touchy-feely." There are hardly any concrete actions that producers take during a session, however, professionals are known for their abilities to do all these things in one way or another. Now I'll try to get more specific.

DURING THE SESSION

Whether you're producing your own music or someone else's, it is beneficial to think and act like a record producer during your recording sessions. Philosophically, you need to be aware of the big picture but focused on the small details of each part. Psychologically, you need to be critical of the performances yet comforting to the performers. Physically, you need be aware of your own energy as well as the performer's.

Seeing the Forest and the Trees

As a producer you need to be aware of the overall sound and each part separate from the whole — this requires a very attentive ear. Listen on three different levels:

- Listen to the details of each track.

- Listen to how certain tracks interact with each other.

- Listen to how the entire song sounds as one unit.

For example, listen to the guitar part and really hone in on the track, then zoom out and examine the big picture of the song:

- *Listen to the details of each track.* Does the guitar part groove by it-self? Is it in tune? Is it creating a good sound/tone? Is the player into the song? Could the part stand on its own? Is the rhythm tight? Are the chord voicings good? Does the phrasing create the right feel?

- *Listen to how certain tracks interact with each other.* Are the gui-tarist and drummer locking up? Do their parts fit together? Are the bassist and guitarist playing well together? Does the tone of the guitar clash with the bass? How does this guitar part sound with the other guitar track? Do the rhythms and chord voicings of the key-board and guitar fit together, or do they step on each other? Are the bass and drums tight?

- *Listen to how the entire song sounds as one unit.* Do all the parts fit together well? Does each part have its place in the mix? Do they mesh together into one unit, or does one part stick out? What's the intended overall vibe of the tune? Is that vibe actually being cap-tured? Is the tempo right? How does this song make me feel?

Critical and Comforting at the Same Time

Critical and comforting . . . these two terms aren't often used together. However, as a producer you must become skilled at melding both terms into comments you make about your artists' performances. Remember the discussion in chapter 6 on tact and diplomacy during preproduction? Tact and diplomacy are very important during the production phase as well. You need to develop methods for giving critical opinions without hurting the artist's feelings — they'll appreciate your honest opinion, but not if it's given in a harsh way.

I recommend using positive feedback first, then making any critical comments. Also make sure your comments are specific and directed at a particular thing the performer can improve. Let's look at some responses to a typical recording session situation. For example, let's say the bass player is overdubbing a part that was good in some spots, but not so good in others.

1. The producer says, "Let's do it again." This gives the bass player no feedback whatsoever. He doesn't know what was right or wrong, plus it does nothing for his self-esteem.

2. The producer says, "That sucks. Let's do it again." This is even worse than the first response because not only does it provide no specific feedback about the part, it also demeans the performer. This shows little respect for the musician. (You might wonder if people actually say stuff like this in sessions, but I've seen it happen.)

3. The producer says, "That was good, but I think you can do it better." The best response of the first three, but still it lacks concrete feed-back.

4. The producer says, "That was really good. I liked the lick you played in the fifth bar and the feel you had in the last chorus. Try to get that feel for the entire song and put that cool lick in there . . . it really makes the song. Let's roll it again." This is what I'm talking about. Pointed comments, positive feedback. Apply your knowledge of music to the specific comments you make. The musicians you work with will really appreciate your attention to detail and positive energy.

Energy vs. Performance

In any recording session you need to be aware of the "energy vs. performance" curve. That is, the energy level of each person involved in a recording fluctuates, which affects their performance. Some people are best on the first take, therefore, you'd better be ready to record when they're ready to lay it down. Others need a number of takes to warm up. In this case be wary of the performer's energy level — once you've crossed a certain threshold the performances will start to degrade. If you notice this happening, take a break. This is particularly important for vocalists, whose voices can tire after just a few takes of a demanding song.

The same things apply when you're producing yourself.... If you feel you're losing energy, take a break and come back after some rest and relaxation. Your performances will be better after you recharge your battery.

Taking a break is also an effective method for easing the nerves of musicians who have little recording experience, or who generally get freaked out when the Record button is lit. People get nervous, they try too hard, they forget parts, they lose the groove. It's your job to ease the stress of studio recording, so after a few takes let the musicians "take five." When they return they'll be more relaxed and probably perform much better.

As the producer it's also up to you to help the artist focus their energy so you can capture the best performances. You must understand that your words and actions in the studio directly influence their playing or singing — you need to say or do whatever it takes to elicit their best. If you inspire them to turn in killer tracks, they'll want you to produce on their next project.

Making Decisions

As I've said many times throughout this book, the producer is responsible for everything in a project. While in a recording session the producer must make creative decisions about performances as well as new ideas that come up. I recommend recording every take, from the warmups to the last licks to any impromptu jam in the middle. However, that doesn't mean you need to *keep* every take. Make creative decisions so that your hard drive isn't cluttered with a thousand takes of the same thing. Commit to some ideas and go with them. If new ideas are flowing, keep the juices flowing by recording, but also stay focused on the plan you created in the preproduction phase.

Interacting with an Engineer During a Session

In professional studios a producer usually has at least one engineer, and possibly multiple assistant engineers, working during the session. In your home studio you most likely won't have that luxury. You'll probably be the engineer and producer simultaneously (as well as the artist). In the event you're lucky enough to be working with an engineer, you can focus all of your energy on producing. In fact, I recommend using an engineer if you can . . . it will free your mind of the technical aspects of recording and allow you to concentrate entirely on listening and evaluating performances.

Communication between the engineer and producer is extremely important for a successful session. The producer needs to be clear with his ideas and requests. This means being explicit and confident about things like the type of sound you want on a track, how much preroll to give the artist, and where to punch in and out of tracks. I've found that it's also good to keep the mood light by joking around with the engineer, so the session is more fun.

Remember that communication is a two-way street. And while it's great to be confident, you should leave your ego at the door. Good engineers are often a great source of information on recording techniques, the latest sounds, and new styles. Keep in mind that the engineer may have been in (and produced) many more sessions than you – when they talk, it's worth listening. That said, never forget this is your show and you have the right to make the final call.

VOCAL PRODUCTION

One of the most important skills you can learn is how to produce a vocal recording session. Because vocals are often the focal point of a song, they need to be the track(s) you spend a lot of time getting just right. In fact, it's a good idea to spend 30–40% of your recording time on vocals alone so you can capture that killer performance.

When recording vocals there are many things you can do as producer to elicit great performances. First you need to get yourself or your singer into the right psychological space. For a believable vocal the artist needs to feel the emotion of the song. Talk to the artist, help them get inside the song, have them read the lyrics aloud (or slowly to themselves), and delve into the feeling and meaning of the song. You're halfway to a good performance if you can get the vocalist into the right state of mind.

And I cannot stress enough the importance of a good headphone mix! When the singer is comfortable with their headphone mix they'll flat out sing better. Get the levels right, put complementary effects on the vocal track, and tailor the mix to the artist's liking (see chapter 11 for more on headphone mixes). Along with the headphone mix you should be sure that the vocalist is comfortable in every possible way. That is, adjust the lighting, temperature, and any other environmental controls you can that encourage the singer to really open up.

You should have the lyric sheet in front of you when tracking vocals, so you can make comments as you record. Writing down notes is good because you might not remember everything that goes on during a take. Once you start tracking, mark the good spots on your lyric sheet and constantly evaluate the interpretation and pitch of every word – even every syllable – because the smallest vocal inflections can make or break a song. Make sure you get at least one good take of each line.

When you're performing punch-ins, pick a good preroll amount. Vocalists usually like short prerolls so they can jump right in on the vocal line and not have to wait too long to record. Also, I recommend recording vocals onto multiple playlists in Pro Tools, as explained in chapters 2 and 4. Comping a vocal together by cutting and pasting among playlists is an easy way to compose a master take. Just be sure you make notes of which tracks are the best for each line/word/syllable.

As a producer, you should also *know* the words to the song you're recording. In fact, you should know how to sing it. Knowing the words (and their meaning) as well as the melody puts you inside the song right along with the singer. Be as articulate as you can when describing what you want the singer to do. Point to sections where the singer performed well and say "sing it like that . . . you already did it once, you can do it again." And if you can't express how you want a part to sound using words, try singing it. Even if you're not a singer, don't be afraid to sing the melody to get your point across. All of this will help you inspire an emotional and compelling vocal performance.

The amount of critical listening and attention to detail you give to a vocal session should also be applied to all of your other recording sessions. Focus on the fine details of the drum parts, the lead guitar track, the string arrangements, etc. Use the knowledge you gain from every session you produce and apply it to every future session.

Okay, you're armed with many of the techniques that make producers successful. It's now up to you to utilize them. The goal is to have a good relationship with your artist while translating their musical vision by capturing excellent performances. If you can do that, you have achieved your primary purpose as a producer. **‖**

Included on the CD-ROM is a PDF file entitled "Take Sheet." Particularly useful during overdubs and vocal comps, this worksheet can help you to keep track of the names of your files (tracks, regions, and playlists) and be used to quickly make notes about each performance.

PRO TOOLS HANDS-ON

Evaluate Performances

As a producer in a recording session, you've got to constantly evaluate musical performances. This involves making judgments and taking notes quickly to keep the energy of the session moving forward. Print out the "Take Sheet" PDF from the CD and use it in your recording sessions. It will help you keep track of your assessments for each recorded take as they happen so when you listen back later, you know what you've got. Staying organized is imperative when you've got hundreds of files flying around your sessions and hard drives.

Comp a Vocal Track Using Playlists

One of the most important aspects of many music productions is getting the best possible vocal performance for each song. Unless you're working with a very gifted "one-take" vocalist, getting the best overall performance usually involves cutting and pasting parts together from multiple takes. In chapter 4, you learned how to edit one spoken-word track to make a "perfect" performance. Now, I'll show you how to comp several takes together to create one "perfect" master take.

Open up the QuickTime movie titled "compingvocals" from the CD. Watch the process of comping several vocal takes together into a master take. Then, try it for yourself by opening the "Vocal Comp" Pro Tools session and editing a portion of the vocal track in the Electronica song.

When tracking vocals, it's a good idea to record notes about each take on a Take Sheet. For vocals, take sheets consist of the lyrics with large spaces (or grids) between each line for performance notes. You should make a new vocal take sheet for each vocal session. On a vocal take sheet, get very specific about what you like about each performance. Write very descriptive notes. Although several word phrases may be small enough chunks for you to evaluate at one time, don't be afraid to get down to the details of each word and syllable. Sometimes, you might even need to take it down to the specific letter, zooming in on an important consonant or vowel sound.

Create Ear Candy

Adding "ear candy" to a song can be one of the most fulfilling jobs of the producer. The term "ear candy" refers to any special little bit placed in a song that adds extra interest for the listener. Ear candy often comes about by experimenting, mutating an existing idea, and creating "happy accidents" (as Bob Ross would say). Some examples include adding sound effects, reversed tracks, extra back vocals and hooks, and numerous mix techniques like imaginative panning, EQ, and effects.

Listen to the MP3 "Chap10JazzEarCandy.mp3" and check out a few ideas I had for adding ear candy to this song...including panned guitars and stereo shaker tracks. Try it yourself. Add some ear candy to this track or any of your own. Open your creative mind to the immense sonic wonderland possible in Pro Tools.

Production Considerations as an Engineer

CHAPTER 11

In this chapter:

- The duties of a recording engineer
- Recording and miking techniques for different instruments
- Checking sounds, printing effects, and headphone mixes
- Combining tracks (submixes) and rough mixes
- The end of the session

Like the producer's role in a recording session, the role of the engineer is multifaceted. Most people consider the engineer's primary responsibilities to be technical in nature, however, he must also deal with musical issues (e.g., listening to the intonation of the guitar) and personal issues (e.g., making the vocalist feel comfortable) during a session.

In chapter 7 the preproduction engineering tasks are described. To recap: Before a recording session the engineer is responsible for setting up the studio and all necessary equipment, developing a plan for track assignments, creating Pro Tools session templates, defragmenting the studio hard drive(s), and several other clerical duties.

During a recording session the engineer is responsible for much more:

- Setting up microphones: choice, placement, and adjustments
- Establishing sound separation: setting up gobos, baffles, and blankets for isolation
- Setting up and working with Pro Tools: routing, naming tracks, record mode, headphone mix, recording levels, and more
- Syncing Digi 002/001 to an optical or S/PDIF device
- Creating the click track
- Managing outboard equipment
- Recording the artist
- Setting up plug-ins and printing effects on tracks
- Constantly attending to the artist's and producer's needs
- Submixing
- Creating a good rough mix
- Troubleshooting: computer, equipment, signal path, etc.

In this chapter I'll cover microphone technique, attending to the artist's and producer's needs, recording, printing effects on tracks, multiple headphone mixes, submixing, creating rough mixes, and troubleshooting. The other topics have been covered in previous chapters: click tracks in chapter 3; Pro Tools session setups in chapters 2, 3, and 5; sound separation in chapter 7; sync in chapter 8; and outboard equipment in chapters 7 and 8.

PERSONALITY MATTERS: THE ENGINEER'S OTHER SIDE

The engineer often plays a service role during a recording session, and a big part of the job — in addition to all of the engineering tasks — is to constantly attend to the artist's and producer's needs. This means the engineer must first and foremost be a good listener. It requires a flexible demeanor to accommodate input from many people and instruments at one time.

Good recording engineers get good sounds recorded and are responsive to the needs of the artist and producer. Great engineers have these qualities plus a deep understanding of the signal flow of the studio and all of its gear... *and* are generally fun to be around.

RECORDING: MIC CHOICE AND PLACEMENT

Choosing the right mic and putting it in the right place to capture a great sound is an art in itself. There are no recipes for doing this, and many times you have to improvise or compromise, depending on your mic selection and available space. However, if the source sounds great before you even put the mic up, more than half of your work is already done…it's then your job to not screw it up.

There is an infinite number of ways to mic instruments. Everyone has their own techniques and you'll develop yours over time. The techniques I describe below are simply a few that I've learned or created — none of them should be considered the only approach.

MICROPHONES IN DIGITAL RECORDING

When recording to analog tape, engineers often choose microphones that have increased high-frequency response to help deal with the loss of those frequencies during analog reproduction — particularly during mastering and duplication. Digital recording doesn't automatically lose high frequencies on playback, so using microphones with boosted highs could make your recordings biting and shrill. I recommend using mics with smooth high-frequency response when recording to Pro Tools.

Recording Drums

Regardless of what you're recording, I usually recommend listening to the sound source before you put up a single mic — to see what you have to work with. With drums some of the issues to consider include: drum heads, tuning, dampening, rattles/squeaks/buzzes, cymbal choice, and the drummer's playing style and genre of music.

First, listen to the drum's heads. Are they new heads or do they sound dead? New heads can substantially improve the sound of almost any drum, and are usually a good investment before important sessions.

Second, listen to the drum tuning. Is the snare tight (or loose) enough for the sound you want? Is the kick sound deep enough? Are the toms (and kick) tuned to specific pitches that correlate with the key of the song? Try to tune drums so they fit with the particular song you're recording. For example, when recording a song in the key of E, I often tune my high tom to B, my middle tom to A, and my floor tom to E. The tighter the snare is tuned, the crisper it will sound in Pro Tools. As an engineer you should own a drum key in case the drummer forgets theirs, because tuning can make all the difference when recording percussion.

When I record drums I also put a weight in the kick drum. You can use something like a brick or a weight from that old bench-press set you bought ten years ago. The weight anchors the kick drum, which gives it an unexplainable solidity and seems to add depth and strength to the sound. It also holds dampening material in place.

Third, consider dampening any drum that's producing an ugly ring or that decays too slowly. Use a little tape, a cotton pad with some tape, a Zeroring plastic head ring strip (from Noble and Cooley), Moongel Damper Pads (from RTOM), a cloth strip, or even your wallet on any toms or snare, and use a pillow or blanket that touches the head(s) of the kick. Be careful, though. Dampening a drum can take away a lot of its character and easily make it sound worse than it did before you tried to fix the problem. Often you'll find the ringing of a particular drum may not even be noticeable when the entire kit is played or when other instruments are added to the mix.

Fourth on the list is getting rid of any rattles, squeaks, and buzzes that shouldn't be present. Drummers are notorious for having squeaky kick drum pedals and various rattles coming from their rackmounted toms. Use a little oil (WD-40 is always handy) to lube up a squeaky kick pedal. Also make sure all lugs, wing nuts, and screws are tightened, even if they're not being used to hold anything in place. Remember, hitting one drum in the kit can cause sympathetic vibrations in other drums (and sometimes in other instruments or objects across the room).

Fifth, listen to the cymbals. Do they ring forever? Do they sound similar in frequency to each other? Does the ride cymbal have enough of a "ping" sound to cut through a mix? Does the hi-hat have the right sound for the song (high and tight, low and rumbly)?

For stereo imaging purposes, consider having two different-sounding crash cymbals near the overhead mics. When you pan the overheads you'll create a cool stereo image of the two crashes. Cymbals with long decays can make a mix sound washy, so you might consider using cymbals with shorter decays for recording. For instance, washy ride cymbals can lose their ability to cut through a mix if they have long decays — not only a sonic problem, but also a potential time/groove-keeping killer. Also consider the sound of the hi-hat and how it fits with the snare drum sound. These two instruments must work well together to create a unified rhythmic palette.

Finally, all drum miking decisions should include considerations for the drummer's playing style. For example, hard-hitting players may require different mics and techniques than lighter players. Sticks can dictate mic choices as well: Different sounds come from nylon-tip vs. wood-tip sticks and thick vs. thin sticks. Also, different types of music are often recorded different ways. For example, I usually mic jazz drum kits differently than rock kits due to (a) the sounds distinctive to each genre of music, (b) the characteristics of the drums and cymbals used in each genre, and (c) the amount of control I want over the sounds during mixing.

There are two basic methods of miking drums: ambient or close miking. Ambient miking uses a minimal number of mics (e.g., two overheads and a kick mic) to capture the full drum kit sound. Close miking means putting one (or more) mics on each drum and cymbal. Using a combination of these two techniques is common, but which one you choose could be dependent on the number of mics you own. I'll list a number of options that cover most drum miking possibilities.

MIC TYPES AND PICKUP PATTERNS ON DRUMS

Generally, condenser mics are best used for ambient miking applications (e.g., overhead mics) because they're better at reproducing transients and usually have a more even frequency response. Dynamic mics are best used for close-miking drums, because they can handle large amounts of volume before distorting and often have frequency responses tailored to accentuate a drum's attack.

Typical ambient drum mic setups

OPTION 1: two overhead mics + one kick drum mic (three mics total)

OPTION 2: two overhead mics + one kick drum mic + one snare mic (four mics total)

In these setups, the overhead mics are placed above the drums and cymbals and are used to pick up everything but the kick drum (hence the need to mic the kick separately). Be sure to listen to the balance between toms, snare, and cymbals in the overhead mics. Moving the cymbals higher or lower can improve this balance. The overhead mics can be placed anywhere from about one foot to ten feet above the drum kit. However, be aware that the farther away you move the overheads, the more room ambience you'll capture.

There are different ways to position overhead mics. I usually use a **spread pair**; that is, two mics that are spread apart from each other using the 3:1 rule (so there's no phase cancellation — see chapter 8 for more on 3:1). You can also use an **X/Y configuration**. To make an X/Y configuration put the two overhead mics (with cardioid patterns) together at a 90-degree angle, making an X shape (see figure 11.1).

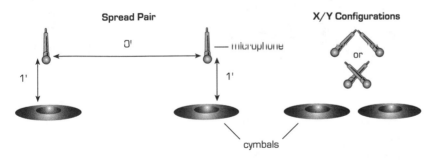

Spread Pair   **X/Y Configurations**

0'

— microphone

1'   1'   or

cymbals

Fig. 11.1.
Spread pair and X/Y mic configurations are often used for drum overheads.

When using an ambient miking technique the sound of the room can make all the difference in the overall drum tone — the natural room reverb will be captured. If you record in a deadened room, this isn't as much of an issue as you can add reverb to the tracks later in the mix.

However, if you record in a very reverberant room the room reverb will be recorded on the tracks forever. That's not all bad, though: The late John Bonham (of Led Zeppelin) was recorded several times in a castle using three mics on his drum kit, and it sounds incredible!

A kick drum mic can be put in several different places. It may be put inside the drum against the beater head (right where the beater strikes the head) — this will capture the most attack. Or it can be placed just *outside* the drum in the hole of the resonant head (the back drum head, if the drum has one). In this position the mic will pick up a good amount of the air movement from inside the drum — the sound is powerful but has less attack. Placing the mic somewhere between these two extremes also works and combines the effects of both aforementioned techniques. (More on miking kick drums later in this chapter.)

The snare mic is usually placed between the hi-hat and the first rackmounted tom and is roughly two inches above the drum, peeking over the outer rim. You can also put the mic higher (6–8 inches) above the snare for a more roomy sound. The mic should face the center of the top head if you want to capture the most attack or, to hear more of the drum tone, aim the mic just inside the rim. (More on miking snare drums later in this chapter.)

Fig. 11.2.
Typical kick drum mic configurations.

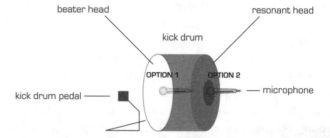

RECORDING A DRUMSET WITH ONE MICROPHONE

Most of us don't have the money to buy a whole closet full of microphones. If you're limited to using one or two mics to record a drum kit, you can still capture excellent sounds. Try one of these options:

- Place a condenser mic (cardioid pattern) about a foot or two in front of the drum kit, at about six feet from the floor, pointed at the kit.
- Place a condenser mic (cardioid pattern) just above the drummer's head, pointed at the kit.
- Place a condenser mic (cardioid pattern) about four feet directly above the cymbals, pointed at the kit.
- Place a condenser mic (cardioid or omni pattern) about six to ten feet in front of the drumset, pointed at the kit.
- If you're desperate you can also use a dynamic mic placed above and to the side of the kick on the opposite side of the snare drum. I used this technique early in my 4-track recording days.

- If you can spare two mics, you can create "earrings." That is, put one mic next to each of the drummer's ears, pointed at the kit. Two mics are also effective if you place one in the kick drum and one directly over the entire kit.

Minimal close miking drum setups

OPTION 3: option 2 (above) + one mic for each pair of toms (five+ mics total)

OPTION 4: option 3 + one mic for each individual tom (six+ mics total)

OPTION 5: option 4 + one mic for the hi-hat (seven+ mics total)

If you use one mic to capture two toms, you should try to use a mic with a wide cardioid pattern in order to get the most attack from both drums. It should be placed directly in-between the toms. However, having mics on each tom gives you more control over capturing the right sound. As with snare mics on the top head, these mics should be aimed at the center of the drum out of the way of the drummer's stick motion. I like to use the Shure Beta 98s, because they're so small that they never impede a drummer from playing a tom fill.

In close-miking applications, the hi-hat mic is usually aimed at the middle or center (bell) of the top hi-hat cymbal. For more sound separation, I recommend pointing the mic away from the snare drum. That way, if you want to bring the hi-hat up in the mix, the snare level won't rise as well.

BUILDING A KICK DRUM TUNNEL

A technique often used with good results is building a "tunnel" for the kick drum. What on Earth does that mean? First you need to take the resonant head off the kick. Then you set up two mic stands and extend the booms about three or four feet perpendicular to the ground, at the height of the drum. Place a condenser mic just inside of the mic stands at the far end of the drum, about a foot off the floor, aimed at the kick. Cover the mic stands with blankets, creating a tunnel for the kick drum sound to travel through the mic. (The blankets isolate the mic from the other drums and cymbals.) Why is the tunnel cool? It gives you a more distant and roomy kick sound, but without picking up any other drums in the room.

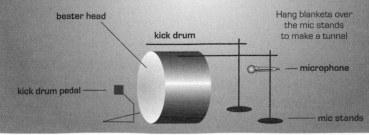

beater head

kick drum

Hang blankets over the mic stands to make a tunnel

microphone

kick drum pedal

mic stands

When using electronic
drums, you may want to
overdub real cymbals
*if you want a more
realistic sound.* Although
electronic drums are
sounding better each
year, electronic cymbals
are lagging behind and
still sound rather fake.

More extravagant drum mic setups

OPTION 6: option 5 (above) + room mics (nine+ mics total)

OPTION 7: option 6 + multiple mics on drums (ten+ mics total)

Room mics are often omni-directional, to capture as much of the room's sound as possible. They can be placed close to the drums for less room ambience or very far from the drums for more. Often these mics are pointed at the snare drum, no matter where they are in the room, and are used in pairs to create a stereo image.

As I've gotten deeper into the art of miking drums, I've found I like certain sounds from different mics and enjoy using mics together on one source. Yes, using multiple microphones on one drum can be extravagant — especially if you have limited mics to choose from — but the sounds you capture can be worth it. For example, I like using two (or more) mics on my kick drum . . . a Shure Beta 52 to pick up the meaty bass boom and a Beta 91 to capture the upper attack frequencies. And for my snare I like combining the sound of the Shure Beta 56 and SM57 (or Sennheiser MD 441). Usually I put the Beta 56 on the top head and the SM57 on the bottom head, but sometimes I use the 56 and 57 on the top alone, or with another 57 on the bottom. To save track real estate you can bus these multiple mics to record on just one track, or simply bounce to one track after you've already recorded them on separate tracks (so you can really be sure of the mix and their sound relationship).

Everyone has their own way of miking drums and there are many techniques I haven't listed here. I've included these because they're some of the common techniques taught at the Berklee College of Music. Regardless, you can use these miking options as foundations for your own sonic experiments.

My favorite drum mic setup, that captures the best sounds from my Yamaha Maple Custom drum kit, consists of:

Kick drum — Beta 52 placed either at the beater head inside the drum or in the hole of the resonant head. Beta 91 placed inside the drum lying on a weight and a pillow.

Snare Drum — Beta 56 placed at the top head about two inches above the head, aimed at its center. SM57 (or Sennheiser MD 441) on the bottom head, facing the snares, about eight inches away.

Hi-hat — Shure SM81 (or AKG 535) on the top cymbal, pointed away from the snare.

Toms — Beta 98s with drum mounts (or Sennheiser MD 421s) on each tom, about an inch or two from the head, aimed at the center of the drum. Many condenser mics also sound great on toms.

Cymbals — A pair of Shure KSM32s (or AKG 535s) about a foot above the cymbals, placed strategically to capture all of the cymbals, implementing the 3:1 rule.

Room Mics — A pair of omni-directional condenser mics (like the Earthworks TC40s) placed away and equidistant from the kit, usually pointed at the snare drum.

Note: The Shure mics mentioned here provide great starting points for capturing excellent sounds without spending tens of thousands of dollars on mics. Your budget and sonic preferences will dictate your mic choices. Top-drawer mics can often yield superior sounds—but proper mic technique allows you to capture high-quality sounds with almost any mic.

I've recorded drums using 22 microphones and I've recorded drums using one mic. However, if the drums sound bad and the player isn't very good, it really doesn't make a difference how many or what kind of mics you put up. Likewise, if the player is killin' and the drum kit sounds great, then you just have to avoid screwing it up . . . any of these miking techniques will help you capture good sounds.

Note: On my drum set I've also used a Neumann TLM 170 on the kick drum in a tunnel, AKG 535s and Neumann KM86s as overheads, and a Sennheiser MD 441 on the bottom of the snare with great results. These, and the aforementioned mics, are my personal favorites for home studio recordings.

FUN WITH MIC TECHNIQUES

Experimentation with mic placement and usage is a fun learning experience. Each time you try something new you can learn whether the technique works or not, and you'll soon develop recording tricks that contribute to your "sound." For example, one time a friend and I were recording drums for some loops and had a whole slew of mics on the kit . . . several on the kick, snare, and hi-hat, one for each tom, and a number of overhead and room mics. Just for the heck of it we set up one Shure SM81 far behind the drummer's chair; in fact, the mic was head-high in a corner of the room with a gobo in front of it. (A gobo is a movable wall used in the studio to isolate a sound.)

When we finally listened to the SM81 we found that it sounded terrible. The frequency response due to the mic's placement behind a gobo in the corner of the room was really bizarre, making the track's tone totally gnarled and distorted. But at the same time, it was sooo cool . . . it captured the sound of the kick and snare in a very unusual way. It was naturally lo-fi, but with a sound that we might have never thought to create using EQ. In the end, we made more drum loops with the signal from that one SM81 than from all of the other mics we used on the drums.

RECORDING ELECTRIC GUITARS AND BASSES

As with drums, there are several issues to consider before you start recording a guitar or bass, including tuning, strings, intonation, pickups, rattles/hums/buzzes, the genre of the music, and the guitarist's or bassist's playing style. In this section you can assume, unless stated otherwise, that any references I make to guitar also apply to bass.

The first aspect of getting good guitar and bass sounds is recording an instrument that is (a) in tune with itself and (b) in tune with the rest of the instruments on the track. Tuners are cheap and you should own one, but you can also tune to other instruments with fixed pitches (like synths) or to instruments that are difficult to tune on your own (like pianos). However, it's usually a good idea to tune with a tuner, so that when you have to go back and do overdubs later you'll have a common reference pitch to match. Also, guitars and basses can go out of tune quickly! Have the player retune often during a session so you avoid getting the perfect performance only to find out the guitar was out of tune. Retune even more frequently if the player put new strings on before the session.

Second, listen to the guitarist play and have him cycle through all of the pickups. Listen for noisy pickups and for any irregularities in the sounds. If you notice one pickup is getting more of the low strings than the high strings, the pickup might not be level (it's angled slightly toward the low strings). With a couple twists of a screwdriver, you can make the pickup parallel with the strings and even out the response.

Third, as the player is warming up, listen for any rattles, hums, and buzzes . . . these noises can come from a variety of places. Check that the input is secure in the body of the instrument. Check the instrument cable and its connections — guitar cables are notorious for giving out in sessions. Hums and buzzes often come from electrical grounding problems; if the guitar is going through a direct box flip the ground switch, or if you're using an amp, get the amp up off of the floor. Active pickups require batteries, and batteries low on power often make noise. (It's a good idea to replace all batteries before the session, anyway.) Also watch for interference from your computer screen. Finally, if you're still getting unexplained noise, try having the guitar player face a different direction or move to a different location in the room. This will often get rid of the problem.

Finally, consider the guitarist's playing style and the genre of the music you are recording before putting up any microphones. Will the guitarist be playing with a pick, fingers, a slide, or some other device? Will the bassist be slapping, popping, tapping, or using some other non-standard technique? Will the guitarist be using an amp, a direct box, a combination of these two, or will the guitar be miked? Is the guitarist playing through any pedals, effects units, or other devices? As with drums, mic techniques differ for different genres of music and playing styles.

There are several ways to record electric guitars: direct, mics on an amplified speaker, or a combination of both.

Direct: Plugging a guitar or bass directly into your 002/001/Mbox or an outboard mixer usually provides the most noise-free input signal and zero leakage from other instruments being recorded at the same time. To record direct you need a preamplifier to boost the signal. Any of the Digi 002/001/Mbox's mic preamps with Neutrik connections accept 1/4" guitar cables, as well as mics and other line-level instruments. To record a guitar or bass direct, use these inputs so you can obtain good recording levels.

You can also record direct using a direct box (commonly called a "DI" for "direct injection"). A **direct box** transforms line-level input signals into mic-level signals so you can plug the cable into a mic preamp. To use a DI, plug the 1/4" cable from the guitar or bass into the direct box and connect a mic (XLR) cable from the direct box to a mic preamp on your mixer. Signal processors can be inserted between the guitar and the DI.

Bass parts are often recorded direct. However, guitar parts are often written using a particular sound from an amp and/or signal processors, making it better to use amps and processors to capture the part, even if the signal isn't as clean as a direct in.

Miking an amplified speaker: There are several ways to mic an amplified speaker. Close miking is the most common technique and, as the term implies, it consists of putting a mic within a foot of a speaker cabinet. Often I put a dynamic mic up against the grill of the speaker (though not touching it) to capture the sound right at its source. On electric guitars Shure SM57s are popular for this application, as are Sennheiser MD 421s. Shure Beta 52s work well on bass cabinets. Some engineers like to use a combination of close mics and EQ them differently to create a thicker or more exciting tone. Experiment with different mics to see which ones sound best together.

Where you point the mic will determine the type of sound you'll get. If you want an edgy sound, point the mic at the center of the speaker to pick up more of the high frequencies. If you want more of a warm and smooth tone, point the mic toward the outer edge of the speaker cone. Also, if the cabinet has more than one speaker, make sure to put the mic in front of the one that sounds best. Have the guitarist play and listen to each speaker to find the one with the most impact, cleanest signal, and least amount of rattle and buzz.

Natural ambience can add a lot of character to a guitar sound. Placing a condenser mic several feet back from the speaker will give you a detailed recording of the amp sound interacting with the room ambience. Blending this distant mic with the close mic(s) will produce a fuller overall guitar track. Experiment with different rooms or spaces . . . you may find that recording in the bathroom or the kitchen could add a cool vibe to your track!

Some effects processors (like the Line 6 Pod Pro) act as direct boxes because they have both line- and mic-level outputs. In addition, they have S/PDIF outputs that you can plug directly into your Digi hardware S/PDIF input. To me, the S/PDIF connection is the most convenient way to use devices like this in a home studio, yet I prefer the sonic quality of the XLR analog outputs from the Line 6 gear.

Any time you put a microphone in front of a loud speaker cabinet, be careful not to overload it. As discussed in chapter 7, some mics have pads that can reduce the incoming volume and allow the mic to handle louder levels.

When recording a band all at once, it's a good idea to separate the loud guitar speaker cabinet from the rest of the band. If you have the space, put the cabinet in a different room than the drums. If your studio consists of only one room (like mine), put the cabinet in the closet and deaden all the space around it. That is, set up the mics the way you want them, then put absorptive materials (like blankets or pillows) all around the amp. Although not as clean as going direct, this technique will sufficiently isolate the guitar signal from the other instruments. Also don't forget to deaden the floor so you don't encounter reflections that might cause phase cancellation. I sometimes use laundry for this purpose (which of course gets picked up immediately after the session).

Combining direct and miked signals: An effective way to make a more interesting guitar or bass sound is to combine the direct input with the miked signal. If you have the track real estate, use two or more tracks for different guitar inputs and mix them down later. You may want to add a special effect to the dry direct signal and then combine it with the close-miked and distant-miked speaker tracks.

Current amp modelers (e.g., Line 6's Pod series) allow you to combine (or keep separate) the direct signal and the amp model signal. It's very cool to have the direct signal available on a track during the mix session, because later you can add different effects that you might not have thought of during recording.

Recording Acoustic Guitars and Basses

Although some acoustic guitars and basses have electric pickups, I often find that miking these instruments with condensers sounds better than recording them using their built-in pickups. I've gotten great sounds using Shure KSM32s and SM81s on acoustic guitars and KSM44s on acoustic basses, as well as other condenser microphones like AKG 414s. I also like combining the direct signal with the miked signal to add character to the overall sound.

Assuming the guitar or bass sounds good, mic placement is the key to getting good acoustic recordings. For acoustic guitars you'll get more high frequencies the closer the mic is to the neck, more mids the closer the mic is to the bridge, and more low frequencies the closer the mic is to the sound hole. I like using two mics, one placed above the sound hole toward the bridge and one placed below the sound hole toward the neck. When panned left and right they create a nice stereo image, since each mic is picking up slightly different frequencies. But this setup is only the technique I've been using lately. I've tried many others and there are numerous positions in which you can capture great acoustic guitar sounds. Experiment, and try rolling off the low end if it gets too boomy.

I've found there are three main ways to mic an acoustic bass. The first is to place a condenser mic anywhere from 6–30 inches away from the strings, just above the bridge where the strings are being plucked. The distance will determine how much room ambience is included in the sound, as well as how much isolation you'll have on the track. This technique will capture a good amount of the attack on the strings when they're plucked and is also good for bowed parts.

The second technique is miking the F hole at anywhere from 6–30 inches away. This technique will provide increased bass and low-mid frequencies, but will lose some of the attack. The last technique is putting a mic under the bridge, wrapped in padding – I've gotten the best results using this technique. It simultaneously captures the attack and a wide frequency range in a crisp yet bassy blend.

A note on bass compression: Most bass parts need compression to even out the volume of the notes so that the bass track sounds more constant in the mix and provides a solid foundation for the recording. Besides helping to control loud sounds, compression also allows the softer nuances of the bass track to be heard. You can compress bass on the way in to your computer using an external compressor, or you can use an insert (plug-in) on the track in Pro Tools, or both.

But there's a difference between these two signal paths: Compressing bass before it gets to the computer means you'll be recording the compressed signal, which can't be undone later. However, inserts in Pro Tools are applied after a signal has been recorded. That means that you won't actually be recording a compressed bass track. If you put a compressor plug-in on the bass track while you record, you will hear what the bass sounds like *after* being recorded and processed. This allows you to tweak the bass track later, which may be preferable unless the bass track could really benefit from compression on the way into Pro Tools. You can find more information on printing effects (like compression) onto a track later in this chapter, and on compression in chapter 12, as well as in the *DigiRack Plug-Ins Guide.*

RECORDING PIANO

Although most home studios aren't likely to have a grand piano I'll briefly touch on recording techniques for those that do, or for those that might have an upright or console piano.

One basic technique for recording piano is using two condenser mics, one aimed at the low strings and the other aimed at the high strings, both about six inches or more from the strings. When panned left and right these two mics will create a large and pleasing sound that captures almost all of the piano's frequency range. To use only one mic, center it at the opening of the piano's lid. And to make your piano sound even better, try to write parts for it in its best-sounding range(s).

Experiment with other miking techniques such as putting the mics close to the hammers or using an X/Y configuration. Listen to the differences when you move mics closer or farther away from the piano and note how the lid height interacts with the sound. If you need to isolate the piano, put blankets over it so that little outside noise gets into the mics.

If you find that a singer is singing slightly out of tune, try having them take a headphone off one of their ears. That way, they can hear the track in the phones and their own live voice in the room.

RECORDING VOICE

Technically speaking, recording vocals seems like it should be one of the easiest jobs in the recording process. Just put a mic in front of the singer and let the singer do his or her thing. Right? Well, this couldn't be further from the truth. Vocals are often the most important tracks you'll record as an engineer, and they require an attention to detail that surpasses all other instrumental tracks.

To capture an emotional and energetic vocal performance, several factors must be considered besides mic choice and placement. The physical environment should be to the vocalist's liking. That is, adjust the lights, temperature, and decor to suit the mood of the song or the personality of the singer. Your goal is to make the singer feel comfortable in their surroundings . . . the environment and *your* mood will help set the tone. Remember, energy is contagious, whether positive or negative, and the energy you give off will have an impact on the artist, the producer, and everyone else.

A good overall vibe for the session is extremely important, and creating an excellent headphone mix with a somewhat flattering vocal sound enhances that good vibe. Be sure to listen to the mix that the *vocalist* is listening to as you're creating and tweaking it – that way you'll know of any problems immediately. I recommend boosting the keyboard or guitar tracks in the headphone mix so the vocalist has a solid pitch reference. To further enhance this, keep the effects on those tracks to a minimum.

Interact with the singer as you're adjusting the level of their voice in the mix. Have them sing along with the track at full volume to accurately assess a good level for their voice, and ask them how they feel about the sound. Note that vocalists tend to go flat if their voice is too high in the headphones and sharp (because they try to push their voices) if they're too low in the mix. Also be aware that most vocalists like hearing some reverb on their voices when recording, so have a reverb plug-in in place or an external unit set up on their track solely for this purpose. Because very subtle differences can have huge benefits, a good headphone mix might make the difference between recording an average track and capturing an outstanding performance. (More info on setting up headphone mixes later in this chapter.)

If you have a home studio like mine, you have one of four places to record a vocal: in your bedroom, in your closet, in the hall, or in another room (e.g., bathroom). As with all other instruments, the voice interacts with the acoustics of its environment. The size and shape of the space as well as the reflections from the material on the walls, floor, and ceiling will influence the overall sound of the vocal track. Listen carefully to the "core" sound of the space where you'll be recording your vocals.

Condenser mics often yield the best vocal recordings because of their flat frequency response and ability to capture sonic detail. Since they are recording in a cardioid pattern, these mics should be placed

The diaphragm of a condenser microphone is a micro-thin metal plate that moves in response to air flow, generating an electronic signal that represents the sound it's recording.

about six inches to two feet from the vocalist, depending on how much ambience you want to include in the track. Close miking a vocalist with a condenser often creates proximity effect (i.e., bass boost). Sometimes used for effect or to indicate intimacy, this bass boost can also create a muddy vocal sound. If you really need to close mic a vocalist with a condenser, you can use the bass rolloff to eliminate some of the boomy low frequencies. Also use the microphone's pad if the vocalist is very loud so you won't get distortion, and to protect the mic's diaphragm.

But don't rule out dynamic microphones for vocals. There are some voices that sound great utilizing the non-flat frequency response of a particular dynamic mic. It might accentuate the best part of the vocalist's sound or may boost a frequency that's lacking in their natural tone. However, experimentation is the only way to find engineering gems like these. Dynamic mics are also useful for creating vintage vocal tones or other interesting sounds. When using a dynamic mic keep the vocalist within six inches of the mic, otherwise the signal will sound thin because low frequencies will be lost.

There are many possible positions for a vocal microphone, but I'll recommend only two here. The first is directly in front of the vocalist's mouth as the vocalist is standing up straight. This position provides the most natural vocal sound but might pick up more breathing and plosives than desired. The second and probably more useful mic position is slightly above (2–4 inches) the singer, pointed down at their mouth. This forces a vocalist to really open up his or her throat, which is useful when they have to hit some high notes, and also decreases the amount of recorded breathing and plosive sounds. This position can, however, be uncomfortable to some singers.

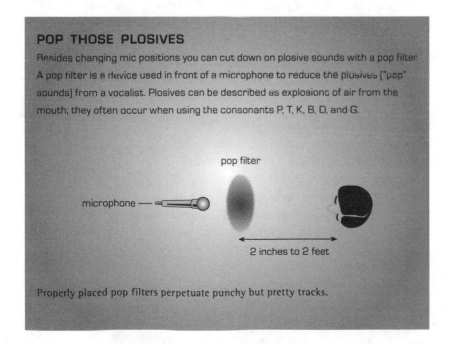

POP THOSE PLOSIVES

Besides changing mic positions you can cut down on plosive sounds with a pop filter. A pop filter is a device used in front of a microphone to reduce the plosives ("pop" sounds) from a vocalist. Plosives can be described as explosions of air from the mouth; they often occur when using the consonants P, T, K, B, D, and G.

pop filter

microphone

2 inches to 2 feet

Properly placed pop filters perpetuate punchy but pretty tracks.

Notice that for all vocal mic positions, the mic should be placed so that the vocalist must stand fully erect. Standing while singing helps expand the chest and elongate the throat, which creates a better vocal sound. It also ensures that the singer isn't bending their neck downward, which can block air passage though the throat. Although not recommended, sitting while singing can work as long as the singer is sitting up straight without having to bend their neck down.

Volume Riding and Compression

Vocal parts are often very dynamic — the volume of a singer's voice can vary between a wide range of levels. As you're setting up the mic, creating a headphone mix, and getting sound from the singer, ask the vocalist to sing as loud as they think they'll sing during the loudest part of the song. Make sure you're not peaking on the input meters in Pro Tools. (Be aware that although the singer thinks that's the loudest they will sing, they'll usually sing even louder once they get into the emotion and energy of the song, so make sure you have some headroom for the additional volume.)

Veteran studio singers know when to back off the mic for loud notes or get closer for softer parts, which makes your job as an engineer easier. However, volume riding and/or compression are often still needed on charismatic vocal parts, especially if the vocalist has little recording experience or microphone technique. If you know the song well and are familiar with the vocalist's interpretation, you can adjust the input level to Pro Tools by riding the input volume level from the mic.

If your vocal mic is plugged into a preamp on your Digi 002/001/ Mbox, you can ride the level using the preamp's Gain controls. The same goes for other mic preamps (like the PreSonus Digimax). If you're recording through an external mixer, use the mic trim or channel fader to ride the volume. Basically, you want to adjust the gain so the track doesn't get digitally clipped — watch the track's meter in Pro Tools and make sure it's not peaking. (Note: The fader in the Mix window of Pro Tools adjusts the output level of the track only, so riding that fader while recording won't affect the input level . . . remember your gain stages?) Also be aware of the input levels to your microphones and mic preamps . . . they can distort as well!

Riding the volume of a track can even out the input level, and is beneficial because it reduces the amount of compression you'll need to control the dynamic range of that track in the mix. However, many times you may need compression on the track anyway, so if you aren't *extremely* familiar with a track I recommend against volume-riding the input signal. (See "Printing Effects to Tracks" later in this chapter to learn more about vocal compression.)

Your goal as an engineer, producer, and artist should be to get the best vocal take possible — one that includes style, emotion, inspiration, and a great sound. There's much more to it than just recording clean audio.

I recommend recording every take of the vocal, whether you're recording an entire run through the song or line by line. The early ones might be rough around the edges but the energy is often the best. By later takes the singer usually gets into the flow of the song and sings more evenly, but the energy might start to fade. At any rate, there's usually some part of every take that's worth keeping. You and the producer should take notes about where the keeper words/phrases/ sentences are so you can find them later. As mentioned in chapter 10, use the file titled "Take Sheet" on the CD-ROM for this purpose. It's also a good idea to have the lyric sheet so you always know where you are in the song. If the singer says they want to redo the second line of the third verse, you should know what that line is and where to find it in your Pro Tools session.

Give the singer some preroll before they have to sing a line, but not too much. You don't want them waiting long because they might lose the energy of the line. As an example, for mid-tempo songs I often start with two bars of preroll before any punch-in, then ask the vocalist if he wants more or less. In Pro Tools you set the preroll time in the Transport window (see figure 11.3).

Fig. 11.3.
Setting preroll in the Transport window (preroll shown engaged). Work with the singer to make sure they're getting the right amount.

When doubling a vocal create a comp of the *first* vocal on one track — that is, assemble the best parts of every take into a master vocal track. Then have the vocalist double the comp. This is easier for them because the interpretation of the song is already done . . . they just need to copy it.

And be constantly aware of the vocalist's energy level (even if you're the one singing). Take breaks to rest the singer's vocal cords and to relax from the stress of tracking. Some vocalists can sing for hours while others need breaks often. Be ready for either of these types or anyone in-between.

As an engineer you really need to be on your toes in a vocal recording session. Vocalists can lose their energy, emotion, intensity, or inspiration very quickly, so you need to be able to work fast. If it takes a long time to set up tracks, playlists, or punch points, you'll lose the session's momentum and energy. So, being able to move quickly through these actions helps the vocalist stay in the mood to give you a captivating performance.

Background Vocals

If you're recording one backing vocal track at a time, use the same microphone techniques as described for lead vocals. However, if you want to record more than one backing vocalist simultaneously there are several effective techniques you can use.

First, I recommend using no more than two mics at one time — regardless of how many background singers there are — to avoid phase problems. One mic with an omni-directional pattern works well for a group of singers positioned in a circle around the mic. Here, creating a good vocal blend is the key. If you want the background voices in stereo you can record two tracks like this and pan them as wide as you'd like — on the second track try moving the singers around for a slightly different sound that will give more dimension to the stereo image. Or if you want to use two mics to capture a stereo image try putting two condensers in cardioid patterns back to back (a foot or more away from each other). Split the vocalists into two groups and have them face each other.

Fig. 11.4.
A stereo background vocal mic setup.

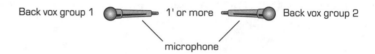

Back vox group 1   1' or more   Back vox group 2

microphone

Experiment with your own techniques as well, but watch out for phase problems and stay focused on getting a good blend of voices.

RECORDING OTHER INSTRUMENTS

Synths: Although recording directly into Pro Tools from your synthesizer is the easiest and most effective way to track synth parts, experiment with running synth tracks through amplifiers or speakers and miking them. If you combine the direct and miked signals you might come up with some interesting timbres.

Horns: Woodwind instruments (e.g., saxophones) usually sound best when recorded with dynamic microphones (such as Electro-Voice RE20s or Shure SM57s) whereas brass instruments (e.g., trumpets and trombones) are often recorded with condenser microphones (such as Shure KSM32s, AKG 535s, etc.). Be careful about not putting condenser mics too close to brass instruments, though. Keep the mic at least ten inches away from the bell of the horn so its diaphragm isn't destroyed by a stray triple-forte note. A pair of condensers works well for a stereo horn section, or a section with many players to capture. You just need to be sure you're getting an even blend of the different instruments.

Strings: In most home recording situations synthesized string parts will do the trick. However, if you do decide to record real strings, use condenser mics. Position the mics close to the players if you want little room tone or further away if you want more. Consider double-, triple-, or quadruple-tracking the string parts to make them sound more full.

Percussion instruments: As with the drum kit, use dynamic mics if close miking and condenser mics when ambient miking.

USING ANTARES MICROPHONE MODELER

Antares makes a cool RTAS plug-in called Microphone Modeler. This plug-in takes the input from your source mic (e.g., a Shure SM57) and sonically alters the signal to give it the characteristics of another mic (e.g., a Neumann U 87). For more information on Antares, check appendix D.

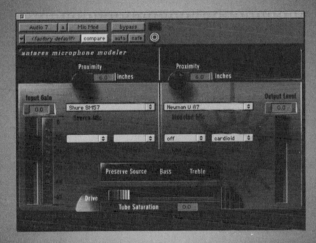

Antares Microphone Modeler plug-in.

If you own and plan to use the Microphone Modeler plug-in in your mix, you should write down all the information about what mics you used on what instruments and where they were placed in relation to the instrument. Also note what pickup pattern you used and if you used a pad or rolloff. This will help you use the Microphone Modeler plug-in more effectively during mixdown.

RECORDING TURNTABLES AND SERATO'S SCRATCH PLUG-IN

Recording turntables through a DJ mixer is really straightforward. Just connect the mixer to any two line inputs on your Digi hardware. Often, there are a number of ways to adjust the output volume on a DJ mixer. Just be aware of the signal flow, and don't overload the inputs to Pro Tools.

A new way to record turntables in your Pro Tools sessions is by using Serato's Scratch RTAS plug-in. Within Pro Tools, Scratch allows you to scratch any digital sample or sound file on your computer using your existing turntables (or even your mouse without the turntables) as the controller. Special vinyl records included with Scratch contain a control signal that allows your computer to track the motion of each record, simulating the same movement within the digital sample. Check it out . . . it's really amazing!

The recording setup for Scratch is a little different than the standard turntable setup described previously. The output of the turntables (i.e., the control signal) is routed into Pro Tools by plugging the turntables directly into the line inputs on your Digi hardware. The selected audio sample is then routed out of Pro Tools to the DJ mixer for crossfading, cutting, etc. Audio from the DJ mixer can then be routed directly to your speakers, or back into Pro Tools for recording. For more information on Scratch and Serato, see appendix D.

CHECKING THE SOUNDS

Once you've set up microphones on a particular instrument, record a sample clip and listen back to the track(s). Think about issues like:

- Does it sound good?

- Are you capturing the sound you heard from the source?

- How are the recording levels?

- Is the signal path correct (from mic to Pro Tools)?

- Are there any unexplained noises on the track?

If the track *doesn't* sound the way you want it to, ask yourself these questions:

- Is anything along the signal path malfunctioning?

- Should you be using a different mic?

- Should the mic be moved to a different place?

- Should you use a different pickup pattern?

- Should you use the mic's pad and/or rolloff?

- Are you getting too much leakage from other instruments?

- Are you getting too much or too little room ambience?

- Do you hear any phase cancellation?

TROUBLESHOOTING THE SIGNAL PATH

If a signal from an input isn't getting into Pro Tools, check all points along the signal path. Start with the mic or the instrument input: Check to see if the cable is plugged in properly, and try giving it a jiggle. If that connection seems fine, it could be a bad cable. Try a different cable. Then move on to the input on your Digi hardware, your mixer, or your outboard mic preamps. Is the connection good between the cable and the input? Is the input gain high enough? Is phantom power on? Check any other connections that route your signal to your computer. Finally, make sure Pro Tools is configured properly. Is the correct track record-enabled? Are the right input and output paths chosen?

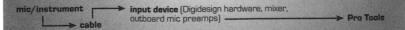

mic/instrument → input device (Digidesign hardware, mixer, outboard mic preamps) → Pro Tools
cable

Always follow the signal path when you're trying to track down a problem.

■ **Fig. 11.5.**
Printing effects to a track through an aux track. Notice that bus 3 takes the effected input and sends it to an audio track for recording.

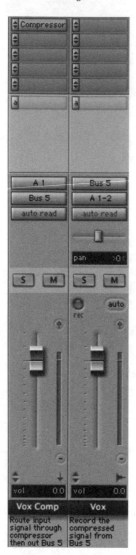

■ **Fig. 11.5.**
Printing effects to a track through an aux track. Notice that bus 3 takes the effected input and sends it to an audio track for recording.

■ **Fig. 11.6.**
I/O setup for printing effects from an outboard processor.

PRINTING EFFECTS TO TRACKS

Sometimes you may find it appropriate to record (or "print") effects to a track. For example, you might want to compress a vocal on its way into Pro Tools, or you may really like a particular effect that you're sure you want to keep for the final mix. However, if you put a compressor plug-in as an insert on the vocal track, remember that inserts effect tracks *after* the signal has already been recorded to disk; they are "post-disk." Therefore you won't actually be printing the effect.

To actually record effects (e.g., to print reverb, compression, etc.) on a track using plug-ins, you need to create an aux input and route the input signal through it. Figure 11.5 shows an Aux input (mic 1 of Digi 001) that's routed to a compressor plug-in, then through the output onto bus 5. Bus 5 (which has the compressed vocal on it) then becomes the input for a mono audio track. In this case, the compressed vocal signal is "pre-disk," so it's recorded.

To record compression using an outboard compressor you would first patch the vocal mic through a preamp on your Digi 002/001 and create a "send/return" setup using outputs and inputs of your 002/001. The setup is similar to the one shown in figure 11.5, but instead of using an internal Pro Tools bus you'd select an output and input for the inserted compressor. For example, you would plug 002/001 output 7 into your compressor input and the compressor output into 002/001 input 7. (Note: The output and input don't have to be the same number.) Then select output 7 on the aux track and input 7 on the lead vocal, as shown in figure 11.6.

If you are using an analog piece of outboard gear with Digi 002/001 mic preamps, this setup introduces some delay due to D/A/D (digital/analog/digital) conversion. If you are using a digital piece of outboard gear, there is no conversion delay, but you will still experience the tiny amount of delay that always happens when routing through the internal busses of Pro Tools.

To use an outboard compressor with the Mbox, a mixer, or an outboard mic preamp, you should connect your compressor to the Insert patch point. In the signal path, it comes before the A/D conversion, thus you won't experience the extra conversion delay found in an 002/001send/return setup.

Note: When printing effects to disk be sure you're not overloading the signal path at any point. For example, if you're recording vocals through an outboard compressor you might not see clipping in Pro Tools software, but the mic preamp could be distorting on loud notes. Watch your levels at all points in the signal path and use your ears to detect any worrisome sounds.

HEADPHONE MIXES

If you're recording using microphones, 99% of the time you'll want to turn off your studio monitors and track with headphones on so you don't get leakage or feedback from the speakers. To do this you'll need to create a headphone mix (sometimes called a "cue mix" or "foldback"). A good headphone mix allows the performer to clearly hear their part along with the other instruments and voices while recording. Often you can use the mix you're already listening to (i.e., the main stereo mix) and simply plug everyone into that signal (depending on where you have your headphone feed in your home studio, as discussed in chapter 1). Usually you can adjust the levels of each track in this one headphone mix so it's good enough for everyone. This gets more difficult the more people you're trying to track at once. However, with Pro Tools LE you can create multiple headphone mixes and tailor each one to an individual's liking!

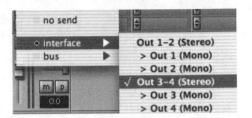

Fig. 11.7.
Select send outputs to create multiple headphone mixes in Pro Tools.

There are two main ways to create multiple headphone mixes in Pro Tools: sends and multiple outputs. On your Digi 002/001 there are four stereo analog output pairs. You can listen to up to four different stereo headphone mixes. (In fact, Pro Tools LE can create up to 12 different stereo headphone mixes using busses and multiple output assignments, though you can only listen to four at a time through your Digi 002/001.)

As you've learned in previous chapters, a **send** is simply a way to route a copy of a signal. Besides creating separate headphone mixes, sends can be used to route signals to any internal mix bus or outboard effects units. Pro Tools allows for five sends per track; that is, five copies of the original track can be sent somewhere else. (You can find more information on sends in chapters 3, 9, and 12.)

Fig. 11.8.
A multiple headphone mix setup.

Included on the CD-ROM are Pro Tools sessions titled "Multiple HP Mixes Sends." Check out the track setups in those sessions to learn how to create multiple headphone mixes using sends.

Included on the CD-ROM are Pro Tools sessions titled "Multiple HP Mixes Outputs." Check out the track setups in those sessions to learn how to create multiple headphone mixes using multiple outputs.

When creating multiple headphone mixes you can use your 002/001's main outputs (outputs 1–2) as the main headphone mix and each stereo output pair as an additional mix. For example, you may want to send only the drums and guitar on a stereo output to the vocalist. To do this, choose outputs 3–4 on the same send (e.g., send "a") from each drum and guitar track. Do this for all of the tracks you want to go to that headphone mix, then set the volume level and panning for each track in the submix.

Create a stereo master fader and choose outputs 3 and 4 (in its output section) to control the overall level of the send. Just like any other track, a master fader that controls a separate submix can have automation and plug-ins. And another positive note about master faders: They don't consume any CPU power.

To sum up sends: You control the volume and panning of each track by its individual send volume and pan. You control the overall send level, panning, automation, and effects with the send's master fader. All you have to do now is connect the outputs (e.g., outputs 3–4) of your 002/001 to a headphone amp, mixer, or some other piece of equipment that allows musicians to listen to your separate headphone submixes. Figure 11.8 shows how the volumes of each track in the main mix (outputs 1–2) can differ from those in the separate headphone mix (outputs 3–4). Note the volume numbers.

Using multiple outputs for creating multiple headphone mixes is easier to set up than using sends, however you don't have as much control over the volume and panning of each track. Say the drummer only wants to hear guitar and bass in his headphones, with no drums. Without the work involved in creating a send, simply assign the guitar and bass tracks to multiple outputs (e.g., outputs 1–2 and 7–8). This will create a copy of the track (with the same volume, panning, plug-ins, etc.) and send it to both assigned stereo outs. To do this you must first assign a main output path, then press Control and click to select an additional output. (Notice the check marks next to the two selected output paths in figure 11.9.) Option + Control + click (Mac) or Alt + Control + click (Win) to add the assignment to all tracks, or Option + Shift + Control + click (Mac) or Alt + Shift + Control + click (Win) to add the output assignment only to selected tracks.

▌ Fig. 11.9.
Selecting multiple outputs is easier than creating sends, but less flexible.

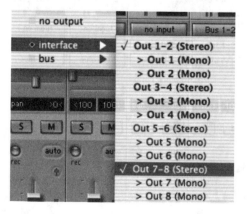

COMBINING TRACKS — SUBMIXES
If you think you might come close to filling all available tracks in Pro Tools, you should consider combining some tracks to free up space for additional comping or overdubs. There are three ways to record submixes to new tracks in Pro Tools: using sends, recording to tracks, and bouncing to disk.

I like to use sends for submixing in the same way as the previous headphone mix examples. One advantage of using sends this way is you can control the volume, panning, and mutes of each track from the send controls instead of the main track fader and its controls. Another big advantage is that you can mute the individual tracks and hear the combined (submixed) track easier than by other methods of submixing in Pro Tools.

The signal that's sent on a bus from a track's send includes inserts (plug-ins) but does not contain effects from other aux tracks. In other words, all of your plug-in effects on each bussed track will be sent to the submix. But if you want to include the effects from an aux track, you also need to assign *its* output to the submix bus.

When you combine tracks in a submix be careful of the effects you use – they'll be printed on the files permanently! Depending on the tracks that you're combining, you might want to wait to add effects until the mixdown. Regardless, you should probably make backup copies of the files you're going to combine in case, at some point later, you're not happy with the submix and you want to bring back the original tracks.

A slightly different way to create a submix is called "recording to tracks." Using this method you assign the outputs of the tracks you want to combine to a bus, and then assign the input of the *new* track(s) to that bus. This is easier to set up than the sends method and allows you use any automation you've recorded on the submixed tracks (though you *can copy* automation data to a send). However, recording to tracks doesn't allow you to hear only the combined track: If you mute a track it'll be taken out of the bus, and won't get to the submixed track, or if you solo the submixed track you'll hear nothing. That's the reason I usually use the send method for submixing.

Both of the above submixing methods require at least one open track (to record the submix). However, if you've already filled every track but need to free up some more, the only option you have is to bounce a submix to disk. You don't need to reserve any tracks when you bounce to disk, and it does offer some additional advantages including conversion options for sample rate, bit resolution, and file format.

The CD-ROM includes a session called "Submix Using Sends." Check out the signal flow . . . see where each audio signal is routed. Adjust send levels, effects levels, track volumes, etc. to hear the effect on the overall submix.

The CD-ROM includes a session called "Submix Recording to Tracks." Check out the signal flow . . . see where each audio signal is routed. Notice the differences between submixing with sends and recording to tracks.

ROUGH MIXES

Most musicians (including artists, producers, and engineers) like to take something home to listen to after they've recorded all day. The engineer is in charge of making rough mixes for this purpose.

To make a rough mix you should do the following:

1. Create a master fader track assigned to your main outputs (e.g., 1–2 002/001 Outs).

2. Assign all channels to the main outputs.

3. Adjust your channel faders to create a good relative balance of the tracks.

4. Pan each channel as you want and add some preliminary EQ or effects, if desired.

You'll probably be tweaking the sounds and levels while the session is going on, so often you can simply bounce each session directly to disk using the Bounce to Disk command. All audible tracks with their inserts and sends are included in the bounce and all read-enabled automation is performed. To bounce to disk, select the portion of audio you want to record (using the Selector Tool) and choose Bounce to Disk from the File menu. The window shown in figure 11.10 will open.

Fig. 11.10.
The Bounce to Disk function is useful for rough mixes at the end of a session.

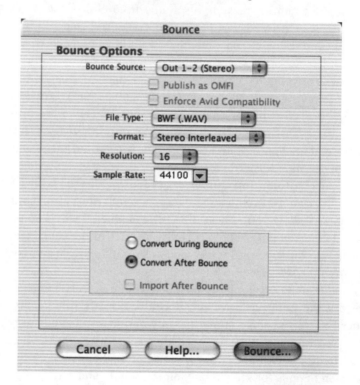

If you want to take the bounce and burn it to a CD-R immediately, select Stereo Interleaved as the format, 16-bit as the resolution, and 44100 as the sample rate. Bouncing takes place in real time – Pro Tools will play through the entire audio selection. Once it's done bouncing (and converting), the file will be ready to burn to a CD-R. (Consult chapter 13 for more information on this topic.)

Many engineers like to do some amount of mixing for their "roughs." That is, they like to add EQ, effects, and other processing to make the best sounding tracks in a short amount of time. That makes the producer and artist happy and adds value to the recording they're taking home. It also makes the engineer (you) look good and can save time at the beginning of a mix session (because all of your settings are saved in

Pro Tools' total recall mixer). Consider performing some basic mixing before making the final bounces for the session. And if you recorded your files at 24-bit, I recommend creating a stereo master fader for the final output of the session (if you don't already have one) and inserting the Digidesign Dither plug-in on that track. That way your 24-bit stereo track will be dithered while it's converted to a 16-bit file. (Chapter 13 explains the dithering process fully.)

AT THE END OF THE SESSION

Once you're done with the session, be sure to save your files and make backups! Nothing is worse than losing files you worked on all day — or worse, an artist's once-in-a-lifetime performance. And finally, cleaning up the studio after the session and doing any preventative maintenance on equipment (from dusting to defragmenting) keeps your studio in good working order. It also makes it more pleasant to come back to the next day. ▌▌

▐ PRO TOOLS HANDS-ON

Capture Good Sounds – Multiple Mic Techniques

There are thousands of ways to capture great sounds. As you were experimenting in chapter 7 with mic placement and technique, did you compare the sounds of different mics on one sound source? Sometimes using multiple microphones to record one sound source will yield a better overall recording, because the frequency response curves of each individual mic combine in a sonically pleasing way. Although you could try to predict what mics might sound good together by evaluating their frequency response curves, what fun is that? The true test is how they sound together.

Open the Pro Tools session "multiplemics" in the BookProjects folder and listen to the sounds of several mics on a kick drum and on an electric guitar. Listen to each track individually and in combination with any or all of the other mics. Check out the Comments section for each track to see how the track was recorded and then critically evaluate the sounds. Which sounds do you like best?

Auto-Tune a Vocal Comp

After you've recorded and comped your vocal tracks, it's common to tune them using Antares' Auto-Tune plug-in. Auto-Tune has two modes of operation: Automatic and Graphical. Automatic mode does the tuning for you as the track plays back. Useful in some cases, this mode is often bypassed in favor of the user-controllable Graphical mode. Graphical mode enables you to see the pitches of each vocal note plotted against the notes of a scale. You can then manually alter the pitch of each note by drawing new pitch lines/curves in the Auto-Tune window. Then you can re-record the tuned vocal on a new track.

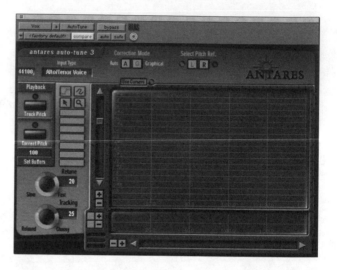

Open the session "Tuned Vocal" and check out the difference between an untuned raw vocal take and the fine-tuned vocal comp track. Also notice how the vocal signal is routed from the original track through Auto-Tune to a new track for recording. Then, try using Auto-Tune for yourself. Use Auto-Tune in Graphical mode to tune a vocal track in any Pro Tools session. If you don't have Auto-Tune, download a free demo version from the Antares Web site (www.antarestech.com) and take it for a spin.

Pre-mix Editing – Preparing Your Tracks to be Mixed

The bulk of the editing process usually occurs after recording and before mixing the final tracks. Although I covered editing techniques in chapters 4 and 5, here are two editing tasks that can help to tidy up your Pro Tools session for mixdown: reducing extraneous track noise and consolidating regions.

Strip Silence and Insert Silence

Stripping out the extraneous noise from tracks by inserting silence can really clean up the sound of your tracks. Use the Clear command, delete and/or mute regions, draw volume or mute automation, or try the Strip Silence or Insert Silence command.

The Strip Silence command examines a selection of audio data, divides the selection into regions based on amplitude, and removes any regions where the amplitude falls below a certain level. In other words, it acts like a noise gate. Any sound below a certain threshold value is replaced with silence. This feature is very useful if your tracks have some low level noise on them, such as fan noise or leakage from headphones. However, if you record your tracks well (that is, without extraneous noise), you may never need to use this feature.

Try it. Select any audio file in a Pro Tools session and choose Show Strip Silence from the Windows menu. The following window will open.

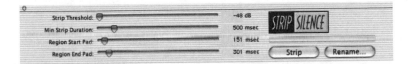

A signal that falls below the Audio Threshold parameter is considered silence. The Minimum Strip Duration is the smallest amount of time that a track has to be under the Threshold for it to be considered silence. (The larger you make this number, the fewer regions you'll create.) The Region Start Pad and Region End Pad specify the amount of time to be added on either end of a new region generated by Strip Silence to help retain musical nuances such as breaths before vocal passages and the natural decay of a sound. Adjust the parameters and experiment to see what values give you the best results.

Aptly named, the Insert Silence command makes it easy for you to insert silence into sections of any audio or automation data. It is particularly useful when you want to move a section of audio or automation to a later part in a song, while keeping the track clear of any extra audio and automation data. If automation data is displayed on a selected track and you insert silence on the automation data, the automation data is cleared but the audio remains. In Grid and Slip modes, the Insert Silence command works just like the Clear command. Select Insert Silence from the edit menu and use it to eliminate a portion of audio and automation from a track.

Consolidating

By the time you're satisfied with an edited track, you most likely have a whole bunch of edits on it. Your edit playlist may contain many regions, like the messy edit playlist shown below.

You can clean up your files and make them easier to mix by consolidating your tracks. Consolidating combines multiple regions into a single region, making the track easier for you to work with, and much easier for your hard drive to locate and process. Because every individual edit consumes precious processing power from your computer, the less edits you have when you go to mix, the more processing power will be available for adding plug-ins to your mix.

When you consolidate an audio track, Pro Tools writes a whole new audio file that combines selected material on a track, including blank space. Muted regions are treated as silence, yet if the track itself is muted, or there is Mute automation on the track, the Consolidate Selection command will not treat the track or the auto-muted areas as silence. Here's what the same track looks like after it's been consolidated.

To consolidate audio within a track, first select the material that you want to consolidate with the Selector or Grabber. (Triple-click anywhere in an edit playlist with the Selector to highlight all the material on that track.) Then choose Consolidate Selection from the Edit menu [or type Shift + Option + 3 (Mac) or Shift + Alt + 3 (PC)].

It's a good idea to copy the edited track material onto another playlist first by choosing Duplicate from the Playlist Selector menu. Then, give the new playlist a descriptive name (e.g., Vox Comp Consol Final) and consolidate it. Using this technique, you still have the original unconsolidated track on another playlist so you can easily get back to it without having to undo the Consolidate Selection command. Try it for yourself on any edited track with multiple regions.

Evaluate the Raw Tracks

Check out the raw sounds in the project songs. Listen to the MP3s "Chap11Rockroughmix.mp3," "Chap11Hiphoproughmix.mp3," "Chap11Jazzroughmix.mp3," and "Chap11Electronicaroughmix.mp3" to hear the raw, pre-mixed tracks I recorded for each song. Use these MP3s as comparisons to the mixed tracks in the next chapter.

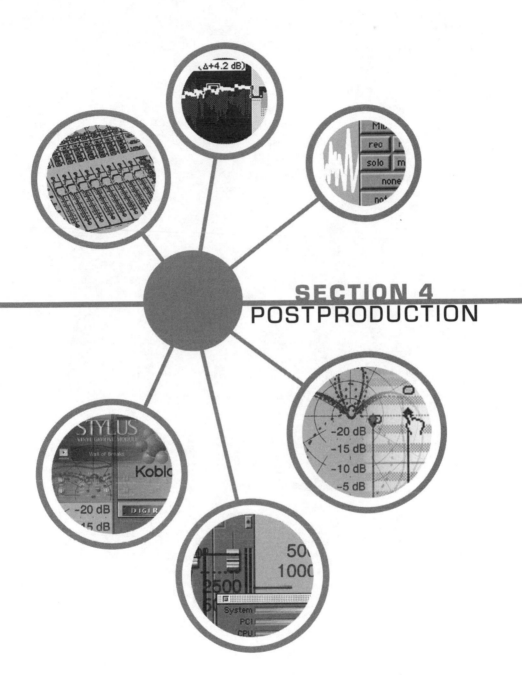

SECTION 4
POSTPRODUCTION

In this chapter:

- **Mix preparation and process**

- **EQ, dynamics, delay, reverb, and other effects**

- **Writing and editing automation, automating plug-ins**

- **Testing and characteristics of a good mix**

- **Surround sound mixing**

With all of the tracks recorded now, you're ready to mix. Pro

Tools provides an incredibly flexible and creative environment

for mixing. You can customize your virtual work space,

insert effects without physical patching, record and draw

automation data, plus much more, and you can save it all in

your Pro Tools session.

BEFORE THE MIX

Once all your recording is finished you can begin to seriously edit and mix your tracks. This is when you formulate ways to make your project sound like it did in your head before you started (i.e., your vision of the music).

Before beginning your mix you should (a) arrange your tracks so they're in the basic song form, if they're not already, (b) edit the tracks,* (c) clean up the tracks, and (d) group tracks to make editing and mixing easier. By cleaning up your tracks, I mean deleting unwanted tracks or regions that have nothing useful on them. (*Editing, usually considered part of postproduction, is covered in chapters 4, 5, and 11.)

And to help mix multiple tracks at once you should set up groups. Highlight each track you want in a group by pressing the Shift key while clicking on the track name, then press ⌘ + G (Mac) or Control + G (Win). Give the group a short and descriptive name, like "Ac Gtrs" for your four acoustic guitar tracks. To link the tracks in both Edit and Mix windows, choose Edit and Mix from the Group Type selector as seen in figure 12.1.

A group is active if the name of the group is highlighted in the Edit Groups or Mix Groups window to the left of your Edit or Mix window. Click on the group name to toggle between making it active or inactive.

Fig. 12.1.
Grouping tracks (like all the backing vocals, or the drum kit) can make mixing go faster.

INTRO TO MIXING

A mix is the combination of all your recorded tracks reduced to two tracks (for stereo playback) or six to eight tracks (for surround playback). The goal of mixing is to create an overall sound that helps support the purpose of the song . . . and doing that well is an art! You want to put the listener in an appealing acoustical space by tweaking individual sounds (volume levels, panning, EQ, and effects) and making sure that every element of the soundscape has its place.

Hearing in Three Dimensions

Humans hear in three dimensions; we can localize sounds all around us. As a demonstration, try closing your eyes and listening to your environment. Right now I can hear my computer's fan humming close to me on the right side and, through a window on my left, I hear a plane flying over my apartment. When mixing we can simulate this three-dimensional sound using only two speakers (stereo) or with surround sound. Most mixes these days are still done in stereo so we'll focus on creating an appealing 3D image for the listener using stereo imaging (panning), EQ positioning, and depth. I like to conceptualize three-dimensional stereo sound as shown in figure 12.2.

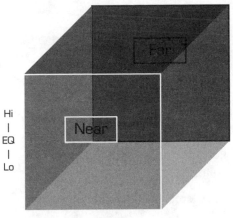

Fig. 12.2.
Think of 3D stereo sound as having three planes: width, height, and depth.

Panning (**width**) is used to place sound sources on the left side, right side, or anywhere between two speakers (see the discussion on phantom image in chapter 1). EQ positioning (**height**) means placing a sound source within one or multiple frequency ranges to separate it from other sound sources. Some call this "carving EQ holes." **Depth** refers to the feeling that a sound source is close to or distant from the listener and is created using reverbs and delays. (Each of these topics is discussed later in this chapter.) It is beneficial to envision a physical layout when placing instruments in this three-dimensional space. Balancing the sound sources visually is a great way to start thinking about your mix.

The Mixing Process

In traditional mixing an engineer receives a tape from a producer and begins to mix from scratch — that is, the mix engineer will get a rough mix on DAT and the raw tracks on 2" analog tape with no set levels, panning, EQ, or effects. In the digital realm this is no longer the case. Using Pro Tools, mixing can be done throughout the recording process, even before the "official" mixing sessions. Track levels, panning, EQ, and effects can be adjusted at any time during tracking and then saved. Thus, you'll probably start each mix session already having a rough mix saved in Pro Tools, allowing you to get right to the creative part of the process.

However, there's still a procedure you may want to follow loosely when mixing. Note that the steps below don't need to be performed in this particular order, and some steps will probably overlap.

- Arrange the tracks: choose best takes, submix tracks, cut/paste/delete tracks, etc.

- Create a rough balance: set starting volume levels and panning assignments, decide what needs to be done to the mix.

- Write mute and panning automation.

Before you start mixing, become familiar with your speakers. Listen to a few of your favorite songs in the genre of the mix you're about to do, and use those songs as reference points for your own mixes.

When starting a mix session you should create a master fader track assigned to your main outputs (e.g., 1–2 001 Outs) and assign all channels to those main outputs.

- Apply equalization and carve EQ holes.

- Add dynamic processing: compression, limiting, gates, expansion.

- Add depth and special effects: reverb, delay, chorus, flange, etc.

- Set final volume levels: add automation on tracks, inserts, and sends.

- Bounce mix to disk in one or more mix passes, save session under new name.

- Check mix(es) on different speakers, at different times, etc., and compare different passes.

- Fix any problems . . . lather, rinse, repeat as needed.

- Bounce more mix passes to create different mix versions (e.g., vocals up mix, etc.).

I'll cover most of these steps here, but please note this chapter is only loosely organized according to the list above. Just like real-life mixing, sometimes things get moved around to improve the flow!

THE PRODUCER'S ROLE DURING THE MIX PROCESS

If you're mixing with a producer and/or an artist who's producing, they are essentially the directors for the mix session(s). Although the mix engineer has a lot of creative input, the producer and/or artist is ultimately responsible for the project, so they're the ones who make the final decisions. It's the engineer's job to create the sound the producer or artist wants — this is true even when you're producing your own tracks. Listen to the producer inside of you. Detach yourself from all the hard work you've put into your mix and listen like you're hearing it for the first time.

Producers and artists tend to use non-technical terms for describing the sound of a mix. (In fact, some even use colors, like "orange," to describe sound.) You should try to learn this vocabulary so you can interpret what they mean. For example, if a producer says "I think the mix should be warmer," this usually means they want you to boost the low end. Likewise, if they want it "fatter" and "more spacious," you might want to add chorus and reverb, respectively. To help you learn the vocabulary some of these terms are listed in the EQ section later in this chapter. (And a hint for working with color-sensitive producers: "orange" is sometimes used to describe the low-mid frequencies.)

ARRANGING THE TRACKS

Often you'll have multiple takes of a song or particular track. So before you begin mixing, you need to make some decisions about what takes are best to include in your mix. You may need to make a comp – a compilation of the best parts of multiple takes – on a track or two. For example, creating a lead vocal track by comping together multiple takes is very common. This is often done with instrumental solos as well, but can be done on any type of track. (I've even comped ten drum tracks together to create a killer rhythm part.)

Another option you should consider is bouncing multiple tracks down to fewer tracks (also called submixing, as covered in chapter 11). Drums are a good candidate for that. For example, I often bounce multiple tom tracks to two tracks (stereo). I also combine many MIDI tracks (recorded as audio tracks, like a MIDI string section) onto two tracks. You can do this for any combination of tracks, provided you plan to treat the combined tracks with the same volume, panning, EQ, and effects.

It's also helpful to place markers in your session to delineate the song. As seen in figure 12.3, I usually label each section of the song (verses as V1, V2, choruses as C1, C2, etc.) so I can jump to those sections easily using the Memory Locations window when mixing.

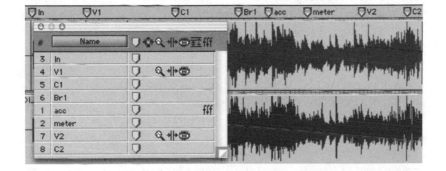

Fig. 12.3.
Markers make it easy to quickly assess your mix at different points in the song.

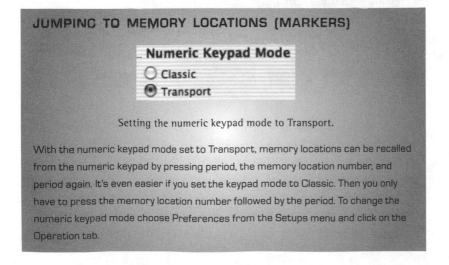

JUMPING TO MEMORY LOCATIONS (MARKERS)

Numeric Keypad Mode
○ Classic
◉ Transport

Setting the numeric keypad mode to Transport.

With the numeric keypad mode set to Transport, memory locations can be recalled from the numeric keypad by pressing period, the memory location number, and period again. It's even easier if you set the keypad mode to Classic. Then you only have to press the memory location number followed by the period. To change the numeric keypad mode choose Preferences from the Setups menu and click on the Operation tab.

CREATING A ROUGH BALANCE

I've seen three basic methods to beginning a mix: In the digital realm many people start with the rough mix from the tracking session(s) and build on that. Others use the rough mix as a guide, but essentially start over building a mix around either the drums and bass or the lead vocal or instrument track. Regardless of how you want to start, you need a solid foundation with the rhythm section; the drums and bass must be mixed well in relation to each other. Also, the lead vocal or lead instrument should be prominent — not covered by other instruments — without sounding detached from the rest of the music.

Allow some headroom for these main instruments! Don't start your mix with them too high or else you'll have no room to raise their levels if required. Try to set them around 0.0 and build your mix from there. Once you've found comfortable levels for the main instruments you can add the rest of the instruments piece by piece, in order of importance. And while you're adding instruments and building a good general balance among everything, pan the tracks to fill out the stereo image. Think of the tracks visually along a line from left to right....

The kick drum, snare drum, bass, and lead vocal/instrument tracks are usually centered in the stereo image. Toms and cymbals are usually panned, but not totally hard left and right because that doesn't sound very realistic. Also, when panning drums think about whether you want them panned from the audience's perspective or the drummer's. Keyboards are often panned left and right for a stereo spread and guitar tracks are often doubled, with each track panned to spread the stereo image nice and wide. Stereo pairs are also common on horns, strings, and even percussion to provide expanded sonic width and balance. However, don't take my word for it. Experiment . . . each song will most likely call for different panning schemes so keep an open mind and try new techniques. Also, once you get further into the mix you can automate the panning of your tracks (and effects) to create more interesting stereo movement.

Fig. 12.4.
Visual placement of instruments in the stereo image.

At this point in the mix procedure you should ask yourself some questions: What kind of acoustical space do you want to put the listener in? Who is this mix for? What kind of overall sound do you want to create? What specific effects do you want to use? Are there any special arrangement issues to consider (long fades, big mutes, etc.)? Try to plan some of these things out before you continue the session.

MONITOR LEVEL DURING A MIX

It's a good idea to keep your monitor level fairly consistent while mixing. That way you'll have a fixed reference level against which to measure any changes that you make. Some people like to mix at loud volumes. This often makes your mix sound impressive, but can be very fatiguing to your ears. *Take breaks to rest your ears if you mix at high volumes!* Mixing at lower volumes won't tire your ears as much, but it may not be as exciting. However, if you mix at a lower volume, crank things up at the end of the session and reward yourself with how cool your mix sounds loud. Check out the "Permissable Exposure to Noise Levels" graphic in chapter 3 for more information on monitor levels.

Note: People will listen to your songs loudly in their cars while they're speeding down the interstate, or softly while they're working in their offices. Your mixes must convey the music at all volume levels so, near the end of your mix session, listen at many different levels and find out if you can hear what you need to hear.

WRITING MUTE AND PANNING AUTOMATION

Once I've got a rough mix I usually record or draw mute automation on any track that needs it. For example, I sometimes mute tom tracks between drum fills so I don't have to use gates on the toms or ride their levels. I'll do the same on guitar tracks to eliminate amp hum. In fact, I might even completely delete a section of the track if I know it contains no useful audio, just to clean things up and make the mix easier. (As covered in the previous chapter, there are several ways to do this including deleting sections manually, using the Insert Silence or Strip Silence command, or writing volume automation data.) In fact, if you find that your mix appears cluttered with too many parts, you may decide to leave some tracks out during parts or even for the entire song. Muting tracks is an effective way to unclutter a mix or create interesting contrast between different sections of a song.

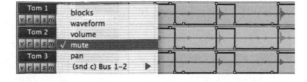

Fig. 12.5.
Writing mute automation makes it easy to silence unneeded portions of tracks.

To write mute automation, I like to draw it in using the Pencil tool on the Mute track view in the Edit window. In the case of figure 12.5, I can see when and where the toms are hit and unmute the tracks. Being able to see the waveforms is probably the biggest time saver in digital editing! On any audio track you can automate the volume and panning the same way. (More info on automation later in this chapter.)

THE DANGER IN MUTING

Be careful when using mute automation . . . sometimes an obvious mute can sound strange. For example, when muting toms you take away some of the ambience provided by the tom mics, only to add it back in when unmuting the toms for a fill. Depending on how the track was recorded, muting may not sound good so you may want to use volume rides or gates instead. Even though you can use your eyes to edit digitally, as always, let your ears be the true guide.

If you find you're running out of CPU power because you have too many plug-ins running at one time, try processing some of your tracks using AudioSuite versions of the RTAS plug-ins. See chapter 9 for more information on how to do this.

USING PLUG-INS IN PRO TOOLS

Since I'm going to cover EQ, dynamics processing, and effects next, a word about using plug-ins is in order. When you add an RTAS plug-in on an insert of a track in Pro Tools, that plug-in is treated as a **prefader insert** on all types of tracks except master faders. This means the plug-in input level isn't affected by the track's volume fader (except when used on a master fader). Therefore, clipping can occur if you boost the Gain parameter in the plug-in. The onscreen track meters are *post-plug-in*, so you can tell if you're overloading the track when the red peak light is triggered. Also note that inserts are processed in series, that is, each effect inserted on a track is processed one after another from top to bottom in the Mix window.

In addition to using inserts you can also use sends for signal processing applications. If you want to apply the same plug-in or outboard processor to multiple tracks, send all of those tracks on a bus to the plug-in (on an aux track) or an outboard processor using the physical inputs and outputs of your Digidesign hardware. This technique saves CPU processing power and is covered in chapter 9 in the "Using Sends, Busses, and Auxiliary Tracks" section.

In Pro Tools LE there are several features that can really improve your effectiveness when working with plug-ins. By deactivating the Target button on a plug-in, for instance, you can open multiple plug-in windows at once.

Clicking the Target deactivates (black Target) and activates (red Target) the button.

Also, Shift-clicking a plug-in opens it with the Target already deactivated (allowing you to open multiple plug-in windows). Option-clicking (Mac) or Alt-clicking (Windows) on the Close box of any plug-in closes all open plug-ins. You can also drag plug-ins from one insert to another on a particular track, or from track to track. Option-dragging (Mac) or Alt-dragging (Windows) a plug-in to another insert creates a copy of the plug-in (with the same settings) in the new position. Pressing Control + ⌘ (Mac) or Control + Start (Win) while clicking on an insert will make the plug-in inactive (the name appears darkened and in italics).

USING OUTBOARD EFFECTS PROCESSORS

In contrast to plug-ins in Pro Tools, many outboard processors can't remember the settings you make during a mix. If you use outboard processors while mixing be sure to write down the parameter settings, or save mix-specific programs so you can recall them later if necessary. Some processors can also be set and controlled by MIDI data. Learning how to use this feature on your gear is invaluable because you can record the MIDI data in your Pro Tools session. See chapter 8 for information on how to connect analog and digital outboard processors to Pro Tools.

APPLYING EQUALIZATION

When you play a musical instrument, that instrument produces many frequencies even if you play only one note. These frequencies make up the **frequency spectrum** of the instrument, and the spectrum gives the instrument its tone quality or timbre. There are several reasons to apply EQ:

- To improve the tone quality (timbre) of an instrument.

- To create a special effect (like a telephone vocal sound).

- To help a track stand out.

- To fix mic choice and placement problems (like frequency, leakage, or noise issues).

- To create a better blend of instruments.

Humans are able to hear frequencies from roughly 20Hz to 20kHz. The chart in figure 12.6 shows the major frequency ranges and words that describe the sound of frequencies within those ranges.

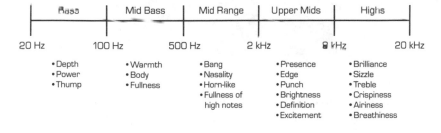

Fig. 12.6.
The major frequency ranges and human perception.

With practice you can learn to identify frequencies and effectively apply EQ to improve your mixes. To help you, I've included a chart (figure 12.7) that shows the major frequency ranges for many instruments.

So what if you want to change a sound using EQ but you're not sure what frequency needs altering? A good methodology for applying EQ in this case is to sweep over a range of frequencies with the gain set to a severe boost or cut to find the sweet spot.

Fig. 12.7.

Frequency ranges for common instruments.

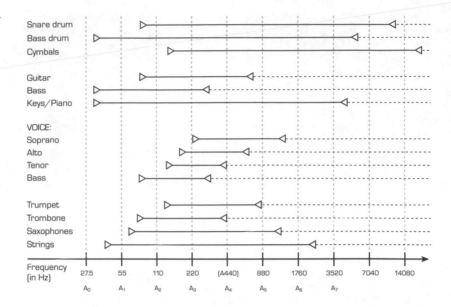

Fig. 12.7.
Frequency ranges for common instruments.

For example, say I want to give the guitar track more of an edgy sound. Figure 12.6 shows that "edge" is found in the upper mid range between 2kHz and 8kHz. So I'd open up an EQ plug-in on my guitar track (like the one-band EQ shown in figure 12.8), increase the gain to 12.0dB, and drag the Freq(uency) slider through the upper mid frequency range.

Fig. 12.8.
The DigiRack one-band EQ. Notice that this plug-in can act as many different types of EQs.

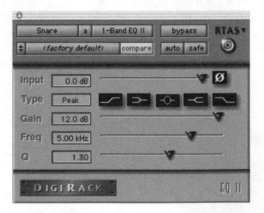

Once you think you've found the right frequency, tweak the sound to your liking then toggle the Bypass button and compare the original to the EQ'd sound. Did you achieve what you wanted? If not, tweak some more.

This DigiRack EQ plug-in provides many EQ options. The one shown in figure 12.8 is a peak equalizer and provides a localized boost or cut at a particular frequency. The bandwidth of the boost or cut (i.e., the other frequencies around the center frequency that are affected) depends on the "Q" value — a higher Q value means the boost or cut is applied to a narrow frequency range; a low Q means the boost/cut affects a wide range. Figure 12.9 shows a Waves Renaissance EQ plug-in with a high Q value (narrow bandwidth), then one with a low Q (wide bandwidth).

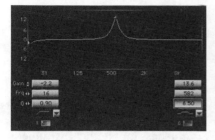 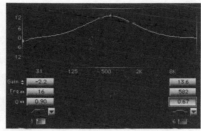

The other types of equalizers are called hi-pass filters, low-pass filters, hi-shelf filters, and low-shelf filters. As the name indicates, **hi-pass filters** allow high frequencies to pass through but cut off low frequencies. **Low-pass** do the opposite — they allow low frequencies to pass through but they cut off the high frequencies. For hi- and low-pass filters, the Q value determines how steep the cutoff curve is. Figure 12.10 shows a hi-pass filter with a low Q value and a low-pass filter with a high Q value.

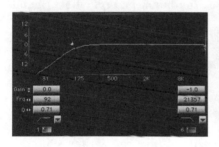 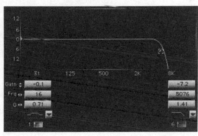

Fig. 12.10.
Hi-pass filter with a low Q value, then low-pass filter with a high Q value.

Hi-pass, low-pass, and shelf filters are useful for rolling off unnecessary frequencies on individual tracks. For example, high frequencies on bass instrument tracks (above 12kHz) are typically useless, and rumbly low frequencies on hi-hat or cymbal tracks don't add anything useful. When trying to clean up a track the use of these filters should be unnoticeable except that they make the track sound more clear. Filters can also be used to create some interesting effects. Try setting up a low- and a hi-pass filter on some of your drum tracks. Experiment . . . there are many cool EQ tricks you can create, especially once you learn to automate plug-ins (covered later)!

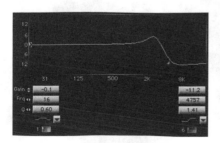 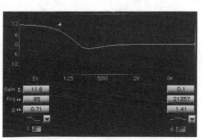

Fig. 12.11.
Hi-shelf filter (cut) with a high Q, then a low-shelf filter (boost) with a low Q.

Carving EQ Holes

Now that you know the many different ways you can affect the frequency ranges of instruments, it's time to think about how that relates to mixing. It is a common practice to "carve EQ holes" for specific tracks. For example, if you want to boost the kick drum and bass tracks, boost different frequencies within each of their ranges. In this case you may want to boost 60Hz on the kick and 100Hz on the bass. Then cut the kick at 100Hz and cut the bass (or another instrument like guitar) at 60Hz. Doing this will carve EQ holes for each instrument and add clarity. (Note: I am *not* saying that each instrument should have its own dedicated frequency range in a mix. Instruments will share frequencies, but clearing a path for the predominant frequencies of certain instruments can "open up" a mix.)

Also be aware that any EQ settings you change on a particular instrument will affect not only *its* sound, but also how the sound of that instrument interacts with all of the others in the mix. When altering EQ don't listen to the track only in solo. You might make the track sound great on its own, but it might not work with the rest of the instruments.

Sibilance

Sibilance refers to the hissing effect, usually found between 6kHz and 8kHz, produced when a vocalist speaks or sings an "ess" sound. With some vocalists this "ess" sound is very prominent (and irritating) and needs to be reduced to improve the overall vocal. Pro Tools comes with a DeEsser plug-in, making it easier to take care of any sibilance problems you encounter.

When you insert this plug-in on a vocal track (as seen in figure 12.12), click on the Key Listen icon and listen for "esses." Adjust the Frequency to find the offending sound and lower the Threshold so the DeEsser will pick up and reduce the "ess" frequency by the desired amount. The Reduction amount is shown as negative values. For more

Fig. 12.12.
The DigiRack DeEsser plug-in can remove unwanted sibilance in a vocal.

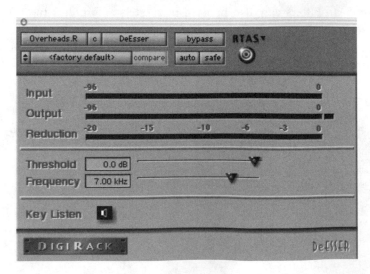

information on this and other DigiRack plug-ins, consult the *DigiRack Plug-Ins Guide* that came with your Pro Tools software.

Watching EQ When Adding Effects

Be aware that every filter or effect you add to a track (EQ, dynamic, and depth processing) will alter your entire mix in some way. So if you EQ a track then add other processing later, the overall EQ on that track and your total mix will change. Therefore, if you find your mixes are getting cluttered (losing definition) in some ranges even though you feel you carved nice EQ holes for each track, you may have to re-EQ them later after you've added your effects — or EQ the effects to combat any unwanted frequency buildups.

ADDING DYNAMIC PROCESSING

The purpose of adding dynamic processing (compression, limiting, gating, expansion) is to alter the dynamic range of a track. This means altering the volume relationship between the loudest and softest sounds.

Compressors

Compressors reduce the dynamic range of signals that exceed a selected threshold (volume level). In other words, they turn down the loudest parts of a track, which helps to manage instruments with wide dynamic ranges like vocals and bass. Using the controls on a compressor, you can tell it how fast to react to a loud signal (attack), at what volume level to start compressing the signal (threshold), how much to compress the signal (ratio), when to let go of the compression (release), and how fast the signal reaches full compression once it passes the threshold (knee).

What does a compressor really do when it's fed a signal? First it looks at the signal and decides if it's above a certain threshold level. If the threshold hasn't been crossed the compressor does nothing. If the signal crosses the threshold, however, the compressor reacts according to the attack speed parameter (measured in milliseconds). It then begins to reduce the volume of the signal according to the ratio and knee parameters.

The ratio dictates how much the signal is compressed. For example, a compression ratio of 4:1 means that an input 8dB above the threshold will come out of the compressor at 2dB. A "hard" knee setting (low number) means compression will take effect very quickly (inflicting the maximum amount allowed), while a "soft" knee means the compressor will ease into the maximum amount. The signal will stay compressed until it falls below the volume threshold. Once the signal is below the threshold it's still compressed until being let go at the release time, and is then allowed to return to its regular, uncompressed volume.

Once a signal has been compressed, the loudest parts are farther away from digital clipping and the overall dynamic range of the track has been reduced. To make up for the lost volume, compressors come equipped with gain controls – because the track's loudest parts have been moderated you can turn up the overall volume of the track. That means the uncompressed softer parts of the track are increased in relation to the compressed louder parts, creating a track with a more uniform volume level. So compression is not only beneficial for controlling loud transient sounds; it's also useful for bringing out softer passages on a track.

Notice the parameter settings in figure 12.13, and the relationship between the Input volume, Ratio, Reduction amount, Gain makeup, and Output volume. Think about the math involved, but let your ear be the ultimate judge for what compression settings yield the best sound for your track.

Fig. 12.13.
The DigiRack Compressor II plug-in.

If you've never used a compressor before, play with all the parameters and see how they affect the signal. If you have any third-party compressor plug-ins check out the presets and compare the settings from one application to the next. Figure 12.14 displays the list of presets for the Waves Renaissance Compressor. Notice the different presets for vocal, drums, bass, and many other applications.

When setting up the parameters of a compressor I recommend adjusting the ratio first. I usually prefer ratios of 3:1 to 6:1 because they yield natural-sounding results. (A ratio of 10:1 is considered limiting, which is discussed in the next section.) Second, set the attack and release times. I usually start with a fast attack time (around 1ms) and a release time of about 500ms. Then I adjust the threshold to give about

3–6dB of gain reduction at the loudest part of the track. (This is simply one technique to get you up and running. Each compression device requires different parameter values to provide its best sound.)

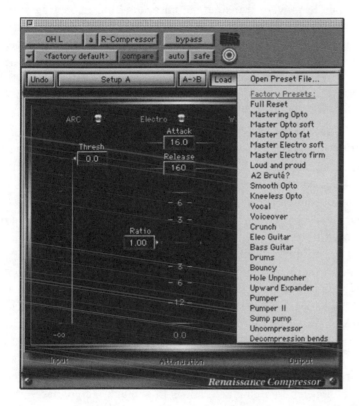

Fig. 12.14.
Presets in the Waves Renaissance Compressor plug-in.

SIDE CHAINS AND KEY INPUTS

Some compressors (like the DigiRack Compressor II) feature **side chain** processing capabilities. A side chain input allows the compressor on one track to "listen" to the varying amplitude of a different audio source, and use that source to trigger compression. The source used to trigger compression is called the external key input. In Pro Tools you can choose any interface or bus as a key input! To activate the key input press the External Key button on the plug-in. If you want to listen to the key source audio and fine-tune the compressor's settings to the key input, press the Key Listen button. Limiters, gates, and expanders often have key inputs as well.

There are many creative mixing techniques that use side chain processing. For example, you can tighten up a bass track by gating it with the kick drum, or trigger a gated synth pad with a click track as the key input. Experiment with side chains to create some fresh effects.

Limiters

Limiters are essentially compressors with ratios of 10:1 or higher. These large ratios set an absolute ceiling on the dynamic range of a signal and are applied to prevent transient signal peaks from exceeding a chosen level. Because of this, limiters (like compressors) allow you to increase the overall track level while avoiding digital clipping. (Note: The DigiRack Limiter II is internally set to a ratio of 100:1 to really clamp down on stray transients, but other limiters may allow you to set the ratio manually.)

Gates

Gates allow signal to pass through them if the signal is above a specified threshold. When the signal is below the threshold, the gate closes, attenuating the signal partially or fully. Gates are utilized to allow the desired (louder) signal to pass through to the output while denying unwanted (softer) signals. Like compressors and limiters, gates can be keyed by a side chain input. They're useful for eliminating unwanted noise on tracks (like guitar amp hum), for creating cool effects like cutting off reverb tails, and many other applications.

What does a gate really do when it's fed a signal? First it looks at the signal and decides if it's above a certain threshold level. If the threshold hasn't been crossed, the gate does nothing (it remains closed). If the signal crosses the threshold, the gate opens up according to the attack speed parameter. The gate stays open for a specified amount of time (the hold time) and then closes after the signal has fallen below the threshold volume, at the speed selected in the decay parameter. The range parameter on a gate determines how much the volume is reduced on a signal that moves below the threshold. The lower the range value (e.g., –80dB), the less volume the gate allows to be heard. Figure 12.15 shows the settings for a gated snare drum.

Fig. 12.15.
The DigiRack Gate II plug-in showing a gated snare.

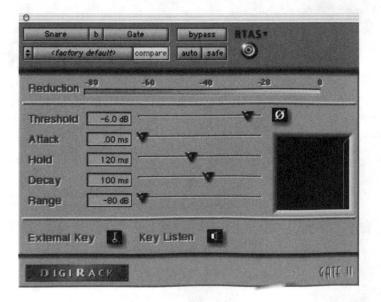

If you want the gate to allow *some* of the volume below the threshold to pass through, increase the range parameter (e.g., –16dB). Gates with medium range values work well when applied to snare drums or toms. A good example is when you want some drum kit leakage on those tracks (below threshold), but want to emphasize the snare hits or tom fills when they're played (above threshold), as shown in figure 12.16. Gates with medium to high range values (–40 to 0dB) are called "expanders," as you'll see in the next section.

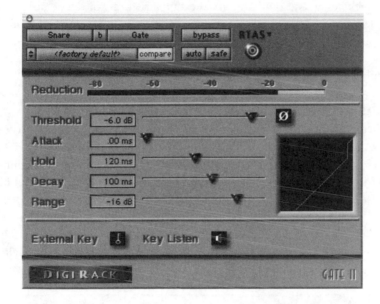

 Fig. 12.16.
The DigiRack Gate ll plug-in showing an expanded snare.

Expanders

Where gates are useful for eliminating unwanted noise between musical sections on a track, **downward expanders** are good for simply lowering the noise, not eliminating it entirely. I prefer using downward expanders to gates in most noise-reducing applications because the level changes aren't as drastic, making them sound more musical. Expanders are also useful for restoring dynamic range to severely compressed tracks. However, because of their function, expanders aren't usually as effective as gates for creating special effects.

Now that you understand the differences between dynamic processors, I hope you experiment with them by shaping your sounds in natural *and* extreme ways. Tweak all of the controls so you hear the processor working and try using the processors on all types of tracks, from individual vocals to your overall stereo mix. Applying dynamic processing can provide power and punch to your tracks while improving the clarity of your mixes. Learn more about DigiRack dynamic processing plug-ins by reading the *DigiRack Plug-Ins Guide.*

Downward expanders turn softer parts down, while upward expanders turn louder parts up. The applications for upward expansion are rare so I'll only cover downward expansion here.

ADDING DEPTH AND SPECIAL EFFECTS

In a three-dimensional mix, we use delay to create the illusion of depth. Delay tricks our brains into thinking that we're in a larger and more interesting listening environment by creating repeats (reflections from the surrounding environment) that combine with the original sound. Short delay times characterize small acoustical spaces, while long delays give the aural illusion of largeness.

Reverb, echo, and chorus effects all revolve around delay. Echo, slapback delay, and doubling are the simplest forms of delay, utilizing a single repeat or several repeats of an audio signal. Chorus (and its brothers the phase shifter and flanger) are short delays slightly varied in time using modulation. Reverb is a complex combination of blended delays that simulate an acoustical environment (like a sports arena or jazz club).

Echo, Slapback Delay, and Doubling

Basically, digital delays (like any of the DigiRack delay plug-ins) record a signal then play it back at a user-selected time delay called "delay time" or "delay length." (A list of effect parameter definitions is included later in this chapter.) A single delay of less than 35ms is called a **double**, because this effect makes the track sound like there are two of the same part being played/sung at basically the same time. A **slapback delay** is a single repeat with a delay time over 35ms. Slapback delay times of 35–75ms are good for thickening vocal or instrumental tracks while delays of 125–350ms are useful for making a vocal or guitar track sound large.

Fig. 12.17.

Delay time calculations with a tempo of 120 BPM.

Tempo (in BPM)	Quarter Note	Eighth Note	Sixteenth Note	Quarter-Note Triplet	Eighth-Note Triplet
D = Delay	D	D ÷ 2	D ÷ 4	D ÷ 3/2	D ÷ 3
120 BPM	500ms	250ms	125ms	333.33ms	166.67ms

It is usually a good idea to set the slapback delay time in relation to the beat and tempo of the song (e.g., eighth note, eighth-note triplet, sixteenth note, etc.). The rhythm you create with the delay can add a nice groove element. To determine a delay time for your song based on a quarter note beat, use the following equation:

60,000 ÷ song tempo (in beats per minute) = D (delay time per quarter note in milliseconds)

For example, say the tempo of your song is 120 BPM. Well, 60,000 ÷ 120 = 500ms. So if you want a sixteenth-note delay on the beat, divide 500ms by four (because there are four sixteenth notes in a quarter note) and you'll have a 125ms delay.

Adding "feedback" to a slapback delay can smooth out the sound of a track. The feedback control sends the delayed signal back into the delay input, creating a delay of the delayed signal. The higher the feedback level, the more delays are created.

Chorus, Phase Shifter, and Flanger

Adding modulation to a delay creates slight pitch variations in the delayed signal. **Modulation**, the varying of delay time, is created using an LFO (low frequency oscillator) and is essential for creating chorus, phase shifter, and flange effects. The LFO speeds up or slows down to alter the playback of the delayed signal, making its pitch rise and fall. These slight variations can actually smooth out pitch problems on a vocal or instrument track.

Remember in chapter 7 when I discussed acoustical phase addition and cancellation? Modulation makes use of these acoustical phasing phenomena. As you recall, total phase cancellation occurs when two entirely out-of-phase waveforms are combined; they cancel each other out to complete silence. Likewise, combining two in-phase waveforms creates a new waveform with twice the amplitude of the original two waveforms; they add together. It follows then that when two waveforms are only slightly out-of-phase with each other, they partially reduce the amplitudes of varying frequencies, while slightly in-phase waveforms partially increase the amplitudes of varying frequencies.

When delayed and slightly pitch-shifted (modulated) signals are combined with each other and the source sound, there is a constantly changing phase relationship between the waveforms. They sum and cancel at varying frequencies. The interaction between the source sound and the modulated delay produces a sound similar to that of several different singers or instrumentalists performing together, and this effect is appropriately called **chorus**. Depth (of modulation) and rate (of modulation) parameters alter the sound of the chorus effect by controlling the amount and speed of the pitch changes. Chorus effects usually have delay times of 20–35ms. Figure 12.18 shows a DigiRack Mod Delay plug-in on a vocal track with modest slapback delay and chorus.

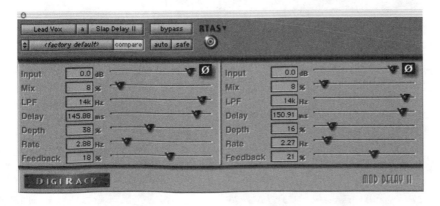

Fig. 12.18.
Slapback delay and chorus on a lead vocal track.

Depth and rate parameters react differently to delay times. If you set the delay time to around 1–3ms you can create a **phase shifter** effect by creating waveforms that are subtly moving in and out of phase. This effect sounds like a mid- and high-frequency EQ sweep and creates an illusion of swooshing motion. Figure 12.19 shows a phase shifter delay effect on a hi-hat track. Flanging is similar to phase shifting, except that it's more dramatic. The delay time for a flange effect is around 10–20ms and the rate and depth can be at a variety of settings according to your taste. Both phase shifters and flangers are useful on guitars, keyboards, and, at times, drums, bass, and vocals. I urge you to play with the parameters of the delay plug-ins just to hear the wacky sounds you can make!

Fig. 12.19.
Phase shifter delay effect on a hi-hat track.

Fig. 12.20.
Phase shifter, flange, and chorus delay times.

Delay Effect	Phase Shifter	Flange	Chorus
Delay time	1–3ms	10–20ms	20–35ms

EFFECT PARAMETER DEFINITIONS

Knowing what the parameters on your effects processors do will help you create the sounds you're looking for.

Wet/dry mix: The mix of the source signal with the effected signal.

Predelay: The time delay before reverb is heard.

Decay time: The time it takes for a sound to disappear (i.e., the total effect time).

Diffusion: The space between reflections/repeats.

Density: The initial buildup of short delay times (reflections).

Feedback: The amount of regenerated signal that's fed back into the processor.

Depth: The amount of pitch variation (in modulation).

Rate: The speed of modulation — how fast the pitch rises and falls.

Room size: The size of the acoustical space.

Plug-ins and outboard effects units might have additional parameters. Consult the manuals for explanations and applications.

Delay Mix Techniques

Putting your delay effects in stereo can really make your mixes sound wide and deep. You can pan your source track to one side and a delayed signal to the other side. Or you can put the source in the middle and pan delayed copies of the source to each side. For this to be effective, select different delay times for each side of the stereo field. Figure 12.21 shows a Waves SuperTap two-tap delay with single delays panned far left and right with delay times of 16ms and 32ms. Different delay times thicken the sound of the source track. You can apply the same technique for chorus, phase shift, and flange. Also, try EQing the delayed signals differently than the source to add more frequency separation, stereo imaging, and character to your mix. And finally, although delay can add much to your mix, *too* much can make your music lose its punch.

Fig. 12.21.
Waves SuperTap two-tap delay showing stereo delay with EQ.

Note: When adding stereo delay effects, sometimes the delayed and original signals can cancel each other out when the mix is summed from stereo to mono. Try routing the tracks with delay to only one output (e.g., output 1 of your Digi 001) through a mono master fader and listen for any cancellation. If the sound is strange or cancelled out in some way, alter the delay times until the effect sounds right in mono.

Reverb and Reverb Mix Techniques

All acoustical spaces (rooms, halls, etc.) have their own sound. The unique sound of a space is created by the combination of reflections from its surfaces: walls, floor, ceiling, and objects. Each individual reflection is a delayed and slightly altered copy of the source sound. When a large number of these reflections are added together, we can't distinguish between the individual signals and they blend together to form **reverb** (reverberation). Some reverbs are created to imitate acoustical spaces (like halls and rooms) and others simulate plate and spring reverbs (which originally were intended to imitate halls and rooms, but eventually took on a sound of their own).

Like delay, reverb is used in mixing to create a sense of depth. When applying reverb to tracks, the wet/dry mix parameter sets the overall amount of depth — how far away a sound is from the listener.

Fig. 12.22.
How the wet/dry percentage affects distance perception.

```
                              Distant
                                 ┬        100% Wet / 0% Dry
         DEPTH                   │
                                 │
         Reverb and Delay        │
                                 ┴        0% Wet / 100% Dry
                              Close
```

Also, the longer the predelay time (the time before reverb is heard), the larger the perceived size of the acoustical space. Check out the reverb parameters on the D-Verb plug-in in figure 12.23.

Fig. 12.23.
Digidesign's D-Verb plug-in. Think about how you'd adjust the parameters shown to emulate the room you're in right now.

Some common uses for reverb are on snare drums, guitars, piano, any group of instruments (horn section, string section, choir, etc.), any lead or backing vocal, and any lead instrument. Like delay, reverb often sounds more impressive if used in stereo. Many plug-ins and outboard effects processors allow mono in/stereo out reverb processing — simply pan out the reverb returns. But be careful! Too much reverb can make your mix less defined and powerful — especially if you apply it to low-frequency instruments like kick drum and bass (which I rarely recommend).

As I stated in the beginning of the chapter, one of the goals of mixing is to put the listener in some sort of acoustical space. That said, try using a combination of different reverb types (like a hall and a room) to add depth and character to your tracks. If you overuse one type of reverb on many different instruments your mix will most likely be less engaging. Gated reverb and reverse (backwards) reverb also have their place, and can sound cool in some applications. And EQing the reverb can be a nice effect as well, differentiating the reverb from the source sound.

Some Final Comments on Signal Processing in Pro Tools

There are innumerable techniques for processing your mixes. I recommend experimenting with all of the parameters of each processor. Also, see how the processors interact with each other when they're used in series (e.g., EQ > reverb > compression vs. compression > EQ > reverb). You'll notice differences that could be very significant to the overall sound of your mix.

Try compressing only certain frequencies. Try using many different tracks or other plug-ins for key inputs on other plug-ins. Keep your mind open to the infinite possibilities of effects processing, practice time-tested techniques, and come up with your own. Your mixes will drastically improve the more you practice and experiment.

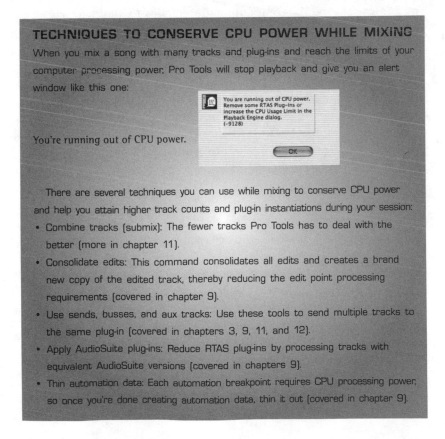

TECHNIQUES TO CONSERVE CPU POWER WHILE MIXING

When you mix a song with many tracks and plug-ins and reach the limits of your computer processing power, Pro Tools will stop playback and give you an alert window like this one:

You are running out of CPU power. Remove some RTAS Plug-Ins or increase the CPU Usage Limit in the Playback Engine dialog. (-9128)

You're running out of CPU power.

There are several techniques you can use while mixing to conserve CPU power and help you attain higher track counts and plug-in instantiations during your session:

- Combine tracks (submix): The fewer tracks Pro Tools has to deal with the better (more in chapter 11).
- Consolidate edits: This command consolidates all edits and creates a brand new copy of the edited track, thereby reducing the edit point processing requirements (covered in chapter 9).
- Use sends, busses, and aux tracks: Use these tools to send multiple tracks to the same plug-in (covered in chapters 3, 9, 11, and 12).
- Apply AudioSuite plug-ins: Reduce RTAS plug-ins by processing tracks with equivalent AudioSuite versions (covered in chapters 9).
- Thin automation data: Each automation breakpoint requires CPU processing power, so once you're done creating automation data, thin it out (covered in chapter 9).

SETTING FINAL VOLUME LEVELS AND EQ

Once you've added the effects you want, begin working on your final mix volume levels and fix any EQ problems that might have been created after adding effects. You've already got a rough mix with decent levels to work from; now it's time to tweak things and create a final blend in which all tracks are heard or felt — but they're not stepping on each other.

When creating your final mix balance, it's a good idea to ride particular tracks to even out the volume of a performance or emphasize a specific section. One of the most important volume rides is on the vocal track: Spend a good amount of time doing this to ensure that every word comes across the way you want it to. This may require such detailed work as boosting particular syllables *within* words to really make the vocal line capture the listener's attention. Also, boost and cut specific tracks when you want to emphasize certain sections (e.g., a bass fill, or a guitar note in a solo that's too low). Subtle volume changes can make all the difference in the effectiveness of your songs. And a necessary tool to create good overall track balance and individual volume rides is automation.

AUTOMATION

You can use several different automation modes to automate volume, pan, mute, send level, send pan, send mute, and plug-in parameter data on audio tracks and volume, pan, mute, and continuous controller data (e.g., sustain) on MIDI tracks. These automation modes are: Auto Write, Auto Touch, and Auto Latch.

Auto Write mode is used for the first time you create automation data on a track, or when you want to completely write over a track's existing automation. After you record automation in Auto Write mode Pro Tools intelligently switches into Auto Touch mode, preventing accidental overwrites on later playback.

Auto Touch mode writes automation data only while a fader or switch is touched or clicked with the mouse. Faders and switches return to any previously automated position after they've been released. (Consult the *Pro Tools Reference Guide* for the behavior of MIDI control surfaces in Auto Touch mode.)

Similar to Auto Touch, **Auto Latch mode** writes automation data only if you touch or move a fader or switch. However, when writing in Auto Latch mode you don't need to keep touching the controls after you've moved them; unlike Auto Touch, they stay in the position where you released them rather than reverting to previously saved data.

Creating automation data: To create automation data, first select Show Automation Enable from the Windows menu and make sure the automation type you want to record is armed. (All types of automation are armed in figure 12.25.) Then choose an automation mode on each

Fig. 12.24.
Dropdown menu showing the different automation modes.

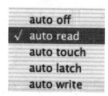

track that you want to automate. Press Play (not Record) and move the automation controls accordingly to write data, and press Stop when finished.

You can mute or solo a group of tracks by selecting Mutes Follow Groups or Solos Follow Groups in the Automation Preferences page. In the same Preferences page, you can have the send mutes and send levels follow groups as well.

Drawing and editing automation data: You can use Auto Touch and Auto Latch to update automation data, or you can edit or draw new automation data graphically. Having worked (frustratingly) with many types of automation systems, I think graphical editing of automation data is one of the coolest features of Pro Tools. Use the Pencil tool to edit or draw new automation data using any one of five shapes: Free Hand, Line, Triangle, Square, and Random. Experiment with each of these . . . try drawing in some cool panning effects for fun. The Trimmer and Grabber tools are also quite useful for editing automation data. (A really effective editing function of the Trimmer tool is presented in chapter 9, under "Eight Features That Can Improve Your Efficiency." Also, see chapter 4 for more information on the Edit tools.)

You can also delete, cut, copy, and paste automation data. When deleting automation data you can:

- Remove a single breakpoint by Option-clicking (Mac) or Alt-clicking (Win) the breakpoint with the Grabber or Pencil tool.

- Remove several breakpoints at once (or all of them) by selecting a range of breakpoints with the Selector and pressing Delete (Mac) or Backspace (Win).

- Remove all automation for all automation playlists on a track by selecting a range of breakpoints with the Selector and pressing Control + Delete (Mac) or Control + Backspace (Win).

In contrast to deleting automation data, removing data with the Cut command creates anchor breakpoints at the boundaries of the remaining data. Note that when you cut, copy, or paste a section of an audio track while you're in Waveform view in the Edit window, all automation data associated with that track section goes with the track.

Turning automation on and off: To play back the automation on a track, put the track in Auto Read mode. Auto Off mode turns off automation for all automated controls on a track. You can also suspend the writing or playback of specific types of automation data on all tracks or individual tracks. To suspend automation writing on all tracks, select Show Automation Enable from the Windows menu and click on

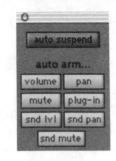

Fig. 12.25.
The Automation Enable window lets you select which parameters will be automated.

Fig. 12.26.
An example of automation drawn with the Pencil tool's triangle shape.

(a) Auto Suspend to suspend all automation writing on all tracks or (b) a specific automation type (volume, mute, etc.) to suspend writing of that automation type. To suspend the playback (and writing) of automation on an individual track, first set the track view selector in the Edit window to display the automation parameter you want to suspend, then:

- ⌘ + click (Mac) or Control + click (Win) the parameter name to suspend writing and playback of only the displayed automation parameter (obeys edit groups except for pan automation).

- ⌘ + Shift + click (Mac) or Control + Shift + click (Win) any parameter name to suspend writing and playback of all automation parameters on that track. (This is the same as selecting Auto Off on a track, and obeys edit groups except for pan automation.)

- ⌘ + Option + click (Mac) or Control + Alt + click (Win) the parameter name to suspend writing and playback of only the displayed automation parameter on *all* tracks.

- To re-enable an automation parameter that has been suspended, perform the same command that you did to suspend it.

Automating plug-ins: Pro Tools makes it easy to automate effects in your mix, opening up many possibilities that are next to impossible to perform on outboard effects processors. The first step is to enable the particular plug-in parameters you want to automate. You do that by clicking on the Automation Enable button in the plug-in window. The window shown in figure 12.27 will appear, allowing you to select the parameters you want to automate for each plug-in on that track.

■ **Fig. 12.27.**
Selecting plug-in automation parameters. Automating plug-ins allows for processing nuances and special effects that are literally impossible on traditional outboard gear.

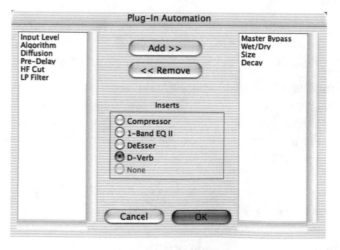

To record plug-in automation, simply choose an automation mode for each track you want to automate, press Play, and away you go. You can edit plug-in automation data in all of the same ways as other track automation by selecting the data from the track view selector (as in figure 12.28).

As you get more familiar with mixing using automation, you'll see how useful each of these features is. The power you have over your music is truly incredible!

In the mix process, you should use automation to create the right volume balance of your tracks, perform any panning moves and track mutes, control your plug-in processing and send levels and mutes, and create fades and other automation on your stereo master fader.

Fig. 12.28.
Selecting plug-in automation data from the track view selector.

I'M BEGINNING TO FADE

Fade-outs are often used at the end of a song as a tool to keep an album flowing and make it appear that the song goes on forever. When creating the fade-out, spend some time to get it right. A short fade-out can sound too abrupt, whereas a long fade loses its effect after a while. Good fade-out lengths are typically 6–16 seconds, depending on the type of music and what's being played at the end. Fades usually start just after the beginning of a musical section (like when a chorus repeats). When fading out, try not to cut a lyric in half (allow it to conclude before fading), and if there's a jam at the end, try to include one last cool lick, sound effect, or vocal phrase as it's fading out. This will make the listener wonder what's happening at the end and turn it up. (For a good example listen to the fade-out of "Every Little Thing She Does Is Magic" by the Police.)

TESTING YOUR MIX

Once you're close to having your final mix levels, panning, EQ settings, and effects, you should test your mix at different overall volumes and on different speakers if you have multiple pairs. Check to see if your mix is effective at low, medium, and high volumes. You might find that the bass disappears at low levels or that the vocal is piercing at high levels. Because people listen to music at different levels, your mixes need to be effective in all volume ranges. Also, people will hear your mixes through all types of speakers, from high-end professional speakers to tiny boomboxes. You might find that the high frequencies really jump out on cheap speakers or that low frequencies are muddy on others. It can be a challenge to make your mixes translate well to all types of speakers.

Often radios have one mono speaker, thus another crucial test for your stereo mix is the "mono compatibility" test. Sometimes stereo signals cancel each other out when summed to mono, obeying the same acoustical phasing principles as discussed in chapters 7 and 11.

As mentioned previously, this cancellation occurs primarily when using stereo delay effects. Before you print your final mix, assign all of your tracks to a mono output (through a mono master fader) and listen for cancellation. In its worst form, cancellation can make entire stereo tracks disappear, or it can simply make your mix sound a little weird.

When you're happy with your mix, bounce down a stereo version and let it be for a spell — don't listen for a while. Try listening again the morning after, in your car, through your friend's home stereo, and/or at a home audio or music store. Listen to it with your eyes closed and from outside your room. Take some notes on how it sounds in each different listening environment. Also, play it for other people to get their response. Then come back to Pro Tools and adjust the mix.

Keep in mind that all the decisions you make while you're mixing are subjective. There is no one perfect mix . . . every person has their own preferences on levels, panning, EQ, and effects. With Pro Tools you can save your mixes to work on them later, allowing you to get away for a while and then return exactly where you left off. The only bad thing about this feature is that now you can mix and remix (and *remix*) the same songs forever and never complete them! Once you get to a certain point with your mix, you need to let it go. If the song is good, a decent mix will get the message across to the listener — you can always improve it later if absolutely necessary. Plus, you can easily make multiple mixes (e.g., vocal up mix) with just a few minutes of work.

CHARACTERISTICS OF A GOOD MIX

Although everyone hears music differently there are some common thoughts on what a good mix sounds like. A good stereo mix has:

- An even balance and nice spread of left and right musical information. The best way to test this is to listen to the mix with headphones.

- Evenly distributed equalization. That means the lows are powerful but controlled, the mids are dispersed well among the different instruments, and the highs are strong yet easy to listen to. EQ holes are carved for each instrument and the overall mix is clean and clear.

- Depth. As we know, delay effects create a sense of three-dimensional space. This means that at least one instrument has to define the close character and one has to define the distant quality.

- Momentum. The song has a flow that the mix enhances by building from the beginning to the end. The intensity and texture of the mix change during the song so the mix isn't stagnant, but rather alive. This helps to keep the listener's attention all the way through the song.

- Consistency. That is, it sounds good on all speakers, in mono, and at all volume levels.

Mix with these characteristics in mind from the beginning, and use the techniques presented here to improve your mixes and create your own sounds. With practice, experimentation, and more practice, you'll begin to create mixes that are exciting, artistic, powerful, and imaginative.

SURROUND MIXING USING PRO TOOLS LE

Although Pro Tools LE doesn't support true multichannel surround sound mixing, there are other ways to mix for surround systems using Pro Tools LE and your Digi 002/001. Using sends, you can build a surround sound mix in the following way. (I'll use a 5.1 surround speaker setup in this example — that is, front left and right, surround left and right, center, and subwoofer.)

First create four paths in the Output section of the I/O Setup window. The first two paths should be stereo paths and the last two should be mono paths. Connect your speakers to the outputs of your Digi 002/001 as shown in figure 12.29.

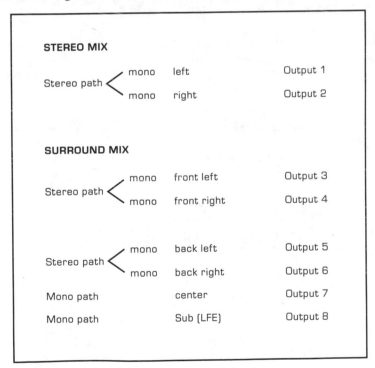

Fig. 12.29.
Connecting your speakers to Digi 002/001 for stereo and surround mixing.

In your session you'll need to create two stereo outputs and two mono outputs in the I/O Setup window. Because routing audio signals in Pro Tools is so flexible, there are several options for creating surround sound setups that make some panning moves easier than others. Figures 12.30, 12.31, and 12.32 show three different options for assigning your outputs. The first setup (figure 12.30) is essentially a glorified quadraphonic setup. You can pan between the front left and right and the surround (back) left and right, as well as feed signal into the center and sub channels simultaneously.

Fig. 12.30.
A quadraphonic-like surround setup.

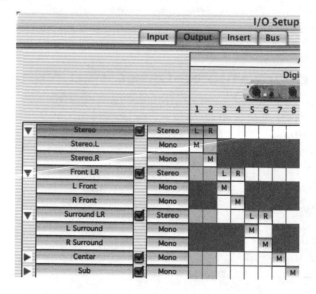

In the second setup (figure 12.31) you can easily pan from front to back on either side, while still feeding the center and sub at the same time.

Fig. 12.31.
Front to back panning surround setup.

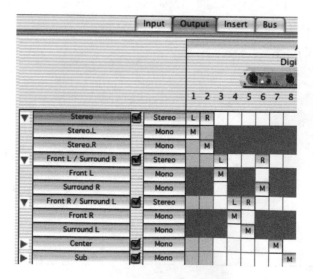

The third setup (figure 12.32) can provide some different and more interesting panning options. With this setup you can pan diagonally (e.g., left front to right surround) and basically anywhere else by adjusting multiple send levels and panning. Try it out . . . it's really cool!

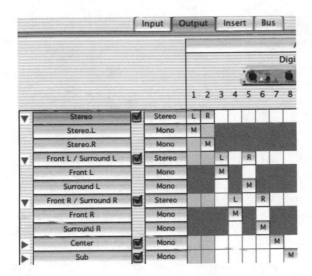

Fig. 12.32.
Diagonal panning surround
setup.

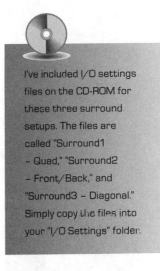

I've included I/O settings
files on the CD-ROM for
these three surround
setups. The files are
called "Surround1
– Quad," "Surround2
– Front/Back," and
"Surround3 – Diagonal."
Simply copy the files into
your "I/O Settings" folder.

What I do is set the output of each audio track to my stereo output pair, while using sends to feed the audio tracks to the surround outputs. That way I can monitor both the stereo mix and the surround mix without changing anything in Pro Tools. The send volume, pan, and mute controls (for each send on each track) manage the surround information. And all of the controls can be automated (and even drawn in) just like any other control information. (Figure 12.33 – taken from the Edit window – shows where to access the send automation data.)

Note: Although my home studio is set up for mixing in stereo and surround simultaneously, I don't recommend mixing in both formats at the same time. A surround mix does not easily translate into a stereo mix and vice versa. I recommend having separate mix sessions (on different days) for your stereo and surround mixes.

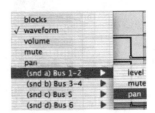

Fig. 12.33.
The send automation selector.

Mix Techniques in Surround Sound

Mixing audio in surround sound is a fairly new art. Only the film industry has logged a good amount of time mixing in surround, and the techniques for mixing music in surround (not to picture) are just now being developed.

With your 002/001 set up for mixing in surround, you can actually mimic a good portion of what true surround mixing systems can do. The main limitation is that it might take longer to create some of the far-out panning moves that are easy to do in true surround-ready applications. In the TDM version of Pro Tools, there's a surround-sound panning control built into each track that allows you to automate the panning control easily. In Pro Tools LE you've got to control multiple send output levels and pan controls at the same time to mimic sophisticated moves.

When mixing in stereo, people use effects processing to create a pseudo 3D space for each track to sit in the mix using reverbs, delays, etc. However, people mixing in surround often find they need much less

■ **Fig. 12.34.**

Here's one method of setting up sends on a channel strip for surround mixing.

Instead of assigning the sends directly to the outputs, you can also route them to aux tracks via busses, then to the outputs. This gives you increased ability to add effects as well as adjust the panning with the horizontal pan controls (instead of the rotary controls on the sends), which I find to be easier.

effects processing because there's much more space to work with – that is, you can distribute the tracks to more than two speakers. Even with songs that have high track counts and that are musically busy, there's room for all of the parts to be heard more easily.

I've mixed in 5.1 surround multiple times. In one of my surround mixes the only processing I used was EQ – I chose to use no other effects. Because the tracks were recorded well and were panned in interesting ways, I didn't need effects to make a great mix. In this case, the room mics were very effective at providing natural reverb when panned to the back. Multiple stereo guitar and vocal harmony tracks filled out the spread of the mix. Sound effects (as in film) provided additional aural appeal when panned in interesting ways. However, creative use of effects in surround mixing can be one of the most captivating aspects to this new art. Experimentation with delays, reverbs, Doppler effects, and flange/phase effects in surround will leave you speechless with a big smile the first few times you try it. It can be absolutely thrilling.

The only other solid technique I've come across for mixing in surround sound is for mixing live concerts. Essentially, the idea is to put the listener in a particular seat at the show (e.g., center stage, row 6), giving them the perspective of actually being at the concert with killer seats. Combined with video footage of the concert, this mix technique becomes even more effective.

Surround mixing is in its infancy and the techniques are just now being developed. Pro Tools LE can help you experiment with surround, and trust me, you'll be amazed by the results. Have fun! ▌▌

PRO TOOLS HANDS-ON

Set Up a Mix Session

The first step for many professional mixers is setting up their mixing environment so that it's organized and ready for quick action. In Pro Tools, this includes grouping tracks, creating effects sends for reverbs and delays, and setting initial volume and panning. When creating the effects sends, professional mixers often have several reverbs and delays ready that are appropriate to the song. For instance, they might place hall, plate, and room reverbs on distinct stereo aux tracks as well as two different delays timed at eighth-note and sixteenth-note intervals to the tempo of the song.

Try it. The next time you begin to mix a song, make groups and setup effects loops for multiple reverbs and delays. Choose the specific effects based on the sound you want to create with the entire mix. Check out how having these in place at the beginning of the mix can improve the flow and speed of your mixes.

Set Up a Side Chain

Setting up a side chain can help you achieve some pretty interesting outcomes if you learn the technique and experiment with it. Open the session "SideChain" and check out how I set up a side chain using a click track to trigger a gate on a synth pad. Notice that the click track is the "key input" for the gate on an aux track. (In the Gate plug-in window, be sure that the output of the click track, Bus 1, is selected as the Key Input.) Press the Key Listen button to hear the click. The synth pad track feeds the aux track via a stereo bus and the click triggers the gate to open and close. In this example, the idea is to create a sixteenth-note pulsing effect on the synth pad. You can then mix this into the unaffected synth pad patch for a more interesting overall sound.

Try it for yourself. Create a side chain to trigger an effect on another track. Tweak the effect based on the key input track by using the Key Listen button. Get creative. There are tons of cool ways to use side chains in Pro Tools.

Automate a Plug-In

Plug-ins can be automated, making them much more flexible than standard outboard analog gear. Try automating a plug-in on any session. Enable the plug-in parameters you want to automate, press Play, make your automation moves, and press Stop. Then, edit your automation data in the Edit window. Check out the QuickTime movie "enablingautomation" from the CD to view this process.

Add a Compressed Copy of the Drum Track to the Mix

A popular mixing technique is to add an effected copy of a track in with the original track. For example, let's say you want to add in a heavily compressed version of your drum tracks into the mix along with the original tracks to beef up the overall sound. Here's a good way to do it that will make sure the two signals are in phase with each other.

First, choose No Output as the output on all your drum tracks. Then, create two post-fader sends on each drum track (e.g., send "a" and send "b") both with stereo bus outputs (e.g., Bus 1-2 and Bus 3-4). Create two stereo Aux tracks, choose Bus 1-2 and Bus 3-4 as the inputs and Outputs 1-2 as the outputs on both tracks, and label the tracks something like "Drum Submix" and "Drums Compress." Add plug-ins as inserts on the "Drums Compress" Aux track to create the compressed and otherwise altered sound of the drums. As you add plug-ins to the "Drums Compress," add the same plug-ins to the "Drums Submix" track, but make sure they're bypassed. Doing this ensures that the same amount of processing delay inside your computer happens for each track, keeping the two signals phase coherent.

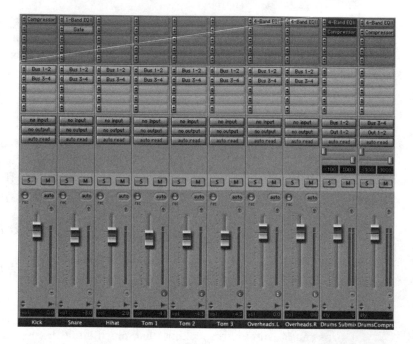

To check the amount of delay on a track, Control-click (Win) or Command-click (Mac) the Track Level Indicator to toggle between Level (which appears on screen as "vol"), Peak ("pk"), and Channel Delay ("dly"). View the delay values (measured in samples) and make sure both Aux tracks have the same amount of delay.

Try it. Create a compressed submix of some drum tracks or several other instruments and implement this phase-coherent technique. You can also try nudging audio regions in time to account for delays instead of doubling up on the use of plug-ins.

For additional mix techniques, also check out Charles Dye's column "A Hard Disk Life" and the Pro Techniques section in Digidesign's DigiZine online magazine.

Evaluate These Mix Ideas

Open the sessions "Chap12Rock," "Chap12Hiphop," "Chap12Jazz," and "Chap12Electronica" to hear the mix ideas I have for each of these songs. I've included submixed tracks of all the major instrument groupings for each song so you can hear the EQ, dynamic processing, and effects choices for each subgroup.

Critically evaluate the sounds, levels, panning, depth, frequency content, and overall energy of the mixes. What can you learn from these mixes that you can apply to your own mixes? What would you change?

I've also included MP3s of all four final mixes for you to compare with the rough-mix MP3s from the last chapter. Listen to "Chap12Rockfinalmix.mp3," "Chap12Hiphopfinalmix.mp3," "Chap12Jazzfinalmix.mp3," and "Chap12Electronicafinalmix.mp3" in comparison to their earlier rough-mix incarnations to truly evaluate the overall mix ideas and sounds.

Note to mix engineers before mastering: Many mix engineers apply plug-ins across the entire stereo mix using the inserts on the master fader. This is a great way to adjust the overall sound of a mix, but you should be careful not to let plug-ins inadvertently disguise an overload on the master fader. If a mix does clip the master fader, use the All Edit/Mix group to bring down the levels of all the tracks and/or adjust volume automation individually. Although this makes your mixes sound quieter at first, once you add compression and/or limiting onto the master fader you can make up the gain on the other side of the master fader. (Remember that inserts on a master fader are post-fader.) Keeping the input signal to the master fader level below the peak will make your mixes sound better and it will impress mastering engineers and enable them to fully maximize your mixes in the mastering process. To learn more about mastering, read on....

Mastering

In this chapter:

- **Final edits and sound adjustments**

- **Setting up a Pro Tools session for mastering**

- **Song order, bouncing to disk, and burning CDs**

- **The step after mastering**

Okay, so you've got your songs mixed and they sound great. You've reached the final step: mastering. Like mixing, mastering is an elusive art form to many. In this chapter I'll try to demystify the process and steer you toward mastering your own recordings using Pro Tools.

In a nutshell, mastering is altering the final mixes of the stereo or surround tracks to achieve the best overall sound and capture the essence of the recording. This includes editing final song arrangements, optimizing each track's volume level and tonal balance, making sure the volume and EQ between each song is consistent, creating the best song order for a demo or full-length CD, spacing the songs correctly, creating and editing PQ subcode, and writing the CD master.

Allowing someone else to master your tracks can be a good idea if you have the money. Professional mastering engineers have great outboard gear and speaker systems, and well-trained ears that can really help identify and fix problems or inconsistencies with your mixes.

FINAL EDITS

The first step when mastering is to determine what the final edits are for each song in your project. If you have final mixes that you're completely satisfied with, you don't have to worry about this. However, some of you might need to put together a radio mix or a dance version from your final mixes. Or you may find you like a part of one mix pass but another part of a different mix. You need to make these edits before you master the recording. Start by loading the final stereo tracks into a new Pro Tools session....

Radio mixes tend to be shorter than album cuts — intros are shaved, the song reaches the chorus sooner and maybe more often, solos are cut out, etc. Dance mixes tend to be longer than album cuts — drums and bass are the focus, melodies are looped, and the song is often totally rearranged. When editing the best parts of two different mixes into one, bring both final mixes into the same Pro Tools session and cut and paste. Make sure the edits aren't noticeable, and spend a good amount of time creating smooth crossfades between the two different tracks. Once you have the final edits of each song ready you can move on to giving the songs a unified sound.

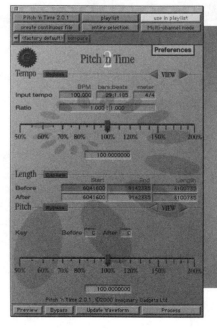

USING SERATO'S PITCH 'N TIME 2

During the mastering stage, you may also want to speed up or slow down a song, or maybe even adjust the pitch of an entire song. Serato Audio Research has developed an amazing plug-in called Pitch 'n Time 2, a high quality time-stretching and pitch-shifting AudioSuite plug-in that enables time compression and expansion from a ratio of half speed up to double speed, independent of pitch. It also enables pitch-shifting of up to 12 semitones (i.e., an octave above or below the original pitch), independent of tempo.

The time-stretching and pitch-shifting possibilities range from simple fixed ratios to complex tempo and pitch alterations that vary over time . . . all with real-time previewing. For more information on Serato Audio Research and their products, see appendix D.

FINAL SOUND ADJUSTMENTS

With final edits made, bounce your final mixes to disk and import them all into one new Pro Tools session. (There's more info on bouncing later in this chapter.)

In your new Pro Tools session, listen and compare the overall sound from track to track. Take notes! You'll probably find that some songs are louder or have distinct EQ curves. Some stereo images may be different, as well (which isn't necessarily a bad thing). Set aside time and create the right environment for super-critical listening.

A good mix is usually mastered so that (a) it's relatively flat across the frequency spectrum with some rolloff at the very top and bottom, (b) it's spread across the stereo field, and (c) it has a volume level that peaks at 0dB at the loudest part of the song.

Waves has a plug-in – the PAZ Analyzer shown in figure 13.1 – that's very useful for analyzing the frequency content, stereo imaging, and overall levels of your mixes. You can use this plug-in (or one similar to it) to assess your mixes and compare them. But even though this plug-in shows you graphically what's going on in your mix, it shouldn't be used in a vacuum. Your ears must make the final judgement.

Note: If you recorded your tracks in 24-bit resolution, bounce your final mixes in 24-bit (with no dither) for the mastering session. You can then add dither and reduce the bit depth during the final mastering session.

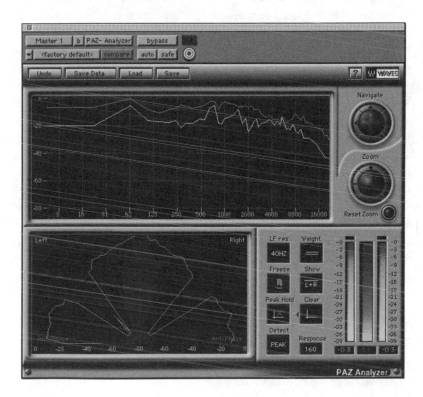

■ **Fig. 13.1.**
The Waves PAZ Analyzer gives you fantastic tools to help visualize things like the frequency makeup of your mix (top) and the relative balance of your stereo image (bottom).

Normalizing

Some people **normalize** their tracks during the mastering process. Applying normalization to a track raises its overall volume level while ensuring that the inherent dynamics of the material remain unchanged. It is useful in cases when an audio file has been recorded with too little amplitude, or where volume is inconsistent for the duration of the file. However, you shouldn't need to normalize your tracks if you recorded and bounced them at good levels. In fact, most professional mastering engineers rarely normalize tracks. They usually receive tracks that have high levels anyway, so they use compression or limiting to make tracks sound louder, if necessary.

Compression and Limiting

As discussed in chapter 12, compression and limiting reduce a song's dynamic range and control sporadic volume peaks, allowing the overall volume of the song to be raised without causing clipping. Compression and limiting are commonly used because people listen to music in their cars and on dance floors, where quieter musical passages can get lost in the surrounding noise. As an example, if you apply a limiter to your final mix and it registers 5dB of reduction at some time during the song, you can actually boost the level of the entire mix by 5dB without clipping – the loud parts of the song will remain loud, while the quieter parts get louder. When applying the right amount of compression or limiting, the overall sound of your mix won't be altered significantly except that it'll be louder and probably more "energetic." This is known as *transparent* compression/limiting.

If you apply compression incorrectly, your mix will have a "pumping" sound…the softer parts will be loud but the loud parts will be compressed too much, making your music actually *lose* power and energy. Also, overusing compression/limiting can make your mixes sound thin and lifeless because the volume level is constant throughout the song and all the contrast you built into your music in the first place is lost.

Instead of applying a compressor or limiter to your entire mix, you may choose to use a frequency-dependent (or "multiband") compressor or limiter. That way you can divide the frequency range into several sections and compress/limit each one differently. Be gentle, though.... As each frequency band is compressed, the different band levels change in relation to each other – this means you could really mess up your mix if you're not careful. However, if used correctly, multiband compression can produce a more consistently powerful master.

SETTING UP PRO TOOLS FOR MASTERING

Import all of your final stereo mixes into a new Pro Tools session for mastering. After you've listened to each track and identified the differences in sound, use inserts to add EQ and compression/limiting plug-ins, or use sends for any outboard gear in the chain. Then use the volume faders to adjust the overall volume for each song (it's important that you do this *after* you apply compression/limiting). Use automation to create any fades you want on your tracks. Create a master fader and apply any plug-ins (like another compressor or EQ) that you want to use on *all* of the tracks. And don't forget to put the Dither plug-in as the last insert on the master fader; it should be applied (with a resolution of 16 bits) regardless of whether you're working with 16- or 24-bit files.

USING T-RACKS MASTERING PLUG-INS

IK Multimedia has developed T-Racks, a suite of RTAS mastering plug-ins that includes a 6-band stereo parametric equalizer, a classic mastering tube stereo compressor/leveler, a multiband mastering stereo limiter, and an adjustable soft-clipping output stage.

All of the effects modules in the T-Racks suite emulate high-end vintage analog gear and have been specifically engineered for mastering final mixes. For more information on IK Multimedia products, check appendix D.

Dither and Noise Shaping

Digital audio's poorest representation of sound exists at the lowest end of the dynamic range (the quiet parts, such as fade outs). Recall the discussion on bit depth in chapter 3: Remember that high bit depths yield more accurate digital pictures of audio signals? Well, low-level audio signals use only a fraction of the possible 16 or 24 bits, meaning that they don't get accurately represented. This inaccuracy creates a kind of distortion called **quantization distortion**.

Dither reduces quantizing inaccuracies by introducing very low-level random noise, thereby minimizing distortion products. Though there's a trade-off between signal-to-noise performance and less apparent distortion, proper use of dither allows you to squeeze better subjective performance out of a 16-bit data format (such as CD format).

Dither plug-ins can utilize a technique known as **noise shaping** to further improve audio performance and reduce perceived noise inherent in dithering. Noise shaping utilizes digital filtering to move noise from frequencies that our ears are most sensitive to (such as around 4kHz) to frequencies we're less sensitive to — making the noise more difficult for us to hear.

The DigiRack Dither plug-in (shown in figure 13.2) allows you to apply dither and noise shaping to an audio track or master fader.

Pro Tools LE processes files internally at 32-bit floating and some plug-ins process files at even higher bit depths. Without dither to process the 24-bit audio files or 32-bit+ internal processing, the extra eight or more bits are truncated (dropped entirely) when written to media or to a device with a 16 bit maximum (like CD recorders).

■ **Fig. 13.2.**
The DigiRack Dither plug-in helps your master make it onto CD while maintaining as much of the original recording quality as possible.

FINAL SONG ORDER

When assembling the final order of songs for your CD, consider the song flow and placement of fades. You should make it easy to listen to all the way through by placing songs so they lead smoothly into each other. Also provide contrast that holds the listener's interest using different tempos, keys, rhythms, lyrical content, and sound texture. Despite the contrast between songs, however, the whole CD should sound like it's one piece of work rather than a hodgepodge of different music. If the songs' volumes and EQ levels are similar and the order is right, your CD will sound professional and the audience will embrace the music more readily.

BOUNCING TO DISK

After you've tweaked your tracks, then listened and tweaked some more, you're ready to bounce the finals to your hard drive. Create a new folder for the mastered tracks. If you're recording to DAT or a similar medium, make sure the inputs of the recorder are connected to the correct outputs of your Digidesign hardware, and enable S/PDIF mirroring if needed. Select an entire song (by highlighting it) or choose only the part you want. Solo the song in the session and select Bounce to Disk from the File menu. Use the settings as seen in figure 13.3 and press the Bounce button. Repeat the process for each song.

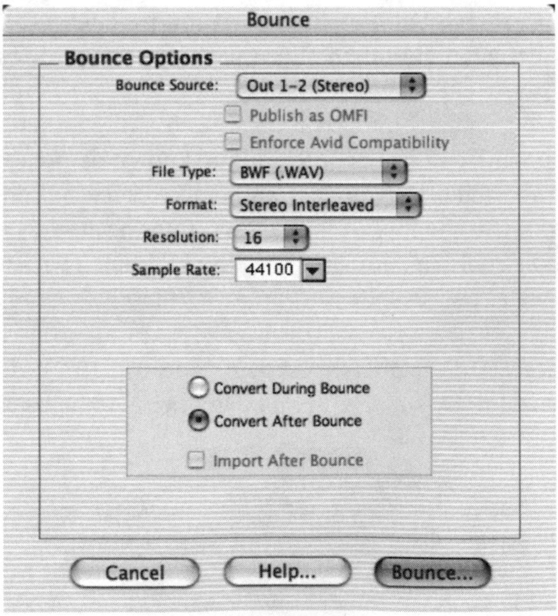

Fig. 13.3.
Bounce settings for your mastered tracks.

Once all of your songs are bounced, use the software that came with your CD burner (e.g., Roxio Toast or Jam) to create a CD by dragging and dropping or importing your bounced files to the software. Assemble the tracks in the right order, adjust times between tracks if necessary, and burn your CD at 1X, 2X, or 4X speed. (I don't recommend burning at anything higher than 4X, because higher speeds are more likely to create errors in your CD, and you definitely don't want errors in your master!) In fact, I burn all my master CDs at 1X speed for safety's sake.

MASTERING SOFTWARE

With many more features than simple CD burning software, simple mastering software (such as Roxio's Jam program) allows you to adjust song spacing, add/subtract gain where necessary, find volume peaks, add crossfades, create PQ subcode data, and make your CD Red Book–compatible (see the box on PQ subcode and Red Book). Because it gives you complete control of your master CD, this software is extremely useful for making your home-produced recordings look and sound like they were mastered by pros.

Here's how mastering software fits into a typical production cycle:

1. Create and edit audio files using Pro Tools.

2. Use Pro Tools to create finished stereo master tracks — compressed, EQed, dithered, etc. — from the original audio files.

3. Import the mastered tracks into your mastering software.

4. Adjust song spacing add crossfades, and edit PQ subcode information.

5. Burn your mastered tracks to CD.

PQ SUBCODE AND RED BOOK-COMPATIBLE CDS

All audio CDs have eight channels of subcode data interleaved with the digital audio data. These channels are named P, Q, R, S, T, U, V, and W. On audio CDs, only channels P and Q are used by the CD player. (Channels R–W are used to store video information in CD+G discs, and MIDI information in CD+MIDI discs.) PQ subcode editing is the process of defining the information that is encoded into the P and Q subcode channels on a Red Book-compatible CD.

The information on the P channel tells the CD player when a track is or is not playing. The information on the Q channel is more comprehensive, describing track and disc running times, disc catalog codes, and many other parameters. You can edit any of the parameters within the PQ subcode, such as the CD track numbers, index numbers, and track start and end times.

Red Book is the name of the CD-DA (CD-Digital Audio) standard as originally defined by Sony and Phillips. It defines the format a CD must have in order to be played on an audio CD player, and what that CD player must do in order to properly play audio CDs. Any CD that's Red Book-compatible should work with any commercial audio CD player.

After you burn the master CD listen to it carefully before you duplicate it. Listen for clicks, false starts, incorrect fades, and the overall sound and order of the songs. Obviously, go back and fix anything before you take it to be duplicated. And remember to check the master that the duplicating company makes to be sure it's as good as what you gave them.

There's an interesting side effect to mastering your projects: as you gain experience you'll apply what you learn to earlier steps in the recording process (recording, mixing, and even writing and arranging). And because you see the final big musical picture, your songs will need less and less mastering as your production skills improve.

THE STEP AFTER MASTERING

What? There's more? Well . . . yeah, if you want to take your music to the next level. With Pro Tools you can create MP3 and RealAudio files to post on the Web. Simply use the Bounce to Disk command and choose MPEG-1 Layer 3 (for MP3 files) or RealAudio in the file type box. (To make MP3 files you can use the 30-day trial option that came with Pro Tools, but you'll need to purchase the full-blown version from Digidesign to retain MP3 encoding.) You should also copyright your songs — go to the Library of Congress Web site at **www.loc.gov/ copyright** to download copyright forms. If you're part of a band, trademark your band name at **www.uspto.gov**.

Create some art for your CD. Disc Makers has CD jewel box templates you can download for free at **www.discmakers.com**. If you want to sell your music in record stores you'll need a UPC bar code to put on your CD case — **go to www.uc-council.org** to get one. Finally, put together a press kit including your CD, a bio, and a picture of yourself or your band. Send it off to clubs and record labels if you're interested in gigging or getting a record contract. There are many books listed in appendix E that discuss these final topics in much greater detail.

Congratulations! You made it . . . you've learned how to produce, record, edit, mix, and master with Pro Tools. I wish you all the best with your future musical projects, and thank you for reading. Now get back to what you really love doing: making music! ▌▌

PRO TOOLS HANDS-ON

Set Up a Mastering Session

When mastering multiple songs for one project, import the final mixes into a new Pro Tools session and place each song on its own track. Then, lay out the songs in the session as you'd like them placed on the master CD. Test out the spacing between songs as well as the order of the tunes to get the overall vibe of the recording. Listen straight through to the entire recording and pay attention to the overall sound and energy from song to song. Does the recording work as a whole? Does anything need to be tweaked?

Open the "Chap13Mastering" session and view the Edit window. Check out the placement of the four final mastered mixes in the session, then play through the songs and evaluate the overall sound from song to song.

Master the Recordings

Although the four songs that we've followed throughout the book are from different genres, probably wouldn't be on the same album, and might be mastered in different ways, I thought of this as a compilation project. That way, these four songs can be mastered together to make one cohesive project.

In the "Chap13Mastering" session, I included the four final mastered mixes in an order and spacing that I like. During the mastering process, I applied various mastering plug-ins primarily from Waves, McDSP, and IK Multimedia, including EQs, compressors, limiters, analog/tube emulators, stereo image enhancers, and dither. As you can see in the Mix window of the session, I set up stereo Aux tracks for each song where I inserted many of the plug-ins. (Although it's not necessary to set up a mastering session in this way, I find it easy to work with this setup.) In addition, I added plug-ins that I wanted to use across all songs, like dither, to the Master Fader track.

I used EQ to enhance the sonic character of each song as well as to adjust for the frequency differences between each mix. This helped to create a somewhat unified final product, while still keeping the individuality of each song. I applied compression and limiting to increase the volume of each mix, making them competitive with music broadcast on radio while retaining much of each song's dynamics. Compression, limiting, and volume automation were also used to help maintain a consistent volume level from one song to the next. I utilized analog/tube emulators to "warm up" the overall sound of the recordings, and I applied stereo image enhancers to widen the stereo image of each song. Finally, I applied dither as the last step in the plug-in processing chain.

Compare these master recordings with the final mixes from the previous chapter and evaluate how the mastering process improved the final mixes. Then try it yourself. Master these songs by first bouncing down a final mix from any or all of the chapter 12 "submix" sessions and then importing the bounced files into the "Chap13Mastering" session or into a new Pro Tools session. Set up your mastering session (as previously described) and use my master recordings as a reference. Try to improve upon my work using the plug-ins (and/or outboard gear) that you have available. Good luck and, more importantly, have fun!

Wow! The songs are done. Take a minute to think back to the beginning of the production process and to the original ideas for these songs. We've come a long way from those initial ideas, haven't we? Now that you understand the entire production process from start to finish, apply that process to your own recordings and you'll see dramatic improvements in your own creations using Pro Tools.

Rock on!

Range Charts

Knowing the ranges of instruments you're writing for is imperative, both for making the parts playable on real instruments and for achieving real-sounding MIDI parts. This chart shows the ranges of instruments relative to a keyboard. The ranges presented here are a little narrower than each instrument's actual limits, but keeping within these boundaries will ensure that your parts sound more authentic.

PICCOLO

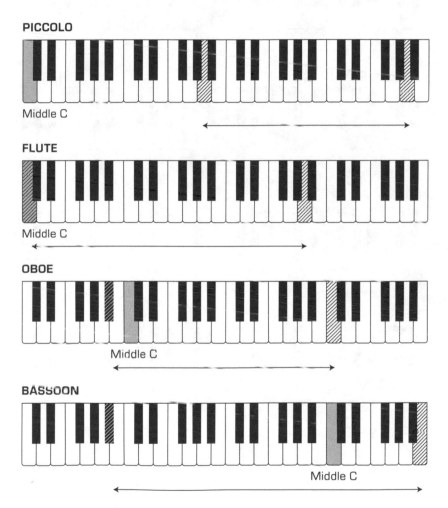

Middle C

FLUTE

Middle C

OBOE

Middle C

BASSOON

Middle C

CLARINET

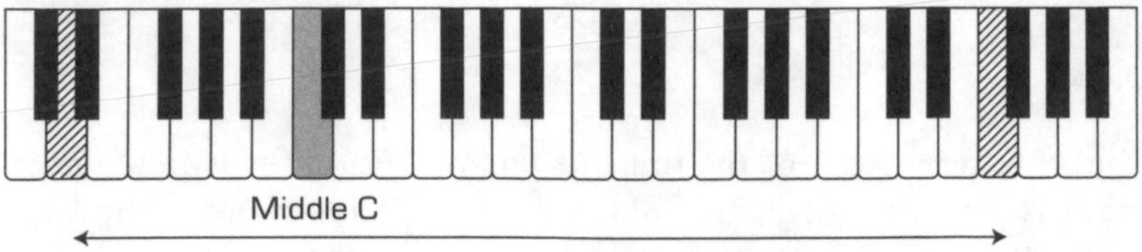

Middle C

BASS CLARINET

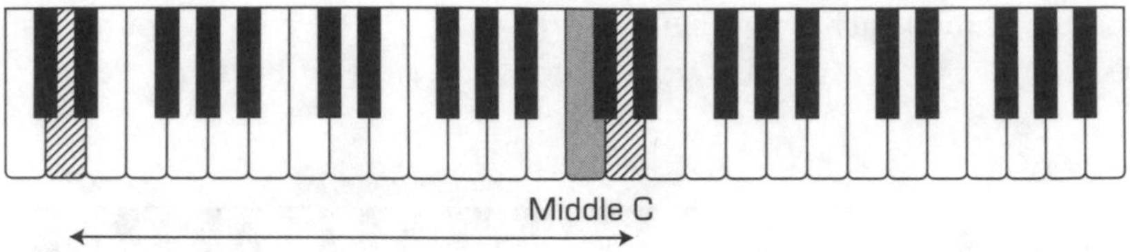

Middle C

SOPRANO SAX

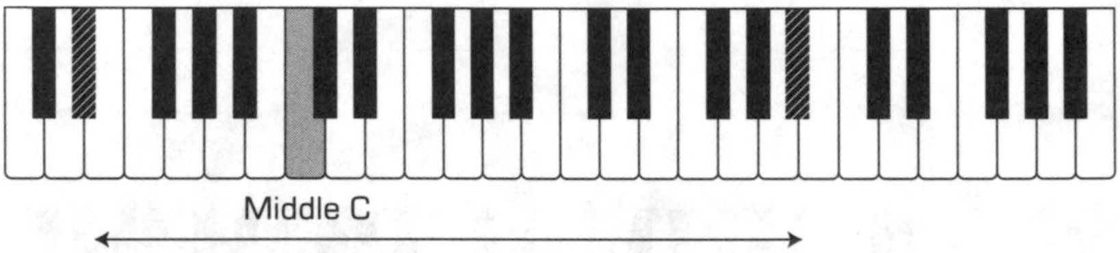

Middle C

ALTO SAX

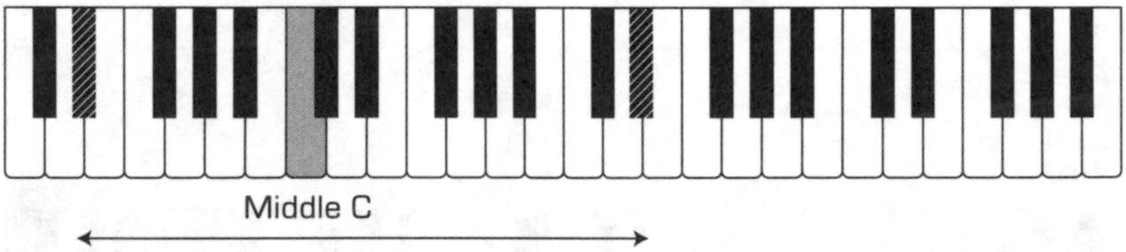

Middle C

TENOR SAX

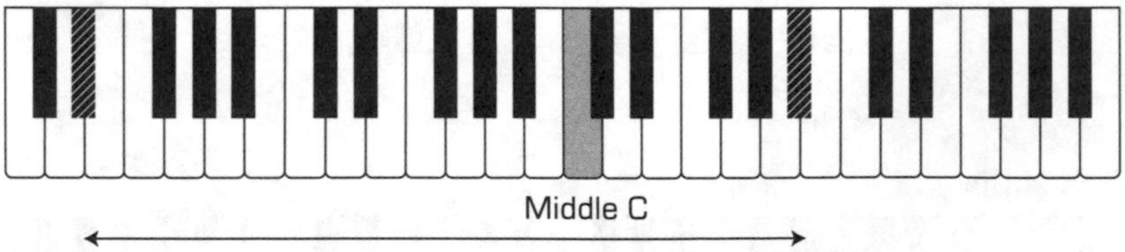

Middle C

BARITONE SAX

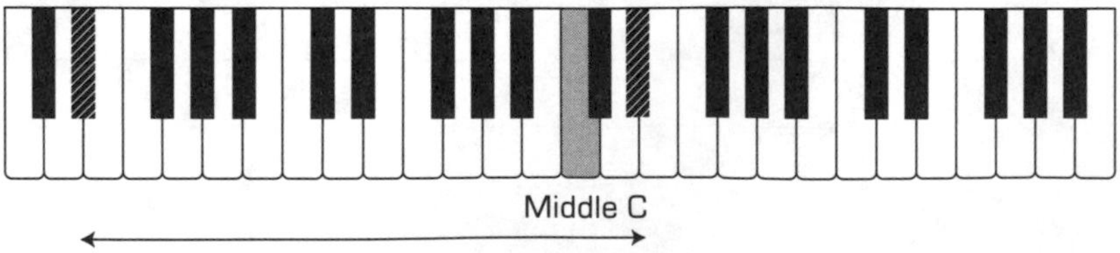

Middle C

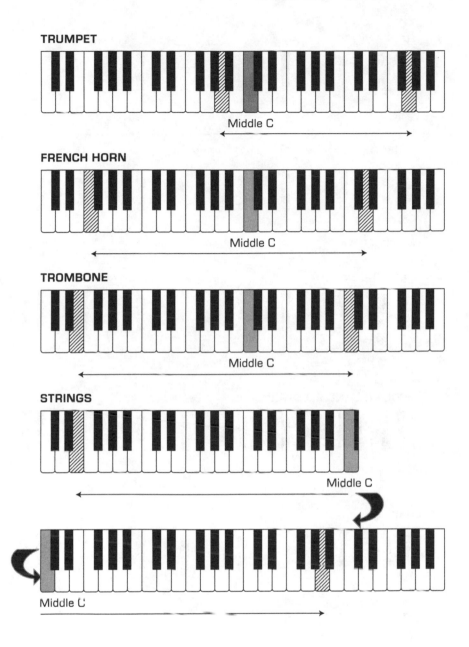

HARP

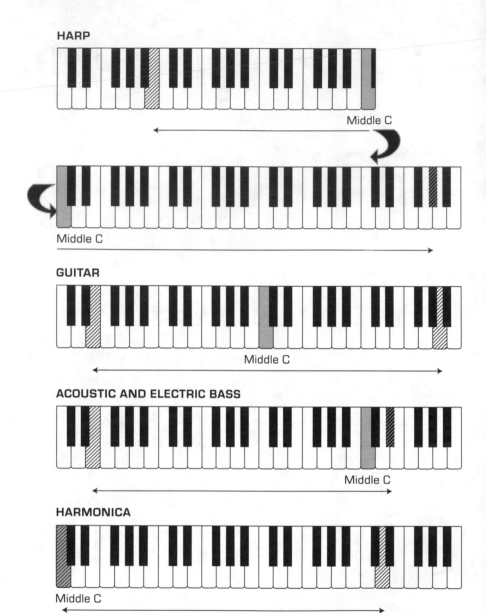

Middle C

GUITAR

Middle C

ACOUSTIC AND ELECTRIC BASS

Middle C

HARMONICA

Middle C

As promised in chapter 6, here's a list of Web sites to help you find musicians for your projects. To build a community of Pro Tools users, try the Digidesign Production Network first at www.digipronet.com.

Berkleemusic (www.berkleemusic.com)

Berklee College of Music has created a comprehensive online training and career networking site for musicians. The site offers musicians instruction and resources to launch, advance, and sustain thriving music careers. The site is divided into four areas: an online music school, a store, a career center, and a musician's network. At Berkleemusic, musicians can find jobs and gigs, network with other musicians, promote themselves, develop their careers, and purchase music books, videos, and other educational products.

Cadenza Musicians' Directory (www.cadenza.org/musicians)

A collection of short biographies and contact details designed to put performers, composers, and teachers in touch with those organizing concerts, those commissioning new works, and those wanting music tuition. The site has information on arrangers, composers, writers, publishers, conductors, soloists, managers, ensembles, orchestras, choirs, bands, instrument makers, musicologists, music theorists and scholars, players, singers, teachers, accompanists, and music typesetters.

Coalition for Disabled Musicians (www.disabled-musicians.org)

The Coalition for Disabled Musicians, Inc. (CDM) is a voluntary, non-profit organization dedicated to enabling physically disabled musicians to pursue their musical dreams. Their Web site facilitates networking opportunities by setting up collaborative projects (bands, recording sessions, etc.) for disabled musicians.

Digidesign Production Network (www.digipronet.com)

This site is Digidesign's own online directory for audio professionals.

Fastdog (www.fastdog.com)

A great source to check for available musicians, or post your own ad for free!

GigFinder (www.gigfinder.com)

A comprehensive musician's service on the Web offering free classifieds, music industry links, and much more.

Harmony Central (www.harmony-central.com)
Harmony Central is the leading Internet resource for musicians, supplying valuable information from news and product reviews, to classified ads and chat rooms.

The International Musicians Trading Post (www.musicians-classifieds.com)
This site has over 10,000 listings for musicians wanted, musicians available, equipment, and other musical services.

Musician.com (www.musician.com)
Besides being a huge resource for all aspects of the music industry, Musician.com's MusicianFinder can connect you with musicians around the world.

Musicians Available (www.musiciansavailable.com)
Musicians Available is the free place to instantly find new members for your band, find a band to join, or simply find other musicians to jam with. All musicians wanted and musicians available listings are completely free and all countries are covered.

Musician's Connection (www.musiciansconnection.com)
This fancy Web site can help you find musicians, clubs/venues, recording studios, producers, and instrument manufacturers.

MusiciansContact.com (www.musicianscontact.com)
The original musicians' contact service that thousands of bands, managers, employers, and agents have used for 30 years.

Musician's Gallery (www.musiciansgallery.com)
This Web site has profiles of musicians and related musical services from all around the world.

Musicians Management and Referral (www.geocities.com/ SunsetStrip/Frontrow/9817)
This is a database of musicians who want to connect with others to create a band, join an existing group, do recording work, or just exchange ideas or information.

Musicians Network (www.musiciansnetwork.com)
A central networking point for the connection of musicians and members of the music industry.

**Music-Tech/Free Musicians' Classifieds
(www.freemusiciansclassifieds.com)**
With Free Musicians' Classifieds you can post ads in a wide variety of categories, including Musicians Seeking Placement, Employment Opportunities, Booking Agents and Managers, Songwriter Opportunities, and even Investors Wanted/Available.

Musician's Web (www.musicians-web.co.uk)
Musician's Web is a great place to find amateur musicians in the UK.

The Music Yellow Pages (www.musicyellowpages.com)
A comprehensive industry trade directory for the music, pro audio, lighting, and entertainment industries.

PrivateLessons.com (www.privatelessons.com)
Use this site to find a teacher, player, arranger, or composer for any instrument.

Taxi (www.taxi.com)
Find and be found by like-minded musicians using Taxi's easily searchable international database. Need a lyricist for your music? A bassist for your band? A studio to record your demo? A producer to produce? A singer to sing? Enter yourself into this database so people can find you, or search the people already entered to find who you're looking for.

The Mode (www.themode.com)
A database of free classifieds for musicians to get gigs, buy and sell equipment, and network with other musicians in their local areas.

Digidesign
Technical Support

Warranty Support

As a registered user of a new Digidesign product you're eligible for complimentary tech support for one year from the date of original purchase. Software upgrade support is complimentary for the first 90 days after purchase.

Non-Warranty Support

Customers in the United States and Canada seeking telephone support for a product that's over one year old, or a software upgrade purchased over 90 days ago, should call the Digidesign ProAxess Line — a priority support service where customers speak with a senior technical support representative. (See the next section for ProAxess numbers.) International customers should call their regional support office.

Be sure to register your Digidesign product because you'll get special offers on upgrades, advance information about new products, and technical support!

PREMIUM TECHNICAL SUPPORT SERVICES

In the United States and Canada: If you only need to call technical support occasionally but require immediate service when you do call, you'll appreciate the "pay as you go" ProAxess Line (PAL). It is available to Digidesign customers and provides expedited access — usually in less than 30 seconds — to a senior tech support engineer for a fee that can be billed to your credit card or telephone bill.

While you may still contact Digidesign for free support during the valid warranty period, the ProAxess Line is designed to meet the demands of users who require immediate help, or for those who need continued technical assistance after their free support has expired (after one year of product ownership).

The ProAxess Line phone numbers are:

888-344-4376 (can be billed to MasterCard, Visa, American Express, or Discover)

900-555-4376 (billed to the caller's monthly phone bill)

Other premium support services: If you need technical support frequently or require extended support hours, contact the Digidesign TeleSales department at 800-333-2137 or 650-731-6102 to learn more about Digi's Pro Tech Passport™ Gold, Silver, and Bronze support packages. They're designed to meet the needs of audio professionals and are available by annual subscription.

For customers outside the United States and Canada: Please contact your Digidesign dealer. Many of them offer premium support programs that extend telephone support hours and provide swift hardware repair services.

DIGIDESIGN SUPPORT NUMBERS

Service	Contact Information	Availability
End User Warranty Support and Customer Service Administration	650-731-6100 (voice) 650-731-6384 (fax)	8:00 A.M.–5:00 P.M. Mon–Thur (PST) 8:00 A.M.–3:00 P.M. Friday (PST) Anytime
ProAxess™ Line (Priority Support)	888-344-4376 (US only) 900-555-4376 (US only)	8:00 A.M.–5:00 P.M. Mon-Thur (PST) 8:00 A.M.–3:00 P.M. Friday (PST)
Digidesign Website	www.digidesign.com	Anytime
Digidesign User Conference	duc.digidesign.com	Anytime
Technical Support Web Site	www.digidesign.com/tsr	Anytime
Customer Service Administration E-mail	csadmin@digidesign.com	Anytime

DIGIDESIGN TECHNICAL SUPPORT AROUND THE WORLD

All listed hours of operation refer to the local time zone for that office.

Country	Telephone Number	Fax Number	E-mail Address	Hours of Operation
Africa, Eastern Europe, and Middle Eastern Countries	44 (0)1753-653-322	44 (0)1753-658-501	ROE@digidesign.com	10-6 M-F (GMT)
Australia, New Zealand, and South Pacific	613-5428-7780	613-5428-7781	infoau@digidesign.com	10-6 M-F
Belgium, Netherlands, and Luxembourg	31 (0)73-613-8080	31 (0)73-612-2044	infobn@digidesign.com	10-6 M-F (CET)
France	33 (0)1-41-49-40-50	33 (0)1-47-57-56-28	support-france@digidesign.com	10-6 M-F (CET)
Germany, Poland, CZ Rep., and Slovakia	49 (0)811-5520-583	49 (0)811-5520-599	infode@digidesign.com	10-6 M-F (CET)
Italy	39-02-577897-81	39-02-577897-25	infoit@digidesign.com	9-6 M-F (CET)
Japan, Southeast Asia, and India	81-3-3505-4762	81-3-3505-3417	infojp@digidesign.com	10-6 M-F
Korea	82-2-543-3062	82-2-543-3063	digidesign@netsgo.com	
Latin America	52-55-5485-1139	52-55-5033-8027	latinamercs@digidesign.com	9-5 M-F (CDT)
Mexico	55-5485-1139	55-5033-8027	latinamercs@digidesign.com	9-5 M-F
Spain	34-93-4233771		soporte@digidesign.com	
United Kingdom and Ireland	44 (0)1753-658-496	44 (0)1753-658-501	infouk@digidesign.com	10-6 M-F (GMT)

SHURE

Shure is a manufacturer of quality microphones, wireless systems, personal monitor systems, and audio processing products. I used Shure microphones to record all audio examples for the CD-ROM and in all of the text examples about microphones. Check out their free technical support (provided by their Applications Engineering department) as well as their significant online information including:

- *Wireless Frequency Reference Guide*

- FAQ/knowledge base: dynamic FAQ function powered by your inquiries and responses, conveniently divided by product category

- User guides and specification sheets: downloadable in PDF format

- Current and discontinued products

- Product selection guides: convenient, application-specific guides offering several product options in order of preference

- Applications bulletins: brief essays on specific audio and electronics topics

- Booklets: useful advice on specific applications and product areas, some available as PDF files

Contact info:
847-866-2200 or 800-25-SHURE; 847-866-2279 (fax)
www.shure.com, info@shure.com

Applications Engineering Department:
847-866-2525, support@shure.com

GLYPH TECHNOLOGIES

With their unique products and incredible focus on customer service, Glyph Technologies has become the dominant provider of data storage solutions for the United States and European digital audio recording and postproduction industries. I used Glyph's FireWire X-Project (30GB hard drive) and their WildFire CD-RW to record, archive, and burn CDs while creating this book and CD-ROM. They also have a FireWire drive called the Companion for the Mbox that's available in capacities of 40GB, 80GB, and 120GB. Check out how these products easily integrate into your Pro Tools home studio.

Contact info:
607-275-0345 or 800-335-0645; 607-275-9464 (fax)
www.glyphtech.com, sales@glyphtech.com

Technical Support and Service:
607-275-0154, tech@glyphtech.com

LINE 6

Line 6 is the world leader in digital modeling guitar products, continuing to offer innovative tools that have forever changed the way guitarists play, create, and record their music. I used the Line 6 Pod Pro, Bass Pod Pro, Flextone II XL amplifier, and Floor Board in the recordings on the CD-ROM. This gear not only sounded great, but it was easy to connect to my Pro Tools home studio equipment.

Contact info:
818-575-3600; 818-575-3601 (fax)
www.line6.com, info@line6.com (product info), sales@line6.com (product sales)

PRESONUS AUDIO ELECTRONICS

PreSonus manufactures extreme audio products packed with high-end components and the latest patented technologies, while keeping these products affordable to home studio users. I used the PreSonus Digimax to record some of the tracks on the CD-ROM. Having the most I/O options of any mic pre on the market, the Digimax is a cinch to add to any Pro Tools home studio.

Contact info:
225-216-7887 or 800-750-0323; 225-926-8347 (fax)
www.presonus.com, info@presonus.com

ANTARES AUDIO TECHNOLOGIES

Antares develops innovative DSP-based audio hardware and software products that provide musicians, producers, and engineers with creative capabilities they may never have imagined possible. I used the AutoTune and Microphone Modeler plug-ins while writing this book. Download fully functional time-limited demos of each of these products (and their audio-controlled software synth "kantos") to try them out for yourself!

Contact info:
831-461-7800; 831-461-7801 (fax)
www.antarestech.com, info@antarestech.com

WAVES

Waves is the leading provider of DSP solutions for audio professionals and Maxx audio processing solutions for consumer electronics. Their award-winning plug-ins are the technology and market share leader for thousands of pros in content creation, utilizing Waves proprietary DSP algorithms. I used many plug-ins from the Waves Platinum Bundle (Native) while writing this book. Try it out for yourself with the demo of their plug-ins on the CD-ROM.

Contact info:
865-546-6115; 865-546-8445 (fax)
www.waves.com, sales@waves.com (product info), support@waves.com (product support)

KOBLO

Koblo builds software synthesizers that integrate fully into all Macintosh Pro Tools production environments. Your work can be quickly edited, mixed, and finalized without any risk of losing your original compositions, sounds, or loops. I used Koblo's Studio9000 software synth while writing this book. Check out the demo of their Vibra1000 synth on the CD-ROM.

Contact info:
Corporate (Denmark) — +45 87 30 14 30/34/35/36; +45 87 30 33 40 (fax)
US (care of Digidesign) — 650-842-7900 ext. 3310/3311; 650-842-7999 (fax)
www.koblo.com

EMAGIC

Emagic is a leader in creating music production tools for computerized studios, professional musicians, and producers. While writing this book I synced Logic Audio Platinum with Pro Tools and used their Unitor8 MkII MIDI interface (which worked quite well).

Contact info:
Corporate (Germany) — +49 4101-495-0; +49 4101-495-199 (fax)
US — 530-477-1051; 530-477-1052 (fax)
www.emagic.de, info@emagic.de

MACKIE DESIGNS

Mackie is dedicated to developing and manufacturing high-quality, affordable professional analog and digital audio products for use in both recording and sound reinforcement. I used the 1604-VLZ Pro 16-channel mixer and a pair of HR824 monitors while writing this book.

The products worked great! Detailed information on the entire Mackie product line is available on their Web site.

Contact info:
US — 800-258-6883; 425-487-4337 (fax)
International — 425-487-4333; 425-485-1152 (fax)
www.mackie.com, productinfo@mackie.com

MULTILOOPS

Multiloops has created Naked Drums — tempo-mapped Pro Tools session documents containing drum loop sample libraries that were recorded using a live acoustic drummer. Pro Tools FREE, LE, and TDM users can open up these sessions and begin working immediately to the Pro Tools tempo grid. The loops are in multitrack format so you can mix them like a real drum kit. There are also fills and single-hit samples so you have the tools to create an entire drum session for your song. This is a great tool for building a solid rhythm track or to quickly assemble a song arrangement. Check out the free Naked Drums demo session on the CD-ROM. You can also download additional free demo sessions from their Web site.

Contact info:
615-646-0150
www.nakeddrums.com, info@multiloops.com

SERATO AUDIO RESEARCH

Serato has developed two amazing products: Pitch 'n Time 2 and Scratch. Pitch 'n Time 2 is a high quality time-stretching and pitch-shifting AudioSuite software plug-in for the Pro Tools platform. Scratch allows you to scratch any digital sample or sound file on your computer using your existing turntables or mouse as the controller. Special vinyl included with Scratch contains a control signal that allows your computer to track the motion of the record, simulating the same movement within the digital sample. I used Pitch 'n Time 2 and Scratch while writing this book. Visit the Serato Web site for demo versions and more information on their products.

Contact Info:
+64 (9) 480 2396; +64 (9) 480 2397 (fax)
www.serato.com, info@serato.com

IK MULTIMEDIA

IK Multimedia has created an innovative range of software studio tools for music creation, including stand-alone and plug-in effects, plug-in instruments, and DJ and remixing tools. Their Pro Tools–compatible products include T-Racks mastering plug-ins, Amplitube guitar amp and FX modeling plug-in, and SampleTank, the first native sample-based sound module available as a Pro Tools plug-in. I used the T-Racks mastering plug-ins while writing this book. Visit the IK Multimedia Web site for more information on their products.

Contact info:

IK Multimedia Production srl (Italy)
+39-059-285496; +39-059-2861671 (fax)
www.ikmultimedia.com, ikm@ikmultimedia.com

IK Multimedia US
866-243-1718; 206-666-6534 (fax)
www.ikmultimedia.com, ikmus@ikmultimedia.com

PACE ANTI-PIRACY, INC.

PACE has developed a portable, convenient, and hassle-free solution to storing software authorizations. iLok, a USB Smart key, enables you to easily and safely move authorization from one computer to another so you can use your software at home, at the office, at the studio, or at a friend's house. More and more software products from a variety of Digidesign Development Partners support the iLok USB Smart Key.

Contact info:

www.ilok.com, www.digidesign.com

SPECTRASONICS

Spectrasonics is a leading developer of world-class sampled sound libraries and new Virtual Instruments. I used Spectrsonics' Stylus and Atmposphere while writing this book. Their Stylus, Atmosphere, and Trilogy virtual instruments are fantastic RTAS plug-ins for Pro Tools.

Contact info:

818-955-8481; 818-955-8613 (fax)
www.spectrasonics.net, info@spectrasonics.net

GRM TOOLS

GRM Tools of Paris, France is the result of 50 years of cutting-edge research and experimentation by the Groupe de Recherches Musicales de l'Institut National de l'Audiovisuel (Ina-GRM). Designed by composers for use by musicians, their plug-ins take sound design to new heights. I used many of their RTAS plug-ins from the the Classic and Spectral Transform packages while writing this book. Take a tour of their Web site and I'm sure you'll be amazed by their products.

Contact Info:

888-749-9998; 518-434-0308 (fax)
www.grmtools.org, grmtools@emf.org

There are many books about the music business, songwriting, producing, and engineering on the market today, but these are just a few of my favorites. Check them out in addition to the new releases from Berklee Press!

Beatles, The. *The Beatles Complete Scores*. Milwaukee, WI: Hal Leonard, 1993.

Braheny, John. *The Craft and Business of Songwriting*. Cincinnati, OH: Writer's Digest Books, 1988.

Gibson, Bill. *The Audio Pro Home Recording Course*, volumes 1–3. Emeryville, CA: Mix Books, 1999.

Keating, Carolyn (editor), and Craig Anderton (technical editor). *Digital Home Recording*. San Francisco, CA: Miller Freeman Books, 1998.

McIan, Peter, and Larry Wichman. *The Musician's Guide to Home Recording*. New York: Asmco Publications, 1994.

Passman, Donald. *All You Need to Know About the Music Business*. New York: Simon and Schuster, 1997.

Rumsey, Francis, and Tim McCormick. *Sound and Recording*, 3rd edition. Oxford, England: Focal Press, 1998.

Schulenberg, Richard. *Legal Aspects of the Music Industry*. New York: Billboard Books, 1999.

You'll also find many useful articles in these magazines: *Mix, Recording, EQ, Tape Op, Home Recording, Keyboard, and Electronic Musician*, among many others.

ABOUT THE AUTHOR

David Franz is a songwriter, record producer, engineer, multi-instrumentalist, arranger, orchestrator, performing artist, studio musician,

author, and instructor. After earning a bachelor's and master's degree in Industrial and Systems Engineering from Virginia Tech, he attended Berklee College of Music and studied music production and engineering.

David has been writing and producing music in home and professional studios for more than twelve years, humbly beginning with 4-track cassette recorders and Studio Vision software. Currently, David runs his own studio and production company, produces and engineers records for bands and singer/songwriters, and writes and records his own music for artistic and commercial distribution. He also plays drums and guitar for studio projects and live performances.

He is the author of an online Pro Tools course available through Berklee Media (**www.berkleemusic.com**). Visit David's Web site at **www.davidfranz.com**, and his new studio Web site at **www.undergroundsun.com**.

Also check out **www.protoolsbook.com** for special offers and more.

Feel free to contact David at dfranz@berkleemusic.com